The Sense of Structure

The Sense of Structure

Writing from the Reader's Perspective

George D. Gopen
Duke University

PEARSON
Longman

New York San Francisco Boston
London Toronto Sydney Tokyo Singapore Madrid
Mexico City Munich Paris Cape Town Hong Kong Montreal

Senior Vice President and Publisher: Joseph Opiela
Vice President/Publisher: Eben W. Ludlow
Executive Marketing Manager: Ann Stypuloski
Production Manager: Douglas Bell
Project Coordination, Text Design, and Electronic Page Makeup: Electronic
    Publishing Services Inc., NYC
Cover Designer/Manager: Wendy Ann Fredericks
Cover Photo: Copyright © Jim Wehtje/Brand X Pictures
Manufacturing Buyer: Roy L. Pickering, Jr.

Library of Congress Cataloging-in-Publication Data

Gopen, George D.
   The sense of structure : writing from the reader's perspective /
George D. Gopen
        p. cm.
Includes index.
   ISBN 0-205-29632-7
   1. English language—Rhetoric. 2. Report writing. I. Title.
PE1408.G613 2003
808'.042—dc22

                                                        2003055624

Please visit us at http://www.ablongman.com

ISBN 0-205-29632-7

For Sarah and Xander

Contents

Chapter **5**

"Write the Way You Speak" and Other Bad Pieces of Advice   149

P A R T   T W O

Mark My Words: A Reader's Perspective on the World of Punctuation   157

Preface

This book is different from most writing textbooks. It does not prescribe rules to be followed. It does not try to help writers figure out how to think up things to say so empty pages may be filled in accordance with the demands of a writing assignment. Instead, it looks at writing from the perspective of the important person where writing is concerned -- the reader.

Once we have graduated for the last time and are catapulted into the working world, almost no one will care how hard we worked at a piece of writing nor how much better a job we did this time compared to last time. Those are school-bound concerns. In the working world, one question alone dominates where the quality of a piece of writing is concerned: Did the reader actually get delivery of what the writer intended to send? If the answer is "yes," the writing was good enough; if the answer is "no," then no matter how strong or confident or even dazzling the writing might sound, it was not good enough.

This text, therefore, will investigate how readers of English tend to make decisions concerning what a given sentence or paragraph or document "means." We have discovered, fairly recently, that there are recognizable *patterns* in the interpretive process of most readers of English. That should come as no great surprise. If there were no patterns, how would we know how to make clauses and sentences and paragraphs make sense consistently? But there *is* a surprise: We have discovered that readers take the greatest percentage of their clues for interpretation not from word choice but rather from the *location* of words within the structure of a sentence or a paragraph. In other words, *where* a word or phrase appears tells us a surprising amount about *what* it is supposed to mean to us. Thus, for most readers, the words of a sentence, rearranged, may significantly alter how that sentence is interpreted.

We look in particular *places* in the sentence to find the answers to the following crucial questions:

-- What is going on here?

-- Whose story is being told?

-- What is most to be emphasized in this sentence?

-- How does this sentence link backward to the sentence that preceded it?

-- How does this sentence lean forward to the one that will follow?

We look in particular *places* in the paragraph to find the answers to the following crucial questions:

-- What is at issue in this paragraph?

-- What is the point of this paragraph?

-- Is this paragraph merely telling a story, or is it trying to make a point?

Since everyone who will read this book is presumably a reader of English, everyone will already "know" most of what this book has to say about readers' responses to the structural location of information in sentences and paragraphs; however, we "know" all of this intuitively–somewhere in the back of our mind or the pit of our stomach. This book attempts to take that which you already know *intuitively as a reader* and make that knowledge available to you *consciously as a writer*.

For example, as a reader you already tend to give extra emphasis to material that appears at the end of a sentence. You may never have realized you were doing that; but most of us do it, most of the time. By becoming conscious of that interpretive habit readers have, you can begin to manipulate the placement of information to invite the largest percentage of readers possible to emphasize precisely what you want emphasized in every single sentence you write.

This is no matter of mere housekeeping; it does far more than merely clean up your prose. It helps you clarify your own thought process. It will help you, for example, to discover whether you yet *know* what you think is most important in any given sentence. If you look at a sentence you have written and find that *nothing* is worthy of special emphasis, then you know you have not thought enough for a full sentence. Or perhaps you will discover that the word or phrase you most want emphasized is not at the sentence's end. No matter how well *you* (the writer) understand how this sentence is to be interpreted, far fewer of *your readers* will be likely to get the message. Some will emphasize what is at the end of the sentence instead. Others, seeing that the end position is filled with something unimportant, will go back through the sentence and make the wrong choice of what else should be emphasized. Or perhaps you will find *too many* candidates for emphasis in the same sentence. You can be fairly sure that different readers will make different combinations and permutations of interpretive choices.

By placing various kinds of information in the structural locations where most readers are most likely to look for them, you accomplish a number of important objectives:

1. You send clear reading instructions. ("Dear reader, I am indicating to you that this information should be emphasized because I am putting it in the place you are most likely to exert your sense of emphasis.")

2. You cut way down on the amount of reading energy a reader must use to figure out *how* this all goes together to make a logical sentence or paragraph, leaving that reading energy available for the far more important task of discovering *what* this sentence or paragraph is supposed to mean.

3. In the process, you get a much clearer notion of how you really want your thought to be formed and connected.

In learning this approach to investigating text and controlling readers' interpretive processes, you will probably apply it first as a revision technique. First you will produce a piece of writing. Then you will review that writing by asking certain important structural questions of it (e.g., "Is the important piece of information at the end of the sentence, where most readers are most likely to emphasize it?"). But soon you will be combining that revision process into your "invention" process -- the process of thinking up what to say. While you are in the midst of constructing a sentence, you will note that the important bit is languishing in the sentence's middle. Knowing that you will later have to go through the pain of revision if you leave it there, you will shift its position before you finish the construction of that sentence. It will not be long thereafter before you will find that this new approach will have melted wholly and imperceptibly into your invention process; you will find yourself naturally leaning toward the end of the sentence as you try to tell people what is most important in your mind.

You will note as you go through the examples in this book that the revised, structurally "better" version of the example often may not sound any better than the original. It may sound no better, but it will *function* significantly better. I will be urging you to rely less and less on your *ear* and more and more on your *eye* and your *mind*. Turn your ear back on after you have manipulated the structure so it will tell your readers to do what you want them to do. Your ear can then neaten up what is left.

As strong as the reader expectations about information placement may be, they must not be allowed to generate a new set of rules for writing. "No rules! No rules!" I will insist, again and again. Sometimes knowing that a reader emphasizes the end of the sentence will caution you *not* to put certain potentially upsetting information there. (Example: "Dear Sir: You are fired.") Sometimes it's just not nice. Sometimes it's off-putting. Sometimes it's impolitic. Sometime's it's overemphatic. What you will find throughout this book are not rules but rather *predictions* of what most readers are most likely to do most of the time. Knowing that will allow you to control a great deal more of your readers' interpretive processes.

This book tries to demystify the English language. Its material has been presented to thousands of working professionals -- lawyers, researchers, government officials, corporate officers, and academics. They report it has given them -- in fairly short order -- a new control over their own writing process and over the interpretive process of their readers. The two comments they most commonly make support the claims I have been putting forward in this preface. They say, (1) "I already knew all this stuff, but no one has ever said it to me in this way;" and (2) "Why didn't someone tell me this a lot earlier in life?"

Bottom line: It works.

About the Instructor's Manual

In my role as director of writing programs at Duke University, I taught this approach and these materials to hundreds of graduate students as they began their teaching careers. From observing each of them teaching an hour's class, I have learned untold amounts about what works and what does not, and about the problems one can have in teaching this for the first time.

Having watched all these new teachers try to use this approach for the first time has produced for me pedagogical insights that I have tried to share in an Instructor's Manual to accompany this volume. It has three sections: (1) A general introduction to this Reader Expectation approach; (2) a number of suggestions for teachers, including responses to the dozen most commonly asked questions about assignments, conferences, grading, and the like, and responses to the most common student objections; and (3) comments and suggestions concerning all the Exercises.

Acknowledgments

I have many people to thank and acknowledge. Foremost, and therefore first, is Joseph Williams of the University of Chicago, who was the groundbreaker for this new way of thinking about controlling language. The great influence of his work on mine will be evident to anyone who takes even a quick glance at his oft-reprinted textbook, *Style.* We worked together in the Clearlines consulting group from 1981 through 1990.

I have also learned a great deal from the other two original members of that group, Gregory Colomb and Frank Kinahan. Greg's perspicacity, wit, and deep understanding of rhetoric were always an inspiration and a comfort. Frank Kinahan was a joy to work with and is much missed by everyone who knew him.

I have also benefited more than I can account from the feedback, problem-sharing, support, and complaints of those hardworking and entirely earnest new teachers at Duke. Although I owe something to almost every one of them, I wish here to record just a few of the most memorable names: Mark Amos, Jill Beimdiek, Stan Blair, Chris Chism, Richard Dickson, Rick Fehrenbacher, Brandi Krantz Greenberg, Scott Harshbarger, Lee Ann Lawrence, Scott McEathron, Fred Neumann, Lori Newcomb, Charlie Paine, Anne Scott, Martha Yeide, and Paul Yoder. I offer special thanks for the pleasure of collaborating with Kary Smout (now of Washington and Lee University) and for the research assistance of Wendy Gwathmey. I have also learned from Judith A. Swan, with whom I have worked on scientific writing.

I wish to thank four reviewers of the manuscripts for their cogent and helpful suggestions: Valerie Balester, Texas A&M University; Joanna Gibson, Texas A&M University; Peter Richardson, Public Policy Institute of California; and -- most especially for his multiple readings and detailed responses -- William Vande Kopple, Calvin College.

It is a privilege to work with Eben Ludlow at Longman. He has maintained a confidence and interest in this work for a far longer time than should have been necessary.

Jim Hill of EPS did a masterful job of overseeing the process of transforming the manuscript into a book.

Part of the illumination that has allowed me to do my work happily for the past 13 years has come from my son, Xander. He lights up my life.

I met my wonderful wife, Sarah Duncan Gopen, when her law firm invited my consulting firm to work with some of their young lawyers on an early version of this approach to writing. We therefore met in the Topic position and have progressed through many a Stress position to the point where we now have achieved both cohesion and coherence in our life together.

Exploring the Shape of English

1

The Complexity of the English Sentence

T ools, Not Rules

When we first go about learning how to construct English sentences, we are presented with a great many rules that govern our actions. Rules are extremely helpful in the teaching of children:

Cross the street only at an intersection and only when the traffic light tells you it is safe to do so.

Always begin a sentence with a capital letter.

Never end a sentence with a preposition.

Any rule, however, runs the risk of going too far: That is, in order for it to be a rule, it has to state general guidelines and restrictions that will govern any possible situation. Sooner or later, a situation will arise in which the rule will produce a difficulty, an awkwardness, or even an impossibility. Obeying the rule then will only serve the purpose of keeping the rule inviolable; it will not necessarily produce the best solution to the reading/writing problem at hand. Since these moments of difficulty or inelegance or even illogicality will arise now and again, it becomes harder and harder for people to remember the rule and to obey it.

Some rules for the English language creak and even break because they were passed on to us from another language, usually Latin. Latin was a language whose grammar attended mostly to the sentence level and little to the larger units of discourse. For instance, many of us were taught that one can never use *however* or *nevertheless* as the first word in a sentence. Nevertheless, we can all imagine, without too much difficulty, a sentence beginning with one of these words and still making perfect sense. This rule (if indeed we still regard it as a rule) is directly imported from Latin, where the equivalent words (like *tamen*, meaning "nevertheless") were never allowed to come first. We can construct a reason for this rule easily enough: Since *however* and *nevertheless* always point backward toward that which they are qualifying, there must always be something in back of them in the sentence in which they appear. For example, "This, however, . . ." acknowledges the truth of "this" but signals that a qualification of it will immediately follow. However, any reader of English will recognize that a sentence starting with *however* will be qualifying the whole sentence that immediately preceded it. In English, this rule is useless.

It should come as no surprise that most of these rules were formulated first as conventions. We cannot often pinpoint when the conventions became rules: We can rarely point to the person or persons responsible. No matter how they actually came into being, to most of us they just seem to have happened -- long before us and without our cooperation.

As long as we view rules as restrictions imposed from above, as power plays from a society that preexisted our own arrival at the age of literacy, we will tend to learn those rules by rote, as requirements for our joining a polite and functional society. We might as well chant in chorus, "We will never split our infinitive or end a sentence with a preposition." If, however, we visualize these rules as controls over text that allow us to influence the reading process, to heighten the probabilities of communication, or even to create for our readers (and ourselves) a better understanding of what we are trying to say, then the rules, for a change, begin to serve us. We can embrace the ones that make sense and isolate for memorization those few that affect only our social acceptability.

We should stop trying to see these rules as controls and begin to seem them as tools. The phrase "tools, not rules" might be a handy, jingle-like device for keeping this concept conscious. The more we fear them -- the more we fear we are constantly being graded or judged on the basis of them -- the more we perceive them as controlling us as writers. Instead, let us view them as significant (and signifying) means to the end of our communicating with and influencing our readers.

Take, for example, the two simplest sentence rules, which rarely give us problems:

1) Every sentence must begin with a capital letter.
2) Every sentence must end with a period.

Why do they not bother us? Perhaps it is because we as writers can so easily understand the need for our readers to know when our sentences begin and end. Perhaps that in turn has something to do with our own desire, as writers and thinkers, to know when we have finished one sentence/thought and can begin another. Where these two rules are concerned, the needs of the writer and the needs of the reader coincide; at the very least, they do not clash.

Contrast that to the annoying rules, so difficult to remember, concerning the use of *which* and *that*. Which of the following are "correct"?

A. Please go out to the garage and bring me the rake, which is broken.

B. Please go out to the garage and bring me the rake which is broken.

C. Please go out to the garage and bring me the rake that is broken.

D. Please go out to the garage and bring me the rake, that is broken.

"Correct" was in quotation marks because there is more going on here than mere correctness. Sentences A and C are grammatically correct; B and D are grammatically erroneous. *Which* always must be preceded by a comma; this kind of *that* must not let a comma separate it from its rake. Far more important than the mere existence of this "rule" is the reason for it and the result of it. Sentence A -- ". . . the rake, which is broken" -- signifies that there is only one rake in the garage. And, by the way, it's broken. The *which* introduces information that is not essential to making sense of the sentence as a whole. The presence of the comma indicates that you could get rid of this "additional" information and still have the sentence make sense. "Go bring me the rake. (By the way, just for your information, -- it's broken.)"

The *that*, on the other hand, introduces information that is essential to the sentence. It therefore tells us that there are multiple rakes in the garage; but only one of them is broken. I do not want you to bring me any old rake; I want you to bring me "the-rake-that-is-broken." That is what that *that* means. And it therefore makes sense to have no comma separate it from its rake.

This distinction, as significant as it can be on occasion, is not easy to keep at the front of your mind while writing. Even the bible of grammars, *Fowler's Modern English Usage,* was once guilty of a which/that error, appearing only a few pages after the page on which the which/that rule itself was articulated. Why is it so hard for so many of us to keep the distinction between the two words in mind? The reason, I suggest, is that in this case, the needs of the writer and the needs of the reader sometimes are in conflict. The writer knows full well whether the phrase or clause in question is restrictive or nonrestrictive -- which are the terms we use to refer to the functional difference between *which* and *that;* it may not occur to the writer that the reader needs to be let in on that distinction as well. (See the section on "The Comma" in Part II, Chapter 6, for a fuller discussion of restrictive versus nonrestrictive.)

The same restrictive/nonrestrictive distinction can sometimes be indicated by punctuation alone. In the following two sentences, what difference is created by the presence or absence of the commas?

1. My sister, who plays the violin, will be home from college next week.

2. My sister who plays the violin will be home from college next week.

Although both sentences are potentially grammatically correct, they are by no means interchangeable. It depends on how many sisters this particular writer happens to have: If there is only one sister, #1 is correct and #2 incorrect; if there are two or more sisters, but only one who plays the violin, #2 is correct and #1 incorrect; and if there are two or more violin-playing sisters, both #1 and #2 are incorrect. My point here, aside from getting an early start on explaining this grammatical concept, is to demonstrate that this writer already *knows* how many sisters, with or without violins, the writer has. It seems a bit of a fuss for this all-knowing author to have to choose a grammatical structure based on the needs of ignorant readers. But it only seems that way if writing is looked at as an academic task to be undertaken only because it has been assigned. If, on the other hand, the writing has to function as communication with real-world readers, then the extra effort is justified.

Once we are out of school for the last time, it soon becomes more apparent that real writing is usually done almost entirely for the sake of the reader. In the world after the final graduation, no one much cares how hard the writer worked or how much the writer has improved since last time. In school, those two concerns can usually be depended upon to save the writer from failure. If you fill enough pages and have followed the instructions of the assignment -- and especially if you have improved since last time -- you cannot fail. You can get a lower grade than you would like -- but you cannot fail.

In that world after graduation, however, we fail a great deal. An example that might give us pause, even for those of us who care nothing about the sport of baseball, is that of baseball's annual batting championship. At the end the baseball season, the champion hitter often is batting about .333; that is, he has succeeded in getting a hit at a rate of about one out of every three batting opportunities. This also means that the champion has *failed* to get a hit in *two* out of every three opportunities. That is more like real life: We fail a good deal. Can you imagine a judge looking at a · lawyer's brief and saying, "This is a real mess; but it is so much better than the last one you turned in, you win the case." Or can you imagine the National Science Foundation responding, "This grant proposal makes no convincing arguments whatever; but we can see you worked very hard on it and filled the right number of pages, so here is two million dollars."

Where writing is concerned in that world after graduation, there is a single, bottom-line question: *Did the READER actually get delivery of that which the writer intended to send?* The important person is not the writer; it is the reader. Once the needs of the reader are accepted as the controlling concerns for writing, then the need for understanding how sentences are likely to function overcomes the more student-centered concern for how we can turn out sentences that will indicate we did the task assigned.

This book, then, tries to revisit the time-weary structural and grammatical concerns of the English language from a relatively new perspective -- that of the reader. It continually keeps in mind the single, controlling question of *how* a reader goes about perceiving meaning from a written text. Part II will treat the *grammatical concerns* of writing as *a system of clues* for the reader. Punctuation sends the reader a great deal of information:

-- when to start;

-- when to stop;

-- when to breathe;

-- how to perceive modification, qualification, and subordination.

Even more importantly, Part I will treat a number of *structural concerns* of rhetoric that allow a reader to answer a good many questions of significance:

-- Whose story does the sentence tell?

-- What is going on?

-- How does this sentence link backward to what has just been said?

-- How does this sentence lean forward to what is now about to be said?

-- What information in this sentence is most to be emphasized?

By its end, this book hopes to demonstrate that there is no essential difference between the grammatical concerns and the structural/rhetorical concerns. This book can therefore be considered either a Rhetorical Grammar or a Grammatical Rhetoric.

·· EXERCISE A ···

Let us ask the five questions of structural concern just mentioned of the following sentences. For each, determine

a) Whose story does the sentence tell?

b) What is going on?

c) How does the sentence link backward to what has just been said?

d) How does the sentence lean forward to what is now about to be said?

e) What information in the sentence is most to be emphasized?

1. Given the difficulty of this problem, Gibson argued at great length that nothing further could be done without consulting the President.

2. Compared to that, the surgery he would have to undergo seemed no more threatening than an appointment with the dentist.

We can make some helpful distinctions between grammar and rhetoric; but a moment later the two would begin to intertwine and lose their distinctiveness. We could point out, for example, that grammar has to do with fashioning perceivable patterns, while rhetoric has to do with forging persuasive connections. We could suggest that a reader's perception of the grammar of a sentence can precede a reader's understanding of the meaning of the sentence, while perception of its rhetoric is continuously unfolding before, during, and after the words of the sentence are read. Those are interesting concepts; but it is simpler and more empowering for us to think of the two as working together as tools and strategies for convincing as large a percentage of our readers as we can to interpret our prose the way we intend it to be interpreted.

Language theorists have long argued that every sentence can be infinitely interpreted. I, for one, agree. Meaning depends on context. Take the briefest articulation we might deign to call a sentence -- a single exclamatory word like "Fire!" That sentence, if it be a sentence, means one thing if it is uttered in answer to the question, "Name the single greatest cause of damage to homes in Wake County in the first three months of this year"; it means quite another if it is uttered with great energy in the middle of a crowded theater. Context controls meaning. Since there are an infinite number of possible contexts for any sentence, it must have an infinite number of possible meanings.

That just states the problem. This book is concerned with shaping some responses and possible solutions to that problem. Since any sentence could mean an infinite number of things, how can we best go about limiting the possible meanings of a particular sentence so that it means what we *want* it to mean at a given moment? We cannot nail it down to stay; no matter how well written any given sentence might be, there will always exist a reader -- whether through incompetence, imagination, past experience, or sheer perversity -- who could give it an interpretation the writer never intended. We cannot make even a single sentence mean only one thing to all readers; the trick is to make it mean pretty much the same thing to the greatest possible percentage of readers who are trying their best to understand what it is you have to say.

As readers, we must constantly read between the lines; we read into things; we read based on our own experiences, many of which are unknowable by the writer; we read with our own axe to grind. While recognizing all this, this book tries to help you get a handle on that which is handleable -- trying to get across that which you mean to get across, as fully and precisely as possible.

Let us begin, then, by briefly investigating just how complex an experience the reading of a sentence must be. Do not be dismayed by this quick tour of the grammatical/rhetorical insides of the sentence; we shall face the compound difficulties by the divide-and-conquer method. It seems best to begin, however, with an indication of why the rest of our effort would be worthwhile.

The Anatomy of a Sentence's Meaning from the Reader's Perspective

It may seem, at first glance, that the meaning of a sentence for any given reader depends somewhat on word order but more essentially on word choice. It turns out to be a great deal more complex than that. Here is a list -- by no means complete -- of some of the major factors that control a reader's interpretive process, sentence after sentence after sentence.

Diction

Diction, or word choice, can easily head the list. One would assume that choosing the wrong words will destroy meaning; equally evident, it would seem that once the right words are chosen, it is up to the rest of the sentence-building process to forge a home for those words that presents them to best effect -- or at least that does not get in their way. I will argue, however, that word choice is only about 15% of the matter; the other 85% is all structure. In fact, it is often safer to get the word wrong and the structure right rather than to get the word right and the structure wrong. The great majority of the interpretive clues used by a reader in making sense of a sentence come not from which words were chosen but rather from *where* in the sentence the words appear. Still, accurate and powerful diction is an absolute necessity if one is to become a strong writer; and varying the level of your word choices can alter significantly the level of your discourse as a whole.

Communal Agreement and Convention

We use a series of conventional signs, which we call *punctuation,* to tell our readers when to start, to stop, and to breathe. The more correct we are in conforming to these conventions, the less risk we run that readers will be misled or distracted by having to figure out or wishing to rail against our breaches of these conventions. However, we can also create special effects from time to time by skillfully flouting these conventions.

Construction

It makes a great deal of difference in a sentence whether a particular concept or thing is presented as a noun, a verb, an adjective, an adverb, or some other part of speech. Choices of sentence construction can alter dramatically the kinds of attention a reader summons and the relative importance a reader assigns. These distinctions are all the more powerful for their subtlety; that is, the reader is often unaware of how controlling these forces may be, since only rarely is the reader consciously noting distinctions between parts of speech.

It also makes a difference which order of construction has been chosen for the arrangement of the sentence as a whole. Is it active or passive? Is it verb-centered or noun-centered? Is it expansive or compact? These choices have no right or wrong to them; but they usually make a great deal of difference to the reader's interpretive process. For example, note here what different kinds of force and attention are generated by the different parts of speech assigned to the concept of arguing:

A. She argued her point with such power that the Court decided unanimously in her favor.

B. Her argument on this point was delivered with such power that the Court decided unanimously in her favor.

C. The argumentation on this point was delivered with such power that the Court decided unanimously in her favor.

D. Her arguing powers on this point were so great that the Court decided unanimously in her favor.

Even though in all four cases the Court agreed with her because she argued well, the four sentences "mean" differently. They focus on different things.

·· EXERCISE B

For the four sentences above lettered A, B, C, and D, state as clearly as you can *how* the "arguing" differs from sentence to sentence. What force does it have? What kind of attention do we pay to it? Is it an action she is doing? Or a product of hers? Or something that exists apart from her, as if it had a life of its own? Is it merely descriptive?

Relative Complexity

Readers respond with great sensitivity to the rhetorical/grammatical issues of length and weight. How long or short is the sentence? How long or short is this sentence compared to the sentence that preceded it -- or to the several sentences that have preceded it? How long or short is this clause compared to another clause in the same sentence? How lengthy or weighty does this sentence seem by itself, given the clarity or convolution of its syntax and the density of its diction? These concerns will be explored at length in Chapter 3; but for the present moment, consider just a single example. Note how the length of the sentence "There was nothing to be done" differs in its effect in the following two contexts.

A. He could not continue to send telegraphic signals. The phone lines to the house were all down. His cell phone battery was dead. He could not shout loud enough to be heard. No one would be able to see him even if he could manage to get outside. There was nothing to be done.

B. He could neither continue to send telegraph signals, nor use the house phone (since the lines were down), nor use his cell phone (since the battery was dead), nor attract people's attention by shouting, nor make himself visible even if he were able to get outside. There was nothing to be done.

·· EXERCISE C

Write two different paragraphs that end with each of the following sentences, making sure that the sentences given here "mean differently" because of the contexts you have provided for them in the paragraphs you have created.

1) He smashed the glass to smithereens.
2) She simply was not interested.

Specificity

Information must not be confused with idea. The former must be summoned to produce the latter. It makes a good deal of difference whether information is presented as abstract or concrete, as explicit or implied, as general or particular, as highlighted or hidden. In any case, information alone does not constitute an idea; ideas require that information be synthesized. No two writers are likely to make the exact same decisions when synthesizing the same complex set of information into thought. We each process that information through our individual intellectual abilities, with the resulting thought being clearly identifiable as ours.

Reference

Even if a single thought were able to appear to us in a visible form, like a host arising from the Afterlife, no group of writers would be likely to point to it or refer to it in exactly the same way. Each would use the sieve of his or her own individual imagination to present that experience to a reader not lucky enough to have been present at its initial appearance. When we cannot easily build a text in a linear fashion, connecting each new unit to the ones that have prepared for it, we must turn to rhetorical techniques of pointing or referring. Many of these were categorized by the ancient rhetoricians as *figures of speech* or *figures of thought*. Some of these are familiar to you from your study of literature: *Metaphor* refers to one thing in terms of another; *simile* explicitly compares one thing to another. Others you have long been familiar with, even though you might never have noticed them consciously nor heard their technical names. That is especially true of those that rely on repetition: *Anaphora* repeats words at the beginnings of units.

> We shall fight on the beaches. We shall fight on the landing grounds. We shall fight in the fields, and in the streets; we shall fight in the hills. We shall never surrender!
>
> (Winston Churchill, speech given during World War II in the House of Commons on June 4, 1940, after the disastrous loss to the Nazis in the battle of Dunkirk)

Epistrophe repeats words at the ends of units.

> Shall I ask him to do this nicely? No thank you. Shall I grovel and whine and plead and whimper? No thank you. Shall I explain and argue and cajole and weave a complex web of persuasive reasons as if I were the lawyer and he were the judge? No thank you.

Chiasmus repeats two or more elements, but in reverse order.

> Ask not what your country can do for you; ask what you can do for your country.
>
> (President John F. Kennedy's Inaugural Address, 1960)

These are but a few of the dozens of rhetorical techniques available and in common use, both for the high rhetoric of literature and the more mundane business of every day.

·· EXERCISE D ··

Chiasmus (the *x y y x* reversal discussed just above) is a favorite rhetorical tool of journalists, advertisers, and politicians. A company that sells tuna fish used to feature a would-be-artist cartoon fish named Charlie, who was constantly studying painting or music to indicate to the fishermen above that he had "good taste." At the end of every ad, a note was lowered down to him on a fishing hook that said, "Sorry, Charlie," as a voice was heard saying, "Sorry Charlie, Star Kist doesn't want tunas with *good taste;* they want tunas that *taste good.*"

1. Using any widely read news magazine -- including those that deal with sports or gardening or the latest fashions -- find three witty examples of chiasmus. They might be easier to find than you would think.
2. Make up three witty examples of chiasmus by yourself.

Structural Location

This, which might seem the least of all these forces, may well be the single most influential and important. Strange though it may sound at first, *where* a word or phrase is placed has a great deal to do with *how* it will be processed by a reader. Controlling these structural placements may well be the single most important skill a writer can develop. It is through structural placement, much more than through word choice, that readers discover whose story a sentence or clause is to be, what is going on, how it connects backward to what has been going on, how it leans forward in anticipation of what will be going on, and which materials are to be considered the most important, the ones that made the sentence worth composing in the first place. Getting some of the words wrong but the structure right probably is less disastrous for your reader than getting the words right and the structure wrong.

For example, a phrase may well have an entirely different impact on a reader depending on whether it comes first, last, or in the middle of a sentence. No two different constructions of the same pieces of information are likely to have precisely the same effect on a given reader. Compare the following:

a) While this argument makes logical sense, its practical effectiveness may be questionable at this point in time.
b) While the practical effectiveness of this argument may be questionable at this point in time, it makes logical sense.

c) While at this point in time the practical effectiveness of this argument may be questionable, it makes logical sense.

d) Questionable though the practical effectiveness of this argument may be at this point in time, it makes logical sense.

e) Though this argument makes logical sense at this point in time, its practical effectiveness may be questionable.

The pieces of information here remain the same throughout; but the various ways of deploying them produce for a given reader a noticeably different balancing, a noticeably different meaning for each variation. All of the above forces must be kept under control for a writer to keep most readers under control. If there is any real *purpose* for the writing -- like applying for something or arguing for something or communicating something or asking for something, where there are real stakes to be gained or lost -- then controlling the reader's interpretation should be at the heart of your rhetorical agenda.

Note, for example, the different kind of force the simple phrase "since 1981" has when it appears in three different structural locations -- the beginning, the end, and the middle. That placement influences readers greatly -- although subtly -- in their expectation of what will happen in the next sentence.

1. Since 1981, we have seen a noteworthy increase in the production of left-handed widgets.

    Most readers will expect the next sentence to follow through with a chronology: "In 1983 production increased to 1,200,000; in 1985 it rose further to 1,675,000; and by 1992 it had reached the 2,000,000 mark."

2. We have seen a noteworthy increase in the production of left-handed widgets since 1981.

    Most readers would now expect to find out why 1981 was such an important moment in the history of widget production: "In that year, several factors combined to increase the country's need for this important item."

3. We have seen a noteworthy increase, since 1981, in the production of left-handed widgets.

    Most readers will accept the date of 1981 as additional but nonessential information. "Since 1981" will have little or no influence in leading readers to expect what will come next.

We can never write even so little as a single sentence that will control all readers at all times; but knowing where readers generally expect certain kinds of material to show up in a sentence will allow us to control the direction most of our readers will take most of the time. It therefore is essentially important for us to explore how to go about gaining this control. That is the task this book sets for itself.

2

A Structural Anatomy of the English Sentence

T *he Fallacy of "Good" and "Bad" Sentences*

We have to face a hard problem right from the start: No sentence is good or bad in and of itself. It can only be effectively judged in relationship to the sentences that surround it -- and perhaps some that surround those, as well. Hand me the most stunning, elegant, powerful sentence you have ever encountered. I can make it a "bad" sentence simply by dropping it into the middle of a paragraph in which it does not belong. For example, insert a famous sentence by President Lincoln into a paragraph by the eloquent C. P. Snow:

> Scientists are the most important occupational group in the world today. At this moment, what they do is of passionate concern to the whole of human society. At this moment, the scientists have little influence on the world effect of what they do. Fourscore and seven years ago, our fathers brought forth upon this continent a new nation, conceived in Liberty, and dedicated to the proposition that all men are created equal. Yet potentially they can have great influence.[1]

President Lincoln's "fourscore and seven years ago" opening gambit of the Gettysburg address is a "bad" sentence in the C. P. Snow paragraph for a number of reasons, including everything from its being on the "wrong" topic to its suffering from stylistic incongruencies. What is worst, perhaps, is that it almost seems to fit the flow of the thought. Look at the string of time references from each sentence:

. . . . today

At this moment, . . .

At this moment, . . .

Fourscore and seven years ago, . . .

Yet potentially . . .

Readers unfamiliar with the famous sentence would give a good effort at making it fit the thought. They might even become convinced either that they had understood what was meant, or, if not, that the fault lay in their abilities to comprehend.

Conversely (and perhaps a bit perversely), I could transform the worst sentence you have ever read into a stunningly fine one, if you gave me enough time and space to create for it a context within which it would function well. Hand me, for example, a sentence in which you have intentionally committed eleven grammatical errors. To make it a "good" sentence, I would write a 20-page essay in which I would analyze in detail "the eleven most common grammatical errors in English usage today" -- a page or two on each error. At the end of page 19, at the height of my summation, I would include your sentence. Far from being an example of incompetence, it would shine as a stunning triumph of wit -- that in a single sentence I could bring together all eleven errors, singing a final choral hymn just before the curtain comes down. Anyone writing a critique of my essay would be sure to highlight that intensely imaginative, error-ridden sentence. "He was able to get *all eleven* into one sentence!" What had been intended as a disaster would be transformed into a tour de force.

It is entirely possible, of course, to admire or despise a single sentence all by itself, with no context. Every once in a while I will read a single student sentence to a colleague as a delightful example of good prose. More often, colleagues will send me individual student sentences as examples of how badly the younger generation has gone astray. But this book focuses on *text* and *discourse*, where sentences never exist without a context. *Any* sentence can be made better or worse by changing its context.

So be wary, therefore, of looking at any of the sentence examples in this volume as "good" or "bad" writing. Instead of affixing these judgmental labels, we will try to focus our attention on a crucial question: How would most readers go about the job of perceiving the meaning of this sentence in this context? If a great majority of readers, with quickness and ease, make of your sentence what you wished them to make of your sentence, then (and only then) can we judge it to be a good sentence. Conversely, no matter how strong and elegant your sentence may sound, and no matter how well *you* can see in it what you intended it to say, your sentence is a bad one if the great majority of your readers cannot perceive from it what you were trying to say.

This book will try to give you better control over your sentences and over what readers are likely to make of your sentences. We will constantly be involved in making value judgments of "better" and "worse," even though we now realize that such judgments cannot be made out of context. But whatever sample sentence we take for study remains by definition out of context. If I were to give you the two sentences that surround the sample sentence, the three together would still lack context. If I were to give you the entire essay or book from which those three sentences came, that book itself would still have yet greater contexts -- those in which it was written or was being read. We are always confronted, on some level, with a lack of context. So do not be surprised if I suggest a meaning for a given sentence with which you disagree. Certainly do not be surprised if you come up with an interpretation different from the one I suggest. That is always a possibility where language is concerned. The best we can do is to find a way to figure out how *most* readers are *likely* to make sense of your sentences, given the context in which they exist.

The question then becomes, "How can we do this?" How can we judge in advance what most readers are likely to do with one of our sentences? You yourself are too close to your own writing to trust your answer to the question "Does this make sense?" -- or even "Does this make the sense I intended it to make?" When you read your own writing, you cannot approach it from the fresh, unengaged vantage point from which your readers begin. As you struggle to be your own editor, your mind deceives you, robbing you of your intended objectivity. Here is what you *think* is happening:

You look at the words of a given sentence;

you know what each of those words is intended to mean;

you judge that when those words with those meanings are put into that particular sentence structure, then the resultant meaning would be [X];

and since [X] was what you intended to say, you judge your sentence to be a good one.

But that is *not* what actually happens. What actually happens is more like the following:

You see those words;

you *remember* those words;

those are the words you chose and put together when you were struggling to write [X].

Therefore, when you look at this sentence, it seems to mean [X] because it brings [X] back to your mind.

Mere association -- not objective perception -- has produced your approval of that sentence.

This may become clearer if I use an exaggerated example. You are doing some writing at the breakfast table. You are suddenly struck by a stunningly brilliant idea. In your haste to write it down, you knock over your coffee cup. The coffee spills and stains a corner of your page. Forever and forever, I would argue, that coffee stain -- through mere association -- could bring to your mind that brilliant idea; but it is highly unlikely to convey that idea to a reader of that page.

The coffee stain problem is a real one when it comes to judging your own writing, even on the sentence level. Mere correctness will not suffice. Elegant diction, reasonable length, and the sound of importance also will not suffice. Nor will the mere *possibility* that the sentence is *capable* of being interpreted the way you intend. You need ways of judging how readers will most likely go about the job of putting your words together to produce a thought.

You can accomplish this by learning how to perceive and control the relationship between the *substance* of your sentence (what you want to say) and its *structure* (how the words are put together). We now know that readers have relatively fixed expectations of where in the structure of an English sentence to look for the arrival of certain kinds of substance. Knowing consciously what these expectations are will give you a great deal more conscious control over them and therefore over your readers' interpretive processes.

The rest of this chapter will give you an introduction to these sentence-level reader expectations. You need not buy this explanation in order to make use of it. You can use it as a thorough set of principles to investigate your writing and the writing of others; or you can use it as a quick and dirty revision tactic; or you can allow it to expand into a procedural aid in producing and extending your thought; or you can limit it to the force of a metaphor that will help you understand the pieces of description and advice that make up the rest of this volume. I urge you now (and will urge you later, a number of times,) *not* to try to make these reader expectations into a set of *rules* to replace those you have learned earlier in your education. These are tools, not rules. As rules, they will rigidify and break down. As tools with which you can achieve greater control of prose, they will serve you well.

R *eader Expectations at the Sentence Level*

Word Order Counts -- More Than You Might Think

Please read the following:

1a. A because of the the the this to to which expected its most necessary particular single clues English interpretation it language meaning order people readers sentence word convey does gives lacks not.

It is difficult going, to say the least. We would be hard pressed to call it a sentence.

Now please read the following:

1b. This sentence does not convey a single particular meaning to most people because it lacks the expected word order of the English language, which gives readers the necessary clues to its interpretation.

That was a good deal easier, was it not? You may already have figured out the relationship between the two: They both contain exactly the same words, but in a different order. By the way, example (1b) is a falsehood, since it does *not* "lack the expected word order of the English language." (Does that make sentence (1a) a truer statement?)

Of course, this is an extreme example. Everyone who knows English understands that word order has a great deal to do with meaning. Example (1a) seems at first to lack order entirely. On closer inspection, though, we find that there is a great deal of order: All the adjectives are together, alphabetically arranged; all the verbs are together, alphabetically arranged; and so forth. There is a lot of *order* -- but not the *kind* of order that helps us understand how the author wants us to put these words together.

As extreme as this example is, it is also the prototype for all the other examples in this book. In every case, the changing of the *order* of words will change the *likelihood of interpretation* on the part of readers. We all are aware of this intuitively when we play the role of the reader; this chapter will try to make some of that readerly intuition a conscious process for you when you switch to the role of writer. If we could consciously understand where readers expect to find certain kinds of materials, then by putting those things in those places we could raise the probability that our readers would make of our prose what we would have them make of it. This general statement should make a good deal more sense by the time we have finished working through many specific examples.

The Sentence: What's Happening?

Compare the following two sentences:

2a. What would be the student reaction accorded the imposition of such a requirement?

2b. How would the students react to such a requirement?

Putting aside the value judgment of better or worse, we would probably find wide agreement that the second sentence is *easier to read* than the first. Why? Some of the reasons that might first come to mind turn out to be false leads:

-- "Sentence (2b) is easier to read because it is shorter than (2a)." No. If that were the case, then every thirteen-word sentence should be shortened to nine. Thirteen is only half the number of words in the average published sentence. Counting words is no way to guide your writing practices. Short and zippy thoughts need short and zippy sentences; but complex, sophisticated thoughts often need longer, more complex, but still clear sentences. "Shorter is better" is not only bad advice, it is false advice. "Longer is better" also does not work well. A sentence should be as long as it needs to be in order to make its point effectively -- no longer and no shorter.

-- "Sentence (2b) is easier to read because it is written in the active and (2a) is written in the passive." No. We will investigate the active/passive controversy at a number of points later on. Let it be enough at present to note that both active and passive have their excellent uses.

-- "Sentence (2b) is easier to read than (2a) because it contains easier or more direct words." Not really. Most people who can read and understand the words in the second sentence can also understand all the words used in the first sentence. There is no diction or jargon problem here -- even though it may sound like that sort of problem exists.

Something else, then, is responsible for this clearly perceivable difference in reading difficulty. It can be stated in the form of our first reader expectation:

....
Readers of English expect that the action of a sentence will be articulated by its verb.
....

By "English" I mean the language that is currently accepted in the United States for public consumption. These expectations change over place and time; but they change very slowly. American expectations differ somewhat from British, Australian, and others; in America itself, dialectical differences abound; and everywhere the language has changed significantly since the sixteenth century. But as a general insight -- not a *rule* -- the above expectation will serve us well.

By "the action of a sentence" I mean quite simply "what is going on" in the sentence. It need not be strikingly active action. In this regard, no verb is "strong" or "weak" by itself. Every verb has meaning -- and usually lots of them. Every verb by itself is therefore potentially strong and potentially weak; it depends on the context offered by the sentence in which it exists. In this sense, a verb is strong if its apparent meaning is the focal point for what is going on in the sentence as a whole. Conversely, a verb is weak if its apparent meaning has little or nothing to do with what is going on in the sentence as a whole.

We therefore cannot tell if a verb is weak or strong just by looking at it, alone. The verb *to be* (*am, are, is,* . . .) has a number of meanings -- "exists," "equals," or "is labeled as." Whenever one of those meanings is the focus of the sentence, the verb *to be*, weak though it looks, is, by our definition, strong.

-- God is.

-- The argument here is faulty.

Conversely, a strong-looking verb is weak if it is not the focus of its sentence's action.

-- She accorded them the opportunity of leaving.

Accorded would be a weak verb here if the sentence was intended to tell us that she allowed them to leave. If *allow* was her action, then *allow* should be her verb: "She allowed them to leave." *Accorded*, on the other hand, would be a strong verb here if our attention was to be focused not on her *allowing them* something, but on her *according them* an opportunity. The difference is subtle, but important.

With that said, let us return to our two example sentences for a closer look at the verbs. Here they are again, with the verbs underscored:

2a. What <u>would be</u> the student reaction <u>accorded</u> the imposition of such a requirement?

2b. How would the students <u>react</u> to such a requirement?

If you asked a group of twenty people how many words in (2a) denote actions taking place in that sentence, you would get responses of zero, one, two, three, four, probably five, and possibly six. If you further probed the people who answered "three," you would find they had chosen different sets of three; and the "two" people might have chosen different pairs of two; and so forth. Out of twenty people, you would be likely to get between ten and fifteen different answers to the question "What is going on here?" But if you ask the same twenty people the same question of sentence (2b), between sixteen and twenty of them are likely to select a single word, "react." (I speak from experience, having used this example with literally hundreds of groups.)

Why? In reading English, people "lean forward" to the verb, in the expectation that it will announce what is going on. If it seems to do that, readers will generally accept that as the truth and go on from there. If the verb fails to settle that issue, then readers have to poke around to find alternative candidates. In practice, few readers will actually interrupt themselves to do this poking around; they hurtle forward toward the end of this sentence and then on to the beginning of the next. Needing to go back, however, to find out what had been going on, they find their mind going backward and forward at the same time. It is that attempt to have your mind travel in two directions at the same time that produces that fuzzy-headed feeling of noncomprehension that we all have when reading is not easy.

In (2a), it is difficult to figure out how "accorded" or "would be accorded" makes sense as an action; but in (2b), it is not at all difficult to understand how "react" could be the central action. As a result, sentence (2b) is significantly easier to read than sentence (2a), for two main reasons: (1) We all believe more firmly that "react" was the main action, and (2) it took us far less effort to come to that conclusion because the action was stated *where* we expected to find it -- in the verb. This is also a major reason why (2b) and other seemingly well-crafted sentences have shape or flow: It has to do with that sense of leaning forward to the verb and being rewarded there with that which we were seeking.

Notice in sentence (2a) how many possibilities for action compete for our attention:

-- "student reaction" (versus "faculty reaction")

-- "accorded" (that is, "merely accorded" versus "the real thing")

-- "imposition" (the political process of "imposition" versus free choice or open debate between interested parties)

-- "such a requirement" (as opposed to "other types" or requirements)

Note that I have not suggested that sentence (2b) is necessarily *better* than (2a). In most contexts, it probably is; but other contexts might make it worse. That depends on what the author intended it to mean. For example, (2b) is shorter because it leaves out the concept of *imposition* altogether in favor of the focus on *requirement*. What if the author had intended to emphasize the tyranny of this imposition? Then (2b) would be a far worse sentence then (2a), no matter how badly constructed (2a) might be.

In order to make it clear to a reader what is going on in a sentence, make the action or actions into verbs. Here is a rewrite of (2a) that values both the actions of imposition and reaction:

2c. How would the students react if the Dean imposed the new requirement?

Perhaps you can hear the two motions of leaning forward -- from "How" to "react" and from "if" to "impose." If you add the doers of those actions (whom we will be calling *agents*) as the subjects of those verbs, you produce the core of the sentence's thought:

How would students . . . react -- if the Dean . . . imposed ?

Rethinking this sentence (2c), the author might be tempted to be yet more specific, to fill in this picture a bit more fully. Perhaps the particular manner of imposing would make the entire question more pointed. A further expansion might produce the following:

2d. How would the students react if the Dean imposed the new requirement without allowing the student government to debate the issue?

Note that the further modification of the main verb "impose" focuses on a verb form with an "-ing" ending, which in turn is further modified by another verb form that is not a main verb -- the infinitive "to debate."

If, on the other hand, the author was not primarily interested in the political imposing but was more concerned with the nature of the new requirement, the author could have telegraphed that concern by omitting "imposition" altogether, lest it muddy the waters. The sentence could be expanded by using "require" as the featured verb:

2e. How would the students react if the Dean required a 90% attendance record for all students taking courses numbered below 200?

Or perhaps it was not in the author's mind to focus on the action of reacting. Perhaps the next sentence was going to introduce the faculty reaction to the student reaction -- and then maybe throw in the trustees for good measure. In that case, the noun "reaction" should not have been transformed into a verb:

2f. What would be the student reaction if the Dean required a 90% attendance record for all students taking courses numbered below 200? How would that compare to the faculty reaction? And would there be any reaction whatever from the Board of Trustees?

These differences may strike you as subtle; but it is in their very subtlety that their power lies. Readers do not consciously notice that these shifts in focus have been imposed on them; but they experience them all the same. It all seems just to happen. That is powerful. You can control part of that power by controlling what you choose to put in the verb slot of your sentences.

It is most common that when an action is hiding in a sentence -- that is, when it is not being stated as the verb -- it is lodged in a noun made out of a verb. We call such a noun a *nominalization*. Sentence (2a) contains three nominalizations: "reaction," "imposition," and "requirement."

Nominalizations are not bad in and of themselves, but only in the way they are (mis)used. Sentence (a) presents a common problem: Since the verb "would be . . . accorded" does not convince many of us that it is the main action of the sentence, we look elsewhere for that action. We find three nominalizations -- "reaction," "imposition," and "requirement," -- each of which could easily be translated into a verb. We have no clue which of these -- or which combination of these -- might have been the author's intended action. That is why sentences (2c), (2d), (2e), and (2f) are all equally plausible translations of (2a). In general, a nominalization is bad when it usurps the action from the verb. If the action is articulated in a nominalization, then the verb cannot answer the question "What is going on here?" It becomes especially difficult when there are several nominalizations in one sentence that could compete equally for the job of announcing the action.

There are many ways, however, in which a nominalization can be a good thing. It can, for example, be used as a powerful linking device. The action of one sentence (announced as a verb) can be nominalized at the beginning of the next sentence, forging a smooth, logical link. Example:

2g. The Dean <u>required</u> all visitors of the opposite sex to sign in and sign out of any residence hall they were visiting. This <u>requirement</u> incited an immediate reaction from over 700 students, who generated over 70,000 sign-ins and sign-outs in one day in order to bring the new system to its knees.

There are also times when nominalized actions, fuzzy and stuffy as they may sound, might be preferred precisely *because* they weaken the focus on the action. Which of the following seems less harsh, less unfeeling?

3a. Dear Sir: We are firing you because you failed to meet your sales quota, as required by clause IV(b) of your employment contract.

3b. Dear Sir: Discontinuation of your employment contract has become necessary because of noncompliance with clause IV(b).

For many people, the fussier (3b) would be easier to take than the more direct (3a). We hurt more to read that we are "fired" than we do when we read that "discontinuation" has happened to our contract. On the other hand, there are situations in which the more straightforward "We are firing you" will seem cleaner and more honest to a given recipient of the letter. As always with rhetoric, it is essential to know who your readers are and how they will be likely to react.

Nominalizations are also a good way to transform individual actions into general concepts. Twenty-five hundred years ago, anyone could see that all sorts of things *moved*; but it took the philosopher Aristotle to develop the concept of *motion*.

Nominalizations still play major roles in many professional fields -- especially if most of the readers already understand the boundaries of the concepts to which the nominalizations refer. They act as code words. The American colonists who started the Revolutionary War did not always have to say to each other, "We should refuse to pay taxes until we are properly represented in the British Parliament." All they had to say was "Taxation without representation is unlawful." Everyone knew who was being taxed by whom and who was not being represented in Parliament.

···| EXERCISE **E** |···

Here are some well-fashioned sentences by well-regarded writers. Investigate the particular effects created by their choices of main verbs and other verb forms like "-ing" words and infinitives. Then have some fun: Instead of rewriting poor sentences to make them better, rewrite these strong sentences to make them weaker. Do that, in this case, by changing the action verbs into other parts of speech -- especially nominalizations. Note that even the much-attacked verb *to be* can be a strong verb, if its meanings -- existence, equality, or labeling -- happen to be the action at that moment.

This example is a quote from a famous speech by Winston Churchill, the prime minister of Great Britain during World War II. After a disastrous defeat at the Battle of Dunkirk, he lifted the spirits of the British people with his stirring rhetoric. This was one of the speech's high points.

Example: We shall fight on the beaches. We shall fight on the landing grounds. We shall fight in the fields, and in the streets; we shall fight in the hills. We shall never surrender!

(Winston Churchill)

Let us take all the "fighting" and "surrendering" verbs and transform them into nominalizations.

> Fighting shall happen on the beaches. Fighting shall happen on the landing grounds. Fighting shall happen in the fields, and in the streets; fighting shall happen in the hills. Surrender will never happen!

With that kind of rhetoric from their leader, the British might have lost the war.

Here are examples with which you can work:

i) The world will little note nor long remember what we say here. But it will never forget what they did here.

(Abraham Lincoln, dedicating the cemetery at Gettysburg)

ii) I have a dream that one day this nation will rise up and live out the true meaning of its creed: "We hold these truths to be self-evident: that all men are created equal." I have a dream that one day on the red hills of Georgia the sons of former slaves and the sons of former slave-owners will be able to sit down together at a table of brotherhood. I have a dream that one day even the state of Mississippi, a desert state, sweltering with the heat of injustice and oppression, will be transformed into an oasis of freedom and justice. I have a dream that my four children will one day live in a nation where they will not be judged by the color of their skin but by the content of their character. I have a dream today.

(The Rev. Martin Luther King, Jr., at the Lincoln Memorial in 1963)

iii) Over the decades, commercial strips have become the "dirty old men" of the American scene. They are often most criticized and much maligned; yet few writers have actually attempted to describe in detail how they have come to look and function the way they do.

(Larry Ford, "Decades of Design on the American Commercial Strip,"
from *Drive-in Dreams*)

One last question before we move on from verbs and actions: In the following sentence, is the underscored verb strong or weak under our verb/action definition of those terms? (See page 19.)

4. Jack <u>articulated</u> his love for Jill.

If you voted for weak, you are wrong. If you voted for strong, you are wrong. We cannot effectively judge whether the verb is weak or strong because we are presented with no surrounding context: Although "articulated" is surrounded by the rest of the sentence, the sentence itself lacks a greater context. As a result, we do not know what the sentence as a whole is trying to say. For example, consider Context #1 -- an 800-page novel about Jack. Jack is a fine fellow -- a top student, a crack athlete, the president of the student government, and an altogether nice guy. His problem is that he has never experienced any really deep emotions. He meets Jill on page 46. After 700+ pages of tempestuous relationship, on page 752 Jack suddenly feels overwhelmed by a inner sensation he had not yet experienced in life -- a new and unexpected emotion for him. The next sentence reads, "Jack articulated his love for Jill." "Articulated" is a weak verb, since we do not care at the moment about his *saying* anything. The appropriate verb/action might have something to do with feeling or loving or being capable of emotion.

Compare with that Context #2 -- a different 800-page novel about a different Jack. This fellow has felt things deeply since the cradle; his problem is his inability to communicate those feelings to other people. He meets his Jill on page 39. Over 700 tempestuous pages later, on page 749 he finally splutters, "Jill, -- I -- LOVE -- YOU." "Jack articulated his love for Jill": "Articulated" is a strong verb, since the concept of expressing himself through articulation is intended to be the main action of the sentence.

The Sentence: Whose Story Is This Anyway?

Let us continue with the passionate story of Jack and Jill, which will eventually, I promise, extend to sentences of more than three or five words. Consider this pair of statements:

5a. Jack loves Jill.
5b. Jill is loved by Jack.

Which of the following statements are true of (5a) and (5b)?

i) The two sentences say completely different things.
ii) The two sentences are identical in meaning.
iii) The two sentences are different ways of saying the same thing.
iv) The differences between the two sentences are so slight as not to warrant attention being paid to them.
v) None of the above.

The answer to this little quiz is (v), "None of the above." Sentences (5a) and (5b) cannot be saying "completely different things" since they both deal with the same two persons and the same interaction. But, less obviously, the two sentences cannot be *identical* in meaning because the difference in their word order varies *the order* in which the information and therefore the ideas are presented to the reader. Word order, placement, and structure all send important signals to readers concerning the relative emphasis and focus the reader should allow to each word. Even those who would argue the two sentences are "essentially" the same would not make the same claim for the following series of sentences that benefit from the luxury of the artificial emphasis of italics:

5c. *Jack* loves Jill.

5d. *Jill* is loved by Jack.

The italics send instructions to the reader how to weigh and balance the words in the sentence to achieve the proportions, dynamics, or colors the author intended. That seems evident. What is not nearly so well known is the important fact that the *structure* and *order* of words in a sentence send reading instructions of even greater importance.

Let us return to our initial two sentences and ask a different question:

5a. Jack loves Jill.

5b. Jill is loved by Jack.

Question: Whose story is each of these sentences? From whose perspective does each sentence view the scene? A great majority of readers -- not all -- will agree that (5a) is the story of Jack and (5b) the story of Jill. This leads us to the next statement of reader expectation:

Readers of English expect that a clause will tell the story of whoever or whatever shows up first.

This makes more apparent sense if you reread the sentence in ultra-slow motion. The reading mind is constantly trying to synthesize words and concepts *as they arrive*. The order of that arrival therefore will significantly affect that act of synthesis. Here is a possible mental narrative for the slow-motion experience for sentence (5a):

Jack . . .   [Well, what about Jack?]

loves . . .   [Oh, so that's what Jack does.]

Jill . . .   [So Jill is the object of all that affection.]

Compare that to the same process unfolding for sentence (5b):

Jill . . .   [Well, what about Jill?]

is loved . . . [Oh, so that's what's happening to Jill.]

by Jack . . . [So Jack is the producer of all that affection.]

When a sentence is as short as this one, the word order may not seem to make enough difference to justify such careful consideration. But as soon as the sentence begins to grow in length and complexity, the difference between Jack-centeredness and Jill-centeredness makes an increasingly greater impact on the reader's interpretive attention. Note how much time and what sense of weight we devote to each of these people in the following pair of sentences:

5e. Jack, after three years of uncertainty, after the engaging and disengaging, after their working through the difficulties caused by the death of her father and the divorce of his parents, finally and conclusively began to love Jill with all his heart.

5f. Jill, after three years of uncertainty, after the engaging and disengaging, after their working through the difficulties caused by the death of her father and the divorce of his parents, finally and conclusively began to be loved by Jack with all his heart.

Both these sentences are reasonable, and both cover the same facts; but since they tell the story from two different perspectives, they really tell two distinctly different stories. Those two stories are "distinctly different" but not "completely different."

This "whose story" principle is important for any given sentence, but of yet far more importance when experienced sentence after sentence after sentence. If a writer wishes to tell a single, continuous story, the continual placement of the "whose story" person at the beginning of sentences will do much to keep the reader's attention organized and riveted. When a change finally does occur in the "whose story" position, the reader will make that switch in focus quite naturally and smoothly.

Jack. . . .

Jack. . . .

Jack. . . .

Jill. . . .

Because this fourth sentence begins with Jill, it suggests to us (without having to say it explicitly), "And now let us turn our attention to Jill."

You may have heard the advice that you should vary the way you begin your sentences to keep your reader interested. That was fine advice in the sixth grade, when you were composing single-clause sentences of only eight, ten, or twelve words in length. Once you begin to form longer and more complex structures, you should keep "whose story" it is up front for as long as that story continues. Your reader will benefit from the orderliness and sense of development that results.

To demonstrate this, here is a longer story about our Jill. In paragraph (5g) it is told with Jill continually in the "whose story" position up front.

5g. Jill found herself intrigued at first by Jack's reticence. She had never met anyone before who seemed to combine such a confident understanding of situations with such an unwillingness -- or perhaps inability -- to step forward and assert himself. She recognized in him some of what she had long felt and had long considered mystifying about her own makeup. She was further intrigued, then, when she noticed Jack constantly putting himself in a position to make the first move toward engaging her in real discussion -- despite his continual reluctance to carry through on that initial effort. She tried to moderate the forbidding aspect she had nurtured over the past two or three years, taking care to avoid seeming to capitulate or to invite. She watched and waited, but not without a growing sense of anxiety, mixed with impatience.

Paragraph (5h) below repeats all the same information, sentence by sentence, but changes the occupant of the "whose story" position on a regular basis. See for yourself if those structural changes destroy the continuity of the kind of forward-leaning narration expressed in (5g).

5h.   Intrigue was the word to describe Jill's first response to Jack's reticence. The combination of such confidence in understanding situations and such unwillingness -- or perhaps inability -- to step forward and be assertive was completely new to her. Her own makeup she recognized was similar and had long mystified her. The constant effort he made to put himself in a position to make the first move toward engaging her in real discussion further intrigued her, despite his continual reluctance to carry through on that initial effort. Over the past two or three years, the nurturing of a forbidding aspect had received much of her attention; moderation of that aspect was now necessary, without implying a sense of capitulation or invitation. Anxiety mixed with impatience increased in her as she watched and waited.

Paragraph (5h) might have been even harder to read had you not read paragraph (5g) just before it. Most of the sentences in (5h) seem to be well enough crafted *as individual sentences*; but the journey from sentence to sentence is a good deal harder than in paragraph (5g). This problem should be taken care of not after finishing the draft of the paragraph but rather in the constructing of each individual sentence. Keeping "whose story" it is up front, where the reader expects it to be, will keep your story focused in the way you want it to be.

A note of complication: I have mentioned in passing that the "whose story" consideration affects clauses, not sentences. (See the boldfaced statement on page 26.) Readers read individual clauses as being the story of whoever shows up first. If a sentence contains only one clause, then whoever or whatever shows up first answers the question "Whose story is this sentence?" What happens, however, when a sentence contains two clauses, each with a different "whose story" up front? Whose story, then, is that sentence as a whole?

5i. Although Jack never said he loved her, Jill could see it in his actions.

5j. Although Jill could tell from his actions that he loved her, Jack never managed to say it in words.

5k. Jack never said he loved her, but Jill could see it in his actions.

In each of these sentences, one clause tells Jack's story and the other clause tells Jill's. Whose story is each sentence as a whole? In processing a whole sentence, most readers will hear the main story as being that of whoever shows up first in the *main* clause. The other clause -- a qualifying clause -- will merely qualify that main story. (By "qualifying clause" I mean the clauses here that have the "although" or the "but." The main clause says something straightforwardly; the qualifying clause qualifies that statement.) The answer to the sentence-level "whose story" question then is agreed to by a large majority of readers:

> **A multiclause sentence tells the story of whoever or whatever shows up first in the sentence's main clause.**

The examples from above show this more simply than this explanation can state it:

(M) indicates main clause.

(Q) indicates qualifying clause.

<u>Underlining</u> indicates whose story is told by the sentence as a whole.

5i. (Q): Although Jack never said . . . (M): <u>Jill</u> could see

5j. (Q): Although Jill could tell . . . (M): <u>Jack</u> never managed

5k. (M): <u>Jack</u> never said . . . (Q): although Jill could see

Note: I am using the term *main clause* a bit differently from most books that deal with grammar. It is possible to have two clauses in a sentence that most books would refer to as *main*, if (1) they are connected by a word like *and* or *but*, and (2) the two clauses, without the connecter, can both stand as complete sentences.

-- Jack never said he loved her.

-- Jill could see it in his actions.

For the purposes of this book, if that connecting word serves the purpose of *qualifying*, then the clause that follows is referred to as a *qualifying clause*. That would be true of the word *but*, since it makes the next clause qualify the one that preceded it. It is not true of the word *and*, which merely connects the two clauses without making clear how one might qualify the other.

·· EXERCISE F   ··

i. All the sentences in this sample paragraph have only one clause. First, note "whose story" each sentence seems to be by locating its grammatical subject. With just those "whose story" answers in mind, how does the story of the paragraph as a whole seem to develop?

Then, rewrite each sentence to transport different persons, things, or ideas up front to the "whose story" position. Then note how these rewrites make the paragraph as a whole a different (probably harder) reading experience. What has happened to the flow of the paragraph as a result?

> But in the 1970s a few scientists in the United States and Europe began to find a way through disorder. They were mathematicians, physicists, biologists, chemists, all seeking connections between different kinds of irregularity. Physiologists found a surprising order in the chaos that develops in the human heart, the prime cause of sudden, unexplained death. Ecologists explored the rise and fall of gypsy moth populations. Economists dug out old stock price data and tried a new kind of analysis. The insight that emerged led directly into the natural world -- the shapes of clouds, the paths of lightning, the microscopic intertwining of blood vessels, the galactic clustering of stars.
>
> (James Gleick, *Chaos: Making a New Science*)

ii. For the following examples, make two kinds of changes to alter "whose story" the sentence is telling: (1) Switch the positions of clauses; and/or (2) make main clauses into qualifying clauses, and vice versa. How do the sentences "mean" differently as a result of these changes?

Examples:

1) Although the Democrats spent millions more during the campaign, <u>the Republicans</u> eventually won.

   (Whose story? The Republicans. Main emphasis? The Republicans.)

2) <u>The Democrats</u> spent millions more during the campaign, although the Republicans eventually won.

   (Whose story? The Democrats. Main emphasis? Split between the two.)

3) <u>The Republicans</u> eventually won, although the Democrats spent millions more during the campaign.

   (Whose story? The Republicans. Main emphasis? Split between the two.)

4) Although the Republicans eventually won, <u>the Democrats</u> spent millions more during the campaign.

   (Whose story? The Democrats. Main emphasis? The Democrats.)

a) Even though Chris had made every conceivable effort, Pat still said no.

b) Although he was often late for work, he always did a thorough job.

c) Although Fred mistreats his dog, he is otherwise a nice guy.

The Sentence: What Are You Waiting For?

Let me relieve you of some of the guilt you may suffer now and then as a reader. We all have these problems. In struggling to comprehend a particularly challenging sentence, we sometimes find ourselves suddenly shocked by the appearance of the period. It's over, and we're still wondering what's going on. When this happens, we tend to feel bad about ourselves. We are glad our friends and colleagues are not inside our head, because they think we are *smart*. They do not know how many times we finish a sentence and then have to reread it because nothing registered. Sometimes when we reread that same sentence, we once again comprehend little or nothing -- and then we feel *really* bad. Well, when this happens to you, stop feeling so guilty. More often than not, when you have comprehended nothing after a real effort, the fault lies not in you but in the writer. All the right *words* were on the page; but they were not displayed in an *order* that allowed you to make immediate sense of them. The sentence may not have looked like example (1a) above on page 17 (where the words were "ordered," but only alphabetically by part of speech); but it presents the same problem. The structure failed to send adequate interpretive instructions to the reader at the moments when those instructions were most needed.

Sometimes when this noncomprehension happens, the cause is one particular structural problem -- so common in prose of the professional world that it warrants our noting the reader expectation that it violates. Here is a relatively mild example of the problem, borrowed from example (5h) above:

6a. The combination of such confidence in understanding situations and such unwillingness -- or perhaps inability -- to step forward and be assertive was completely new to her.

A reader critical of this sentence might complain that it is too long. Actually, its 25-word length places it dead center at the average length of published sentences. As I suggested above, lengthiness has little or nothing to do with the number of words in a given sentence.

But this sentence does indeed *feel* long. Where does that never-arriving feeling come from? It comes from the violation of our next reader expectation:

> **Readers of English expect that the arrival of the grammatical subject will be followed almost immediately by the arrival of the verb.**

As a result of the subject-verb-complement order of English sentences (S-V-C hereafter), readers have come to expect that when they encounter a grammatical subject, they will almost immediately be handed the verb that completes the S-V core unit. Until the verb arrives, we do not know how to conceive of the subject. Conversely, if by the time the verb arrives the subject has been forgotten, then the verb will fail to make complete sense. The two parts of speech, subject and verb, rely on each other's presence. For the reader, therefore, waiting for the verb to appear is like waiting for the second shoe to drop; eventually that sense of waiting commands all available attention.

Therefore, any information that intervenes between a subject and its verb tends to be read by readers as an interruption, as less important information, as parenthetical. Because we are waiting for the verb to arrive, we tend to read the interruptive material at a lower decibel level and at a faster pace. That by itself can be a problem; but it becomes a major problem when the information that lives in the interruptive location with the "less important" sign on it actually turns out to be the most important information, the stuff that the writer wanted the reader most to emphasize. When that is the case, the reader has been *mis*instructed -- has been told to pass quickly over the very thing that should have most engaged the reader's attention. No wonder most readers feel that this sentence is too long; no wonder, at the sentence's end, most readers feel frustrated by having missed the point.

Look again at example (6a), this time with the subject and its verb underscored:

6a. <u>The combination</u> of such confidence in understanding situations and such unwillingness -- or perhaps inability -- to step forward and be assertive <u>was</u> completely new to her.

Getting subject and verb together at the beginning of the sentence would make life significantly easier and clearer for the reader -- even if they reverse positions:

6b. Completely new to her <u>was the combination</u> of such confidence in understanding situations and such unwillingness -- or perhaps inability -- to step forward and be assertive.

If that opening phrase does not present the author's answer to the question "whose story is it?", then the grammatical subject can be changed to reflect the author's intentions. For our purposes, let us assume the sentence is meant to be *her* story. If the verb *was* fails to state the action of that sentence, we can choose a verb that does. We need to get *her* up front and make the verb say what is going on. The result might be a sentence just like the one in the original (5g):

6c. She had never met anyone before who seemed to combine such a confident understanding of situations with such an unwillingness -- or perhaps inability -- to step forward and assert himself.

Once again, though, we have to be careful not to make a rule that a writer must never separate the subject from its verb, because every reader expectation can be violated to good effect. It turns out that our best stylists are often our most skillful violators; but in order to violate expectations effectively, you have to fulfill them most of the time, so that the violation appears an unusual circumstance, worthy of special note. Here is another look at example (5e) from above, this time with our attention focused on the separation of the subject from the verb:

6d. <u>Jack,</u> after three years of uncertainty, after the engaging and disengaging, after their working through the difficulties caused by the death of her father and the divorce of his parents, finally and conclusively <u>loved</u> Jill with all his heart.

Why does this work well? How does it differ from the more annoying examples of S-V separation? It works, I would argue, because this sentence is all about *waiting*, all about the continual postponement on Jack's part of his willingness to engage emotionally. When the verb finally arrives, we feel like we have ourselves experienced both the sense of Jack's emotional procrastination and the extraordinary force of the arrival of long-awaited love. Any reader expectation can be violated to good effect.

·· EXERCISE G

Rewrite the following sentences to undo the subject-verb separations. Beyond the question of better or worse, what kinds of distinctions in meaning can you make between the originals and your rewrites? For your amazement and entertainment, I offer you some gems from the world of legal and scientific writing. These are real sentences written by real people. I have not doctored them for our present purposes. While some are easier to rewrite than others, all can be made significantly more readable, even if you are not familiar with a good many of the words or concepts used. Pay special attention to example (iv). What additional lesson does it teach us about writing *habits*?

i) The trial court's conclusion that the defendants made full disclosure of all relevant information bearing on the value of Knaebel's stock is clearly erroneous.

ii) All of the proposed work, with the exception of the cross-species look at females of teratospermic species that seems a unique feature of the lack of zona pellucida specificity for sperm binding in the field family, is repetition in the cat of studies in other species preservation.

iii) Significant variations in the process for the initial review of some major grant mechanisms, such as research project grants, First Independent Research Support and Transition (FIRST) Awards, program project grants, Academic Research Enhancement Awards, Small Business Innovation Research grants, National Research Service Awards, Support of Scientific Meetings, and Research Career Development Awards are described in subsequent sections.

iv) First, the mechanisms of development and tissue specific control of the gonadotropin genes in pituitary cells, including the roles of both transcriptional activation and restriction in directing unique patterns of gene expression, will be assessed. Second, the molecular basis of hormonal regulation of gonadotropin gene expression, with emphasis on induction of gene expression by hypothalamic gonadotropin-releasing hormone (GnRH) and repression by gonadal steroids will be determined. Finally, the molecular events determining the developmental lineage of the gonadotrope in the anterior pituitary, utilizing approaches in transgenic mice including targeted immortalization, cell ablation, and ectopic expression of regulatory proteins, will be investigated.

v) The technique for obtaining adequate ultrasonic traces from the posterior left ventricular wall and interventricular septum and the subsequent ventricular volume estimation has been described elsewhere.

vi) Should the "Jobs, Science and Technology Bond Act of 1984" which authorizes the State to issue bonds in the amount of $90,000,000.00 for the purpose of creating jobs by the establishment of a network of advanced technology centers at the State's public and private institutions of higher education and for the construction and improvement of technical and engineering related facilities and equipment as well as job training and retraining programs in high technology fields at these institutions; and in a principal amount sufficient to refinance all or any such bonds if the same will result in a present value savings; providing the ways and means to pay that interest of such debt and also to pay and discharge the principal thereof, be approved?

(From the "State Public Questions" of New Jersey's 1984 General Elections ballot)

If you have done these exercises, you might have fallen back into the belief that these are "bad" sentences that you, through intense concentration and much labor, have now made "better." Remember: No sentence can be judged entirely good or bad outside of its context. Part of that concept of context includes the knowledge and experience of the particular reader. Take exercise example (5) above as an example. A reader deeply knowledgeable about and currently involved with this information might have no problem with it whatsoever. That is, if that reader had just been reading about "the technique for obtaining adequate ultrasonic traces from the posterior left ventricular wall and interventricular septum and the subsequent ventricular volume estimation," that whole difficult phrase might appear to them as simple and recognizable as a single word. Let us call that phrase X. Sentence (5) would then become, "X has been described elsewhere." Piece of cake. No problem.

The Sentence: Save the Best for Last

As demonstrated by the last Jack and Jill example, a long wait can occasionally be a good thing. A short wait, on the other hand, is quite often a good thing. We like to save the best for last. We like to reward ourselves at the end of journeys. Once we have traveled most of the way, we wish to arrive. How many of us begin a meal with the strawberry shortcake and delight in working our way up to the broccoli? Only those of us for whom broccoli is just like dessert.

All of this leads us to our next reader expectation. Readers of English, in general, tend to read with more emphasis whatever is located in a sentence's Stress position. I will offer a fuller definition of Stress position below; but for the moment let us oversimplify and think of it simply as the end of the sentence.

About half a century ago, Bell Labs, the telephone people, did a good deal of research on memory. They demonstrated to many people's satisfaction that (1) one remembers best the ends of things, (2) one remembers next best the beginnings of things, and (3) one remembers not nearly as well that which came in the middle. This seems to hold for readers of English sentences. If readers remember best that which comes at the end, it makes good sense to reserve for the end that which you wish your reader best to remember. Put more simply, it is wise to place the information you wish your reader to stress in the Stress position.

There are additional, perhaps more important reasons. One has to do with the kind of mental energy a reader uses in order to read a sentence. We take a mental breath at the beginning of each sentence, summoning enough mental energy for the job of reading and interpreting the sentence that is about to unfold before us. As we approach the sentence's end, we need to exhale whatever we have remaining of that mental breath; we will be needing to take in a whole, fresh new breath for the new sentence that will be starting soon. There is no holdover effect: One sentence cannot use another's leftover energy. That exhalation at the end of the sentence produces a sense of emphasis; that is what makes a Stress position.

If this mental energy image does not work for you, here is another and perhaps better way to think about the matter. In our Western culture, we have a pressing need and desire -- almost a compulsion -- for closure. It is so deep in our bone marrow that we hardly notice its existence. Perhaps one of the following examples will strike a chord with you.

-- In high school, how did you know when you had finally *finished* a multipage writing assignment? For me, that moment of arrival was always signified by the crunch of the stapler. Once those pages were bound together by metal, I was a free person again. No paper clips for me. I wanted to hear and feel that crunch. It said, "Done."

-- Are you one of those hamburger eaters who silently calculates, about halfway through, how many french fries are left per bite of remaining burger in order for it all to come out even at the end? If you are, have

you ever felt a minor kind of rage when, as you reached for the carefully calculated final french fry, your companion (in an act of true generosity) says, "You can have the rest of mine" and dumps an extra
eleven on your plate? Or what would it feel like if, after all your careful conservation of french fries, somebody whisked the last one off
your plate just as you were about to reach for it?

-- "'Twas the night before Christmas, / and all through the house, / Not
a creature was stirring, / not even a. . . ."

That's all. I'm not going to give you any more. Is it possible for you to
resist leaning forward into the void and producing your very own mouse?
(Were you now somewhat relieved when the word *mouse* finally appeared,
even if a bit tardily?)

-- Can you imagine sitting through your favorite murder mystery film for
the third time and walking out of the theater just before the murderer
is identified? Or coming to the end of a 600-page novel and closing the
book in the middle of the last paragraph?

If you try to think of other examples culled from your own particular
likes and needs, you may well find a great many. We are committed to closure in our society. We crave it. We insist on it. That is not the case in all societies. Philosophies and religions from China, Japan, and India counsel
people to maintain a constant sense of balance or equilibrium. We, in contrast, are taught to set goals, large and small, and then are urged to strive
to achieve them. We check things off on lists; we paint new, increasingly
higher levels of red on publicly displayed giant cardboard thermometers
to demonstrate how near the United Way is coming to achieving its goal;
and millions of us count backward from ten to one just before midnight on
December 31 as we stare intently at a large ball on a TV screen to be sure
not to miss the precise moment the old year will end. We are committed,
perhaps addicted, to arrival, goal, achievement, end, closure.

This functions for us as readers, sentence after sentence. The expectation of a sentence's closure produces just enough sense of arrival and
fruition to create a heightened state of emphasis; it also creates a structural location called the *Stress position*.

> We "think" in a crescendo because it parallels certain psychic and physical
> processes which are at the roots of our experience. The accelerated motion of
> a falling body, the cycle of a storm, the procedure of the sexual act, the ripen-
> ing of crops -- growth here is not merely a linear procession, but a fruition.
>
> (Kenneth Burke, speaking about Western culture)

How far back from the end of a sentence does the Stress position begin? That varies. In some sentences, the Stress position may be only one
word long; in others it can be three or five or eleven; on occasion; it can even
extend to a few lines. Its beginning point is determined by when the reader feels certain that what is now being read is all that remains to be read.

In other words, the Stress position is produced by the act of the sentence running downhill toward its resting place.

In still other words, it is produced by the grammatical structure of a sentence (its *syntax*) finally reaching its resolution. To put it concisely, a Stress position is any moment of full syntactic closure. Full syntactic closure happens in English at any properly used period, colon, or semi-colon. Every moment of full syntactic closure is a Stress position.

A Stress position can never be created by a comma. Unlike all the other marks of punctuation in English, the comma never fully announces its function at the moment of its arrival. We always have to read beyond a comma to find out what *kind* of comma it was trying to be. Note how many different comma uses follow "Sam" here:

-- Sam, the only person who could be . . .

-- Sam, Chris, and Pat . . .

-- Sam, however, . . .

-- Sam, but not Pat or Chris, . . .

-- Sam, it was hard to believe, did not . . .

In each case, we have to read beyond the comma to discover what its function was meant to be. No possibility of closure? No Stress position.

This reader expectation comes with its own corollary:

Readers of English expect that the material most to be emphasized in the sentence will appear at a moment of full syntactic closure, called a Stress position.

and

Readers of English expect that every Stress position will be filled with material intended to receive significant emphasis.

Because *full syntactic closure* is the important element, a sentence may have more than one Stress position if it employs a properly used semi-colon or colon. Both of those punctuation marks require that the clause preceding the mark be capable of standing by itself as a full sentence. Thus there is full syntactic closure both at the period and at the semi-colon or colon. (Suggestion: If you are not as comfortable with the colon and the semi-colon as you are with the comma and the period, now might be a good time to read the sections on the colon and the semi-colon in Part II, pages 171–179 and 161–167)

All of that abstract talk makes a good deal more sense when we begin to look at actual sentences. Let us return to the beginning.

5a. Jack loves Jill.

To the question "Whose story is this?" we can answer "Jack." He appears up front and therefore acts as context for all that follows.

To the question "What is going on here?" we can answer "love." We look to the verb to find the action; this verb fits the bill.

To the question "What is most to be emphasized in this sentence?" we can answer "the fact that Jill is the object of his affection." She appears in the Stress position and is the recipient of the natural emphasis afforded by the syntax's final resolution.

If you know Jill is loved but not by whom, then sentence (5a) is not as effective as (5b), "Jill is loved by Jack." The new information occupies the Stress position.

In such a short and simple sentence, these distinctions may seem arbitrary or unnecessary. With so little to occupy the reader's attention, it is unlikely that much confusion will arise. (Recall, though, that any sentence can be strengthened or weakened by the context in which it appears. We could make this three-word sentence a triumph or a disaster if we wished to do so.) But as information becomes more complex, as ideas begin to intertwine, as length begins to increase, these structural clues become more and more essential to the reader who wishes to understand exactly what the writer meant to communicate.

Let us now complicate the matter just a bit:

7a. Jack has fallen in love with Jill because she completely understands his passion for raising fox terriers.

7b. Because she completely understands his passion for raising fox terriers, Jack has fallen in love with Jill.

The information is the same in both sentences; however, the balance of emphasis has shifted because the occupant of the Stress position has changed. In (7a) -- for most but not all readers -- the emphasis is not as much on Jill as it is on the passion for raising fox terriers. In (7b) -- for most but not all readers -- the terriers play a supporting role to Jill; because Jill understands Jack, Jill winds up the prime recipient of his affections.

Once again, these are tools, not rules. The interpretations I have offered for examples (7a) and (7b) are not the only possible readings but rather the ones most likely to occur to a great majority of readers. Other interpretations, though perhaps not as probable, are still possible. Sentence (7b), for example, could be read with the following sense of emphasis:

7b. Because she completely understands his passion <u>for raising fox terriers</u>, Jack has fallen in love with Jill.

This possible reading, however, is not the most probable one, because nothing in the sentence specifically sends us a signal to stress the raising of the terriers. In fact, the structural forces all persuade us away from such a decision. When we encounter the terriers, we know we are reaching the end of the "because" clause; we are ready to lean across that comma to begin giving our primary attention to the main clause. The passion for the terriers is apparently a given; the passion for Jill is the new news.

It is difficult to explain the power of the Stress position by the use of a single sentence example. The most powerful attribute of the Stress position is the great gift it offers to both readers and writers -- when it is consistently well used. When Stress position after Stress position is filled with the most stressworthy material, then readers can trust that they are following where the writer intended to lead. This proves to be the case even when the sentence structures remain relatively simple.

Here is a paragraph from Lars Eighner's *Travels with Lizbeth*, in which he discusses the potential dangers of encountering botulism if you regularly make your meals on discarded food reclaimed from dumpsters. Note the natural ease of the motion toward the Stress position. Note also how the contents of the Stress positions are allowed to absorb importance without crying out for attention. It is all very natural.

8a. Although very rare with modern canning methods, botulism is a possibility. Most other forms of food poisoning seldom do lasting harm to a healthy person. But botulism is almost certainly fatal, and often the first symptom is death. Except for carbonated beverages, all canned goods should contain a slight vacuum and suck air when first punctured. Bulging, rusty, dented cans, and cans that spew when punctured should be avoided, especially when the contents are not very acidic or syrupy.

Again I want to emphasize that there are no rights and wrongs about what should go into the Stress position. Eighner could have made any number of other, equally correct or even equally powerful decisions; the result would be prose not necessarily better or worse, but just different. If we dewrite his paragraph by changing the occupants of the Stress positions, we get a piece of prose related to the original but producing different effects. (*Dewriting* is a term I use for the reformation of a text that keeps all the original material but changes some of its locations.)

8b. One possibility is botulism, although very rare with modern canning methods. A healthy person rarely suffers lasting harm from most other forms of food poisoning. But death is often the first symptom of botulism, which is almost certainly fatal. All canned goods should contain a slight vacuum and suck air when first punctured, except for carbonated beverages. Especially when the contents are not very acidic or syrupy, bulging, rusty, dented cans and cans that spew when punctured should be avoided.

The individual sentences here *sound* no worse (and no better) than the originals; but we start to perceive that the flow of thought -- both within the sentence and from sentence to sentence -- has been impeded. We cannot depend on the ear to inform us whether a sentence is doing its job or not. We have to rely on the mind. We also need a set of helpful questions -- structural questions -- that we can use in order to judge how a reader will be likely to perceive what we have written.

As sentences become increasingly complex, the occupancy of the Stress position becomes increasingly more important. If there are many potential candidates for emphasis in a single sentence, location in the Stress position is the simplest, subtlest, and most convincing method of signaling a reader which is the MVP (most valuable piece-of-information). Note the occupants of the Stress positions in the following paragraph:

9. If we consider democracy not just as a political system, but as a set of institutions which do aim to make everything available to everybody, it would not be an overstatement to describe advertising as the characteristic rhetoric of democracy. One of the tendencies of democracy, which Plato and other antidemocrats warned against a long time ago, was the danger that rhetoric would displace or at least overshadow epistemology; that is the temptation to allow the problem of persuasion to overshadow the problem of knowledge. Democratic societies tend to become more concerned with what people believe than with what is true, to become more concerned with credibility than with truth. All these problems become accentuated in a large-scale democracy like ours, which possesses all the apparatus of modern industry. And the problems are accentuated still further by universal literacy, by instantaneous communication, and by the daily plague of words and images.

    (Daniel Boorstin, "The Rhetoric of Democracy")

The longer sentences get, more difficult it is for the reader to identify what is of primary importance. If that important material is constantly located somewhere other than the Stress position, two things happen to the reader -- and both of them are bad:

1) The reader arrives at the Stress position only to find something that is old news or clearly unimportant. At that moment, the reader knows he or she has already passed by the important part of the sentence without having given it the reading emphasis it deserved. The reader then either has to go back to rectify the situation or has to continue forward without the knowledge that should have been gained. All too often the reader tries to do both at once. It is, I suggest, that very going-backward-and-going-forward effort that produces that all-too-familiar cloudy, marshmallowy sense of noncomprehension with which our mind is left at the end of reading a badly written sentence.

2) Even worse, the reader arrives at the Stress position only to find something that could conceivably be stressed as the most important element

of the sentence; but, unfortunately, it is not the particular bit the writer wished us to emphasize. In that case, the chances increase dramatically that the reader will stress the information in the Stress position and therefore depart from the sentence with the wrong idea. A wrong interpretation may be worse than no interpretation at all -- especially when the reader has no clue of having missed the boat.

As soon as there is more than one thing/person/concept in a sentence, the Stress position assumes a subtly powerful role. That is true even for sentences that seem relatively uncomplicated. For example, let us say you have written the following:

10a. I hope that you will arrive on time and with all the appropriate information.

This sentence will function well if your primary concern is that they should bring "all the appropriate information"; but it will not do nearly as well if your primary concern is that they *"arrive on time."* If that was your intent, best to get the timeliness of the arrival into the Stress position:

10b. I hope that you will arrive with all the appropriate information and on time."

Once again, you can only judge a sentence *in context*.

A sentence fails to live up to its promise if it is completely devoid of stressworthy information. No matter how many words such a sentence may have, it is too short to be a sentence. It will mislead readers in either of two ways: (1) A reader might feel unfulfilled or annoyed to have read a whole sentence without having been given anything new. If this happens too often, that reader will tend to lose respect for the writer. It's all downhill from there. (2) A reader might be persuaded by the power of closure that the occupant of the Stress position was indeed to be emphasized. That reader will come away from the sentence on the wrong track, having just taken as important something that was of no importance whatever. A sentence is "too short" when it has no viable candidate for the Stress position.

I cannot offer you, by itself, an example of a sentence that is too short because of its lack of a worthy occupant of the Stress position. Perhaps by now you can supply the reason for that: Such a sentence would be read out of context; and context controls meaning. *Any* sentence could be put in a context in which it turns out to contain nothing stressworthy. The same sentence, transferred to a different context, might shine with importance. Consider these two sentences, which are the first two of a much longer paragraph:

#a. The period from 1767 through 1775 proved to be crucial in the process of transforming the American colonies into the United States of America. Prominent amongst the statesmen who would play large roles later on were John Adams, James Madison, and Thomas Jefferson.

Is that second sentence "too short"? It depends on what follows it. If these three names need to be remembered because they will assume great importance in the rest of the paragraph and beyond, then they are well worthy of a Stress position. Their presence there tells us to expect we will hear a great deal more about them, soon.

#b. The period from 1767 through 1775 proved to be crucial in the process of transforming the American colonies into the United States of America. Prominent amongst the statesmen who would play large roles later on were John Adams, James Madison, and Thomas Jefferson. Between them, Adams, Madison, and Jefferson were to alter the course of history in ways that. . . .

But if, on the other hand, this paragraph, and the ones which follow it, never again mention these three patriots but instead concentrate on the political and economic forces that shaped the Revolution, then nothing in this patriot-naming sentence is worthy of a Stress position. If the naming of these names is helpful, but not critical, then they should be transferred to some other sentence and located elsewhere than in a Stress position.

#c. The period from 1767 through 1775 proved to be crucial in the process of transforming the American colonies into the United States of America. Prominent men, amongst them John Adams, James Madison, and Thomas Jefferson, produced philosophical and political writings that were to change the focus of Colonial thinking dramatically. Such an influence would have been impossible without the presence of local printers and book sellers. The printers in Boston around 1767 were. . . .

In the (c) version above, it would have been misleading to highlight Adams and friends by giving them a Stress position. Any sentence that did that -- and only that -- would have to be considered "too short."

Sentences can be too empty; but they can also be too full. We cannot judge when one of our own sentences is "too long" by counting its words. Without much difficulty we can produce examples of ten-word sentences that are impenetrable; we can also create 100-word sentences that are models of clarity and power. That feeling of excessive length can better be measured in terms of how well the structure of a sentence prepares the reader to deal with its length -- whatever that length may be. I would urge you to disregard the all-too-common advice that "A sentence is too long when it exceeds 29 words." Here are two new definitions that function more pragmatically than can any arbitrary word-limit:

-- A sentence is too long when it has more viable candidates for Stress positions than is has Stress positions.

-- A sentence is too short when it no viable candidate for the Stress position.

You can use the reader expectations concerning Stress positions in two complementary ways:

1) Make sure (most of the time -- No rules! No rules!) that everything worthy of special emphasis is located in a Stress position; and

2) Make sure (most of the time) that every Stress position is filled with something that is stressworthy.

These tools can be used in reverse when the situation calls for it. There exist conditions under which you should *not* put important information in the Stress position. One example: If the stressworthy information by itself is obviously important and is likely to cause pain to the reader, that pain can be undercut by keeping that information *out* of the Stress position. We do not like to read "Dear Sir: You are fired." The insult compounds the injury.

The most important use of the Stress position -- its ability to make the reader expect how to lean forward into the next sentence -- will be discussed in some detail in Chapter 3. Skillful control over your Stress positions will help you make individual sentences better, clearer, and more forceful; but it will also give you far greater control over how your readers will most likely connect your sentences one to another.

·· EXERCISE H

i) Rewrite the following sentences at least twice each to locate different pieces of information in the Stress position. How do these structural changes alter the ways in which the sentences can have meaning? (All these sentences are taken from Robin Lakoff's article "We First"; but occasional marks of punctuation have been altered for our purposes. If a sentence seems ungainly, it is probably the fault of the alteration, not of Ms. Lakoff's original prose, which is of high quality at all times.)

    a) People create categories in order to understand both the physical universe outside themselves and the meaning of being human, belonging to a group.

    b) Our belief that the category expressed by the word "tree" deserves to exist gives that concept meaning and form, whereas the physical and visible existence of maples and oaks gives them reality.

    c) Categorization is the basis of science, crucial to human understanding and the growth of our intellect and to our power as a species over the physical universe.

ii) Rewrite each of the following by changing the number of Stress positions to accommodate a total of at least two stressworthy items. (Remember: Stress positions can be created by the proper use of the colon, the semi-colon, and the period.) How do these structural changes alter the ways in which these sentences can have meaning?

a) The making of categories is a creative and synthesizing act that allows us to give meaning to our world and definition to the things within it -- but is always, to some degree, arbitrary and culturally grounded.

b) The existence in our language of superordinate categories permits us to generalize, to talk about what "trees" are like as well as what "this maple" is like, and thus to understand the universe parsimoniously, with the least amount of effort -- and to create abstractions.

(Note: "Superordinate," the opposite of "subordinate," denotes a general class under which a set of subcategories may be included. "Parsimoniously" means "frugally" or "extremely economically.")

Perhaps the language would be easier to read if in order to indicate the various functions of various words we used a color-coding device. Whose story is it? Print that in green. What's going on? Print it in brown. What is the piece of information most to be emphasized? Print it in red. But we do not do this. Instead, we use structural locations to indicate the answers to these questions.

If I were put in charge of changing our publication practices to include such color coding, I know just what I would do. I would have all Stress positions printed in blue; and I would have everything stressworthy printed in red. That way the best prose would be purple prose. There would never be a blue location without red words mixed with it. There would never be red words that were located anywhere else but in blue locations. We should all try to aim for purple prose.

Conclusion

Here, then, are a half-dozen pieces of advice based on the existence of these reader expectations. If you do these things on a regular basis, your readers are highly likely to understand what you were trying to say. *In order to do them,* you will have to discover for yourself what it is you are trying to say. Whenever there is a good, compelling reason, any of these pieces of advice can be reversed or discarded; but those unusual moments should be kept unusual. Constant fulfillment of reader expectations will make the occasional purposeful violation all the more powerful. Constant violation of reader expectations just creates difficult reading or miscommunication.

-- Begin a clause (or a one-clause sentence) with the person, thing, or idea whose story it is meant to be.

-- For multiclause sentences, locate whose story the sentence is at the beginning of the main clause.

-- In any clause, articulate what is going on (the action) by making it the verb.

-- Keep subjects and verbs together, usually toward the beginning of the clause/sentence.

-- Locate all stressworthy information in a Stress position.

-- Make sure that every Stress position contains something worthy of stress.

You may fear that if you follow all the above advice all of the time, all of your sentences will sound precisely the same:

Whose story -- Action -- Stress

Whose story -- Action -- Stress

Whose story -- Action -- Stress

That will not be the case unless all your thoughts are also unerringly similar in shape. We make our sentences sophisticated by increasing the number of clauses, qualifications, and articulated connections. The shape of the sentence should reflect the shape of the thought. We make our sentences clear by taking as much account of the reader as we can. Since the structural location of substance sends the most important instructions to readers for interpretation, fulfilling reader expectations on a regular basis should produce clarity for the reader and for the writer as well.

If after revising a sentence to take advantage of reader expectations your sentence seems empty or insubstantial, it probably means that your thought was more empty and less substantial than you had previously realized.

Understanding reader expectations can give you a relatively objective way to beat the coffee stain problem. It is often of no avail to ask, "Does this sentence mean what I want it to mean?" To you, it does. To your reader? If you are relying only on your ear, you cannot be sure. But it is not as difficult to ask, "Is my most important information located in a Stress position?" That is a relatively objective question, one which can produce a yes/no answer. When the stressworthy material is located elsewhere than in the Stress position, it does not matter that *you* can understand the sentence; the chances are high that not enough of your readers will get the right message.

Practicing these structural changes sentence after sentence will, after a short while, begin to affect your structural choices during the initial drafting process. You should start by using this approach as a tactic for revision:

-- Write like you usually write.

-- Then go back through it and change any sentence that seriously violates reader expectations in any of the ways we have been discussing.

Once you have done that to one or two or perhaps three papers, you will start to recognize your old reader-unfriendly habits as you are in the process of doing them. Your revision tactic will then be available to you as you are in the process of writing sentences:

-- Write a sentence.

-- Before you go on to the next sentence, notice whether reader expectations have been violated.

-- If so, change this sentence now.

By the time you have done this to two or three papers, your awareness of reader expectations will be with you as you draft any given sentence. It will actually help you make logical connections backward and forward that you otherwise might have missed. (There will be much more on this in later chapters.) In other words, what started as a revision technique will end up helping you create the text in the first place. The structural alterations you will be making are by no means merely cosmetic; they go to the heart of thought itself.

Endnotes

1. C. P. Snow. "The Moral Un-Neutrality of Science." From Lee A. Jacobus, ed., *A World of Idea*, 2nd edition. New York: Bedford Books, 1985, p. 416.
2. Kenneth Burke. *Counter-Statement*. Berkeley: University of California Press, 1968, p. 45.

3

Weights and Balances; Motions and Connections

In Chapter 2 we identified a number of places in the structure of the English sentence in which readers tend to expect certain kinds of substance to appear.

Whose story is it? ⟶ Whoever or whatever shows up first.

What is going on? ⟶ Whatever the verb says is going on.

What is most important here? ⟶ Whatever is located in a Stress position.

As important -- crucially important -- as these are, they do not tell the whole story of how a reader perceives meaning. There is, of course, word choice to consider; but most people overrate its importance. I have suggested it weighs in at about 15%, with the other 85% having to do with structural concerns. In addition to the structural locations we have explored already, here are some other indicators that tell readers how to go about weighing and balancing the individual materials in a sentence:

-- the kind of unit of discourse in which it appears (independent clause, dependent clause, or phrase)

-- the location of that unit of discourse within the sentence (beginning, middle, or end)

-- the length of that unit of discourse

-- the presence, if any, of artificial emphasis (underlining, bold, capitals, italics)

Since the last of these is the simplest, let us attend to it first.

A rtificial EMPHASIS: *When to* Use It *and When* NOT *to*

You may often find yourself tempted to use artificial emphasis, like underlining or capitalization, to indicate the importance of the words you wish your reader to notice most. When you feel this urge, you are probably recognizing, half-consciously, that your sentence will otherwise be unlikely to invoke the kinds of emphases you want. It is important to know (1) when to resist this temptation; and (2) under what conditions the artificial indications will serve you well.

(1) If you can, relocate the word or passage you are tempted to underline to the Stress position, where the structure will do the emphasizing for you. The Stress position is a more powerful and more graceful indicator of emphasis than the artificial enhancements. Using structural location rather than underlining, bold face, capital letters, or italics allows you to avoid the condescension to the reader often caused by the artificial indicators: Locating something in the Stress position never says to your reader, "Look *here,* stupid." It also keeps both your mind and your reader's mind more finely focused on the thought process. Here is a delicious example, since it was written by a famous writing teacher, about a century ago, in a book that purported to teach us how to write.

> 1a. Both usage and reason agree in regarding the END of the sentence as the place of greatest strength or emphasis.
> (Alexander Bain. *English Composition and Rhetoric.* Enlarged edition. New York: American Book Company, 1887, p. 4.)

Especially given what this sentence was trying to say, Professor Bain might have done better to rely on the Stress position instead of on capitalization to make his point:

> 1b. Both usage and reason agree that the place of greatest strength or emphasis in a sentence is its end.

The "end" does better at the end.

(2) On the other hand, artificial emphasis is a wonderful tool for highlighting words that, because of their syntactic functions, cannot with ease be transferred to the Stress position and will not otherwise be likely to attract the reader's heightened attention. This is the case especially for pronouns and adjectives, words that are difficult to get to the sentence's end position.

> 2. It matters not *how* you deliver this message, but only *that* you deliver it.

This is even more the case when the sentence is a long one.

> 3. They are so caught up in trying to decide *how* these words could be made to come together to form a coherent unit that they are unable to feel confident in deciding *what* these words might mean.

You can effectively use artificial emphasis when both of the following conditions are present:

a. You cannot conveniently create a Stress position for the word(s) to be emphasized; and

b. If you do not use the artificial emphasis, readers stand a good chance of missing your meaning -- at least on a first reading.

Comparative Weights and Their Uses

A sentence weighs more than a clause. A single-clause sentence usually weighs more than the same exact words were they to appear in a multi-clause sentence. Compare:

2a. A sentence weighs more than a clause.

2b. Whether you are ever conscious of the fact or not, a sentence weighs more than a clause.

Note please that I am not suggesting that *sentence* (2a) weighs more than *sentence* (2b); rather, I am indicating that the *words* "A sentence weighs more than a clause" tend to weigh more when they are their own sentence than they do when they appear in some larger sentence.

Readers expect a sentence to tell them something whole. That wholeness "weighs more" than the very same words acting as a clause in a multiclause sentence. In a multiclause sentence, each clause plays its part in supporting the weight of the sentence taken as a whole. That supporting role is usually not as heavy, as weighty, as the weight of a whole sentence.

An independent clause weighs more than a dependent clause, which weighs more than a phrase. As readers, without ever having to think about it consciously, we assign greater importance to a clause that could stand by itself as a sentence (an independent clause) than we do to a clause that "depends" on the presence of another clause. A dependent clause, although it cannot stand by itself, must have a subject and a verb. A unified group of words that lacks either or both subject or verb we call a *phrase.* Dependent clauses weigh more than phrases.

This point is harder to define than it is to exemplify. Here is an example -- an intentionally creaky example. Why does the following sentence seem so inelegant, so immature, so clumsy?

3a. I went downtown yesterday, and I had a car accident.

(We could, of course, create a context for this sentence that would render it a fine piece of work; but taken by itself, it seems to suffer from inelegance, immaturity, and clumsiness.)

Perhaps the problem lies in the all-too-equal balancing of the two clauses. The car accident gets the Stress position and therefore wins the "Is everybody looking at me?" contest; but both halves of the sentence are independent clauses and therefore have a certain amount of "look-at-me" weight. This sentence could easily be divided into two full sentences:

3b. I went downtown yesterday. I had a car accident.

Now it sounds like the going downtown is intentionally supposed to be weighed by the reader at the same level of seriousness as the car accident.

If we agree that we want the trip downtown to be subordinated to the car accident, then we can accomplish this by decreasing the weight of the unit of discourse in which it appears. We can subordinate it by making it a subordinate clause, which will then naturally weigh less (with a reader) than the independent clause.

3c. When I went downtown yesterday, I had a car accident.

Can you hear how the dependent clause leans forward in expectation of the arrival of the independent clause? The car accident now seems more important than the trip downtown.

But you may still think that that fateful trip, subordinated though it has been, remains too weighty compared to the automotive mishap. It still feels longer or heavier than it deserves. Solution? Demote it once again -- this time from a subordinate clause to a phrase.

3d. Downtown yesterday, I had a car accident.

Now the "downtown" and the "yesterday" are limited to being contextualizers for the car accident. They do not shine by themselves. Yes, we have reduced the unit's size; but far more important, we have reduced its grammatical or syntactical weight.

What if the "downtown" element were the most important thing we had to say? What if this motorist had been warned *not* to go downtown yesterday? To get that across to a reader, we had best demote the accident from its independent clause status and promote the downtownness in its place.

3e. When I had that car accident yesterday, I was downtown.

Note that even though the subordinate clause is longer than the independent clause, the latter still holds sway. It suggests that the driver's presence downtown was a point of some significance.

·· EXERCISE J

A. For each of the following pairs of sentences, turn them into a single, two-clause sentence -- twice. The first time, make one the main clause and put it at the end. The second time, make the other the main clause and put it at the end.

1. I had the flu. I could not go to my senior prom.
2. Capital punishment should be abolished. It is cruel and inhuman.
3. Education is the key to success in later life. It trains the mind and expands awareness.

B. Rewrite each of the examples once more, this time reducing one of the sentences to a phrase.

F red and His Dog: Competition for Emphasis

As readers, we know intuitively how to make all these comparative judgments of the relative importance of the various materials we find in a sentence. We will do ourselves and our readers a great favor if we translate the knowledge that is intuitive in us as readers into knowledge that is conscious in us as writers. Location, location, location: *Where* we put something is a sentence tells our readers *what* to do with it in the interpretive process.

Let us meet Fred and his dog. We will assume the dog is nice. We have to figure out what we think of Fred. Here are four different constructions that all utilize the same information.

4a. Although Fred's a nice guy, he beats his dog.
4b. Although Fred beats his dog, he's a nice guy.
4c. Fred's a nice guy, but he beats his dog.
4d. Fred beats his dog, but he's a nice guy.

For the purposes of investigating this example, I beg your indulgence. Just for the moment, please assume the following:

(1) It is a very bad thing to beat your dog; and (2) it is possible otherwise to be a nice person in spite of having the one bad attribute of being a dog-beater. I do not subscribe to the latter assumption; I just wish to establish an extreme good side and an extreme bad side to Fred, to demonstrate how the two combine with or play off each other in different rhetorical presentations.

I have worked through this example with more than 300 groups of people. The results have been the same in almost every case. Taking each sentence by itself, I ask the participants to determine whether the writer wants us to approve or disapprove of Fred and to indicate their decision by a show of thumbs up or thumbs down. Here are the stunningly consistent results. See how yours compares.

4a. Although Fred's a nice guy, he beats his dog:
    Unanimous or nearly unanimous thumbs-down on Fred.

4b. Although Fred beats his dog, he's a nice guy:

Nearly unanimous thumbs-up on Fred; but some people cannot abide the thought of even a fictional dog being beaten and therefore vote negatively or abstain.

4c. Fred's a nice guy, but he beats his dog:

Some up, some down, many hesitating to vote, and some demonstrating a vacillating hand motion of ambivalence. Overall, somewhat more negative than positive, but definitely split as a group. Some people are split within themselves.

4d. Fred beats his dog, but he's a nice guy:

Same varied response as (4c), except the overall result is noticeably more positive.

The facts, the "data," remain the same throughout the four sentences; yet the votes indicate four different group interpretations. Since the facts do not differ, the "instructions" for these consistently varying interpretations must be sent by the structures in which the facts are differently deployed. In other words, the same facts in differing structural locations will produce differing interpretations.

If your own thumb did not vote with the majorities indicated above, do not feel either that the example is flawed or that you are abnormal. There is always a minority vote. You are therefore part of the normal minority. The structural interpretive clues I am about to discuss do not generate reliable probabilities for any individual reader; but they seem to be remarkably reliable in predicting the response of a community of readers as a whole.

When two clauses compete with each other for attention and emphasis, there are several structural/syntactical factors that influence the reader. Of these, three are dominant:

(1) end placement

Readers tend to give greater emphasis to the final clause because it contains the Stress position.

(2) the "main" clause (as opposed to the "qualifying" clause)

Readers emphasize the "main" clause (an independent clause) because they expect it to contain the main thought. (Again, I put quotation marks around *main* because in technical grammatical terms, a sentence may have two main clauses. By the term *main* I refer to the clause that is not limited by a qualifier such as *but* or *although*.

(3) length

A disparity in length between two clauses invokes a disparity of emphasis given by the reader. More often than not, readers tend to give more emphasis to the longer of the two, perhaps because more reading time and energy is expended upon it. It is possible, however, for a shorter clause to be so comparatively brisk and forceful that it dominates the reader's attention.

The consistency of the communal judgments on Fred and his dog can now be explained. Since the clauses in each of the four sentences of example (4) are of approximately equal length, we need only consider the effects of emphasis derived from end placement and from inclusion in the main clause. The dominance of these two structural indicators explain why there is such widespread consistency in how Fred is viewed.

4a. Although Fred's a nice guy, he beats his dog:

End placement:	dog-beating
Main clause:	dog-beating

Both indicators of emphasis are negative, thus explaining why almost all thumbs are down on Fred.

4b. Although Fred beats his dog, he's a nice guy:

End placement:	nice guy
Main clause:	nice guy

Both indicators of emphasis are positive, producing mostly thumbs up for Fred. The vote is never quite as strong as the previous one because Fred's negative trait is repellent to so many. This is the case even though the vote is based on whether or not the *author*, not the reader, is pleased with Fred.

4c. Fred's a nice guy, but he beats his dog:

End placement:	dog-beating
Main clause:	nice guy

The two indicators point in different directions. This explains the hesitation and indecision of certain individuals and the ambivalence of the group as a whole. Some follow one sign; some follow another; and others cannot decide which to follow. In general, however, the vote is notably more negative than positive. At first glance, it might seem that this can be explained by the moral inequality of the two statements: Dog-beating is a worse negative than being a nice guy is a good positive. However, that turns out not to be the case, as the vote on (4d) will demonstrate.

4d. Fred beats his dog, but he's a nice guy:

End placement:	nice guy
Main clause:	dog-beating

The fact that the emphasis indicators once again diverge in their instructions accounts for another ambivalent response. But the response to variation (4d) as a whole is consistently more positive than is the response to (4c). That suggests that the moral balancing mentioned above is not the controlling factor. Instead, the difference can be explained structurally: Whenever end placement and main clause compete with each other for attention, the slight edge goes to end placement. The attraction power of the main clause is not quite as strong as the attraction power of the Stress position. It is clear that this does not hold for individuals, for that would once again produce a unanimous vote. But it is just as clear (from the consistency of the outcomes) that it does hold for a community of readers taken as a whole. The end placement of a qualifying clause will not eliminate the influence of an earlier main clause; it only results in a higher percentage of influence than its competitor.

Now let us complicate the matter by introducing the factor of length:

4e. Even though he beats his dog, Fred is a good husband, a caring father, a fine colleague, and an altogether nice guy.

4f. Fred is a good husband, a caring father, a fine colleague, and an altogether nice guy, even though he beats his dog.

Audience responses to these are just as consistent as those in the previous four examples: (4e) engenders unanimous or nearly unanimous thumbs up; (4f) engenders great consternation and a good deal of inability to vote at all.

4e: End placement: nice guy
     Main clause: nice guy
     Length: nice guy

All three indicators are positive. The sentence translates into "Although Fred beats his dog, he is wonderful, wonderful, wonderful, wonderful." Fred for President! By the time the sentence ends, the dog has disappeared from view.

4f: End placement: dog-beating
     Main clause: nice guy
     Length: nice guy

We saw before, with sentences (4c) and (4d), that when end placement and main clause compete for attention, end placement wins a narrow victory due to the power of the Stress position. What happens, then, when the influence of length is added to the influence of main clause in that struggle? Does the combination of length and main clause outweigh the end-placed clause, negating somewhat the power of the Stress position? Or does the Stress position maintain a certain dominance no matter what is placed in opposition to it? In practice, neither of these questions receives a clear answer. Instead, reading communities respond most keenly to the turmoil raised by the conflict. They find themselves less able to come to conclusions of any kind. If, after all that information about being a nice guy, Fred ends up beating his dog, then something is drastically wrong with Fred. He needs help. It is the turmoil, the conflict, the sense of friction that wins.

From these experiments we can derive tactics (not rules) for structuring sentences that have two clauses that compete for reader attention. The tactics are based on the likelihood of what most readers will do most of the time. It cannot predict interpretive results for any individual reader.

(1) Let us say you are a member of Congress and must vote on the expensive and highly controversial MRX plan. You poll your constituents and find they are split 50-50 on the issue. With an election coming up, you feel you must take into account both of those strong feelings and demonstrate you are open to both points of view. Tactic: State your decision clearly in the main clause; but do not place that clause at the end. Let the risks attract the attention provided by the Stress position. The conflict between the two structural indicators will convey your evenhandedness to a majority of your readers.

5a. We should invest in the MRX plan, even though the risks are high.

(2) Perhaps instead of demonstrating ambivalence, you wish to indicate the firmness of your positive support of the MRX plan while still pointing out the risks. Tactic: After articulating the risks clearly in a qualifying clause at the beginning, put your opinion into the main clause and place it at the end. The combined strengths of the two structural indicators (end placement and main clause) will make your opinion seem firm to a majority of your readers.

5b. Even though the risks are high, we should invest in the MRX plan.

(3) Perhaps you may wish not merely to state your opinion but also to agitate for it. You still feel the need to identify the risks, but you do not want your audience to weigh the risks nearly as heavily as the positives of the MRX plan. Tactic: State your opinion in the main clause, place it at the end, and beef it up with additional length. The combination of all three structural indicators will give your opinion not only firmness but also a sense of urgency for a majority of your readers.

5c. Even though the risks are high, we should draw upon whatever funds are available and invest in the MRX plan.

Those are the three main structural indicators, but not the only ones. There are at least three others to consider.

i) As we noticed in Chapter 2, anything that intervenes between a subject and its verb tends to be read with less emphasis. Therefore, another way to undercut the power of a piece of information is to place it between the subject and the verb. Compare the following:

6a. Although this all-encompassing scope is a great conceptual strength of the proposal, it might prove to be overly ambitious.

6b. This all-encompassing scope, though it might prove to be overly ambitious, is a great conceptual strength of the proposal.

There is good news and there is bad news. The bad news is the "overly ambitious" quality. In (6a), the bad news is left to burble and fester in the spotlight of the Stress position. In (6b), the same bad news is undercut significantly by being tucked away not only in midsentence but between a subject and a verb. Most people read (6a) as a much more negative statement than (6b).

ii) Nouns weigh more than pronouns. If "Fred" is in one clause and "he" is in the other, the "Fred" clause carries a bit more weight. As negative as (4a) seems to most readers, (4g) seems yet more negative.

4a. Although Fred's a nice guy, he beats his dog.

4g. Although he's a nice guy, Fred beats his dog.

iii) I have mentioned a number of times that structure accounts for 85% of the interpretive instructions sent to the reader, while word choice only accounts for 15%. Eighty-five to 15 is not 100 to 0: Word choice still counts for something. If a word is strong enough or extreme enough, perhaps even inflammatory enough, it can dominate a reader's attention. Let us add something new about Fred:

4h. Even though Fred's a nice guy, he commits genocide.

No matter how I might rearrange the information into varying structural permutations, I would expect a unanimous thumbs-down vote from all of you at all times.

This does not mean, however, that structural variations, even with such outrageous information, will not create differences in interpretation. Compare (4h) with (4i):

4h. Although Fred is a nice guy, he commits genocide.

4i. Although Fred commits genocide, he is a nice guy.

A slow-motion reading technique is helpful in demonstrating the differences.

4h. ALTHOUGH FRED IS . . .

It is Fred's story. The verb *to be* suggests we are soon to hear something about him; but the "although" qualification suggests we will be hearing something quite different about him in the next clause.

. . . A NICE GUY,

So there is Fred -- a nice, smiling, attractive sort, at the moment. But the initial "although" warns us to expect to hear something less flattering coming up after the comma.

. . . HE COMMITS

Uh oh, here it is. Commits what? Adultery? Tax fraud?

. . . GENOCIDE.

Boom! Fred is an unsalvageable moral reprobate.

Now change the structural order.

4i. ALTHOUGH FRED COMMITS GENOCIDE, . . .

What do you mean *"although"* he commits genocide? How can there be any "although" about such a thing?

. . . HE IS A NICE GUY.

"Nice guy" cannot possibly mean here what it meant (momentarily) in (4h). No nice, smiling, lovely Fred can emerge. The label "nice guy" is not descriptive in a simple sense but clearly a term of sarcasm or parody.

So, your task as a writer is to choose not only the right words but also the most efficacious structure, one that will tend to persuade the largest percentage of readers possible to interpret your sentence as you intended.

If, as you read all these Freddish examples, you find yourself *not* interpreting them as I suggest the majority of people tend to do, remember that there is always a minority that hears them differently. You are not strange or dense or incompetent. You are just a member of the minority. But if you are, then it is even more important for you to learn the lesson taught by Fred and his dog: Your ear, if it is your only tool for judgment, will lead you astray.

·· EXERCISE K ···

A. We can see from Fred and his dog that we can control how readers will weigh and balance the simultaneous presentation of good and bad news. Here are four statements in a report of a supervisor on the performance of a new employee. Although you have seen an example like this earlier in this book, please do not review it at this time. Do it again, freshly, now that you have learned all about Fred and his dog. What outcomes are most likely, given each of these statements: (a) Will the employee be fired? (b) Will the employee be rehired? (c) If rehired, will the employee be on probation? (d) If rehired, will the employee be given a raise?

   a. Although he is often late for work, he does a thorough job.

   b. Although he does a thorough job, he is often late for work.

   c. He is often late for work, but he always does a thorough job.

   d. He always does a thorough job, but he is often late for work.

B. Scientific investigators submit grant proposals to the federal government to obtain funding. The government has a team of experts evaluate the proposals, assign scores, and write responses that indicate what was weak and/or strong about the proposals. Here are two sentences that deliver the same good and bad news, but in different structural arrangements. It is fair to say that the difference in sentence structure produces a different effect for the reader.

Example:

a) Overall, although this proposal is scientifically sound, the preliminary results are not persuasive.

b) Although the preliminary results are not persuasive, overall this proposal is scientifically sound.

While neither of these would be considered a rave review, the (a) version will probably make the scientist less happy than the (b) version. In (a), the bad news (the unpersuasiveness of the preliminary results) gets the main clause and occupies the Stress position. In (b), the good news (the overall soundness of the proposal) gets the main clause and occupies the Stress position. To achieve an effect somewhere between these two, split the structural indicators: Give the main clause to the good news and the Stress position to the bad news:

c) Overall, this proposal is scientifically sound, but the preliminary results are not persuasive.

or vice versa -- giving the main clause to the bad news and the Stress position to the good news.

d) The preliminary results are not persuasive, but overall this proposal is scientifically sound.

Recall that when one piece of news has the Stress position and another has the main clause, reader reaction will be split; but more people will tend to emphasize the material in the Stress position. A majority of readers, therefore, believes that of these four, (b) would represent the highest score (out of 100), followed by (d), then (c), then (a).

Sentence	Main Clause	Stress Position	Approximate Score
(b)	good news	good news	70
(d)	bad news	good news	60
(c)	good news	bad news	40
(d)	bad news	bad news	30

What score do you think each of these four sentences represents, and why? Only the top 15% will receive funding. Take into account that the creativity of the investigator is not nearly as important (to the people with the money) as the quality of this particular application.

Ex. 1   This is an exciting but somewhat flawed application from a creative investigator.

Ex. 2   This creative investigator has produced an exciting but somewhat flawed application.

Ex. 3   This creative investigator has produced a somewhat flawed but exciting application.

Ex. 4 This creative investigator has produced a somewhat flawed but truly exciting application.

C. (i) Here is another scientific investigator, Dr. X. She, too, is vitally interested in the score her proposal will receive. When she reads the following sentence, what score (from 1 to 100) would it be reasonable for her to expect? Again, only the top 15% will receive funding.

Ex. 5 Although Dr. X was not able to realize her goals with this interesting protein, considerable progress was made in other related areas.

(ii) Now rewrite (Ex. 5), keeping all the information the same but changing the structural locations of that information in order to produce a sentence that promises a higher score. By using differing structures, undercut the bad news and emphasize the good news.

(iii) Now rewrite (Ex. 5) again, keeping all the information the same but changing the structural locations of that information to produce a sentence that promises a lower score. Undercut the good news and emphasize the bad news.

If you get a word wrong and the structure right, more of your readers will understand what you meant to say than if you had gotten all the words right and the structure wrong. Here is an example of this from a famous moment in the history of American political rhetoric.

The Berlin Wall had been erected in 1963, in the dead of night, by the Soviet Union to separate communist East Berlin from democratic West Berlin. Not only did the Wall pose a logistical problem for the residents of that city but, far more importantly, it stood as a symbol of the great divide between the world's two major opposing political forces. It was the primary symbol of what was called the Cold War -- a war that could destroy the world. Twenty-six years later, on a Saturday in November of 1989, as part of a series of stunning political events in Eastern Europe, the Berlin Wall suddenly stopped functioning as a barrier between East and West. Both the political and metaphorical significance of that occurrence were beyond the hopes and expectations of most people on either side of the Wall. On that historic day, I heard five broadcasts (three on radio, two on television) of President John F. Kennedy's memorable 1963 speech in Berlin: "I can say -- and I am proud of the word -- *ich bin ein Berliner!*" ("I am a Berliner"———→ "We all are Berliners.") The crowd roared, and the hearts of all in the Western world were lifted. The summoning of these words of our martyred leader 26 years later, at the Wall's demise, recaptured not a simple statement of policy but rather a moment of political prophecy.

It came as no surprise that not one of the announcers of those five rebroadcasts pointed out that famous moment's extraordinary and embarrassing mistake. President Kennedy's speechwriter had not been the German specialist the occasion had required. He had gotten the word wrong. In order to say "I am a Berliner" in German, the appropriate phrasing would have been not "Ich bin ein Berliner" but rather "Ich bin Berliner." "Ein Berliner" does not mean "*a* Berliner"; it refers instead to a particular kind of pastry made popular by that city. President Kennedy had actually proclaimed, in all solemnity, "I can say -- and I am proud of the word -- I am a jelly doughnut!" Knowing that, one can discern that half the roar from the crowd was appreciative applause and the other half was derisive laughter.

Why could that misspoken moment legitimately be perceived 26 years later by millions of Americans as a prophecy fulfilled -- a great moment in American political rhetoric? Because although Kennedy had gotten the word choice wrong, he had gotten the structure right. He uttered the famous words in a number of different Stress-type positions simultaneously: They were at the end of a sentence, at the end of a paragraph, at the high point of a crescendo, in the strife-torn city of Berlin, at a serious moment of international tension. Had he reversed it and gotten the words right but the structure wrong, that moment would never have been preserved for our collective memory -- not then, and not 26 years later. Had he said "Ich bin Berliner" but buried it in the middle of a sentence in the middle of a passage and uttered it without a sense of dynamic arrival, it would have been at best a botched job; had he said it at some other place and at some other less appropriate time, it would have been entirely without historical significance.

Once again we see that the majority of interpretive clues offered the reader come not from the choice of words but from the choice of structure. We all know these structures intuitively as readers; let us get to know them consciously as writers.

M oments of Truth: The Shape of the Sentence, Revisited

Language is much more like music than most people think. That becomes clearer when you consider the role that expectation plays in both. Where music is concerned, we could almost define the concept of *meaning* in terms of the fulfillment and violation of expectations. Picture yourself at a concert -- any kind of concert. The performers are in the middle of a piece. Freeze the moment -- just like they do on television when they analyze a figure skater's jump or a golfer's swing. At this frozen moment, every concertgoer has a unique set of expectations as to what the next musical moment will bring. Your particular set of expectations will depend on a number of factors: How well do you know this particular selection? Have you heard it done by these performers before? If you don't know this one, how well do you know others that are like it? How has this group been doing tonight? How hot and tired are you? What have you had to eat or drink to this point in the evening? Did you have an argument over dinner with the person to your left? Now unfreeze the picture and allow the music to continue to that next moment. The meaning of that moment is the sum total of all the ways in which your particular set of expectations were fulfilled and/or violated.

The same is true for words. It does not matter that individual words have dictionary meanings while individual notes do not. If the notes have too few meanings, the words have too many. For example, consider the word *yellow*. It means lots of different things to you. Of course it seems to describe a color; but there are myriad shades and kinds of yellows that still evoke the name *yellow*. (Look around you right now: You may see a number of different ones in front of you at this very moment.) Beyond that, *yellow* brings to mind a number of kinds of associations. It recalls for us the sun, or gold, or our school -- if yellow is one of its colors. But it also brings to mind cowardice, or age -- as of paper or teeth. And it "means" differently if we had just been thinking about red than it does if we had just been thinking about blue. (The yellow after red is tinged with orange; the yellow after blue is tinged with green.) So there are many, many possibilities for our mind to summon up when the word *yellow* appears. How do we go about choosing which one will dominate our thinking at any given moment? We make that choice (in a millisecond) by the context in which the word appears. That which precedes the word -- in this sentence or this paragraph or any other sized unit -- creates expectations of what will or could come next; and when that which comes next is "yellow," the context tells us which yellow to call to mind.

8a. When she backed away for the third straight time from the bullying taunts of the girl across the hall, she was not surprised when her roommate called her yellow.

8b. As the sun rose, it seemed to turn all the white walls in the room a flaming yellow.

8c. His dentist looked down at him in disgust and growled, "I've never seen your teeth so yellow."

8d. After peering into the stream for 20 minutes without moving, the miner suddenly saw an unmistakable glint of yellow.

So words, like notes, have meaning mainly because of the company they keep. The new news in this book is that they also have meaning because of the *location* in which they appear. As you draw near to the verb, you *expect* it to tell you what is going on. As you near the end of a sentence, you *expect* it to tell you what is most important in this sentence.

We tend to expend most of our writing energy in composing individual sentences. But a thought is not limited to the space between a capital letter and a period: It moves and develops and grows from sentence to sentence. A sentence puts before us, we presume, something worth noting. (It works best if that something is located in a Stress position.) The paragraph, however, is the unit of discourse that presents *and develops* a thought. But paragraphs do not spring fully grown from the mind, as the goddess Athena was supposed to have appeared from the mind of Zeus. (She was supposed to have arrived not only fully grown but fully armed.) We will attend in the next chapter to the reader's expectations concerning the shape and function of paragraphs; but before we get there, we would do well to consider what I would argue is the single most important thing to which a writer should attend -- the way to control the movement of thought (and therefore the movement of the reader's mind) as it connects a sentence to the two that immediately surround it.

There are two moments in the reading process, which occur over and over again, that are of paramount importance to both writer and reader: They are the beginnings and the ends of sentences.

We have already looked at the ends of sentences, which I have been calling a Stress position; but the beginning of a sentence is also important, although in different ways. I am now going to label that structural location the *Topic position.*[1]

The Topic position extends through the first few words of the sentence, up to and including the grammatical subject. It stops short of the verb. In the last two sentences, the Topic positions were filled by "The Topic position" and "It." Both of those sentences contained only one clause. If the sentence has more than one clause, it technically has more than one Topic position -- one at the beginning of each clause. To keep things simple for the moment, we will consider only one-clause sentences. Two important reader expectations are raised every time we start a new Topic position in a one-clause sentence. One of these we explored at some length in Chapter 2: We expect the Topic position -- especially the clause's subject -- to tell us "whose story" the sentence is going to be. But the second expectation is also of crucial importance: We expect to find out -- immediately -- how this sentence links backward to the one that preceded it. If a writer takes care of this concern on a regular basis, readers are able to follow the progression of thought from sentence to sentence without stumbling. If the writer fails to do this on a regular basis, the reader is constantly being mystified, hampered, and hobbled.

We will explore this concept of the backward link more thoroughly; but let us first consider what happens when all the reader expectations we have now encountered function together in a single sentence. Here is the progress most readers expect as they travel through an English sentence:

Time	*Question a reader expects to have answered*
Right away	How does this link backward to what I've just finished?
As soon as possible	Whose story is this sentence? (= the grammatical subject)

Immediately thereafter	What's going on here? (= the verb)
Then, at leisure	How will this thought develop? What more do I have to know?
At the end	What is the most important piece of information here?

We can restate this in our structural terms, naming the places and listing what is expected to appear in those places:

TOPIC POSITION: (up through the end of the grammatical subject)

    -- the backward link

    -- answer to the question "whose story?"

VERB:

    -- the action

MIDSENTENCE:

    -- all other nonstressworthy information

STRESS POSITION:

    -- that which the sentence was created to emphasize

This might sound really unreasonable and even threatening to you at first. After all my harping on the "No Rules! No Rules!" principle, it now sounds like I am handing you a template -- no, a straightjacket -- into which you are being told to fit all your thoughts, no matter what shape they might have in your mind. Not to worry. I have not regressed into being your sixth-grade teacher. Here are the (quite reasonable) fears many students have expressed -- together with responses I hope you will find comforting and reassuring.

Some have said, "If I follow this advice, all my sentences will sound the same":

TOPIC -- VERB ————→ STRESS

TOPIC -- VERB ————→ STRESS

TOPIC -- VERB ————→ STRESS

This problem was addressed in Chapter 2, you might recall. If all your sentences do have exactly the same shape, then probably you are trying, all by yourself, to fit every thought into the same mold, no matter what shape the thought would naturally have. Instead, we have to learn to make the shape of the sentence reflect the shape of the thought. Some thoughts have two parts and therefore need two clauses. Some thoughts need to be interrupted in the middle so the end will make sense; in that case, we have to create an interruption in the structure. Some thoughts have two or three moments that need to be stressed; for them, we need to create two or three Stress positions.

Others have worried, "If I follow this advice, my individual style -- and therefore my individuality -- will be suppressed or even obliterated."

That turns out not to be the case; in fact, just the opposite is true. You will be expressing your individuality by using the structure of your sentence to shape the progress of the reader's interpretive process. Many hundreds of times I have given a group of 15 or 20 professionals (lawyers, scientists, government agents, business persons) a thorny sentence or paragraph to rewrite according to the principles of this reader expectation approach. It is relatively rare for two of the rewrites in any group to be exactly the same. Why? Because each person, possessing a unique mind, interpreted the problematic text differently; and each person's revision of that text clearly articulated their particular interpretation.

Some students have complained, "When I do what you say with the Topic and Stress positions, all my sentences sound stupid and empty." Ah well. If, when you have clearly indicated what is going on and whose story it is and how this links back to your previous thought and what here is most important, your sentence sounds stupid and empty, then I'm afraid that particular thought of yours was probably stupid and empty. We all have stupid and empty thoughts on occasion. Knowing consciously what belongs in a Topic or Stress position can help point out to us when that unfortunate moment is upon us. Have you not had the experience (I certainly have had it many, many times) of being sure that you have just come up with a brilliant thought but failing miserably in trying to get it down on paper? When that is the case, I suggest that you have *not* had a brilliant thought; you only had the feeling that a brilliant thought was somewhere nearby. Thinking is hard. Writing is hard. Thinking and writing cannot meaningfully be separated from each other. If you cannot find a worthy occupant for the Stress position of your sentence, then you have not yet got enough material or enough control of your material to fashion that sentence.

One more important thing to remember where this is concerned: Every reader expectation can be violated to good effect. As it turns out, our greatest stylists are also our most skillful violators. But in order to violate expectations with good results, you have to fulfill them most of the time -- so that the violation will appear an unusual occurrence. Constant violation will just produce chaos. .

Let us then take a closer look at the beginnings and ends of sentences, where the two most crucial reading moments occur; and then let us look at a number of structural ways to indicate to readers the relative weights and balances of the writing's substance. If you can control the contents of your Topic and Stress positions, sentence by sentence, you have solved much more than half the problem of writing.

The Backward Linking Function of the Topic Position

In one sense, readers are willfully in charge of whatever shows up in the Topic position: They tend to want to answer the "whose story" question with "whoever or whatever shows up first," whether the writer intended it or not. In another sense, readers are greatly in need of the writer's help in the Topic position, because the primary reader anxiety at the beginning of each new sentence is often the question, "How does this new sentence connect backward to the sentence I have just finished?" The anxiety is so pressing that readers will tend to use the first opportunity afforded them to accomplish this mental task. If something up front in the new sentence *can* be used to forge that backward link, then the chances are high that it *will* be so used. As a result, it becomes essential for the writer to control with great care what kind of information appears at the beginning of every sentence.

We can use this understanding to formulate another reader expectation:

Readers expect the material at the beginning of a sentence to provide a connection backward to the previous sentence.

Writers of English would be well advised, then, to put at the beginning of every sentence the piece of old information that forges the logical backward link to the previous sentence. The term *old information* does *not* refer to things that happened before the year 1800. Rather, it refers to any material that has already appeared in this particular piece of text. Often it will have appeared in the sentence immediately preceding; sometimes it will harken farther back within the paragraph, or even to a previous paragraph. The farther the leap in space, the more tenuous the connection is likely to be.

When do you *not* want to start a sentence with a clear backward link? (No Rules!) Omit that link if you want your reader to be shocked by the arrival of the new sentence. This opportunity will not occur often.

When a piece of old information appears at the beginning of a sentence, it offers the reader the following comforting instructions: "Dear reader," it says. "Of all the information that has come your way most recently in this document, this is the one strand you should use to tie the present moment to its immediate past. This will help you continue to read in a logical and orderly fashion." Having done that, it combines with the answer to the "whose story" question to provide the context in which to consider the new information yet to come.

BACKWARD-LINKING OLD INFORMATION + WHOSE STORY = CONTEXT

This concept is trickier to work with than it may appear at first glance -- which should become more apparent as we look at several examples.

9a. The assignment of supplemental readings -- even if those readings were referred to in texts already approved by the official curriculum, were clearly germane to the subject in general, and could be demonstrated to be related to the core assignments -- would also require the School Board's permission.

Why is this sentence so burdensome to read? Many readers would suggest it is too long. Creators of readability formulas, like Rudolph Flesch (who concluded for us that "no sentence should exceed 29 words"), would probably agree,[2] since sentence (9a) contains 46 words. But instead of relying on magic numbers, let us look closely at the structure of (9a). With the material of Chapter 2 in mind, we can immediately spot one glaring problem: There is a 37-word interruption between the subject and the verb. That interruption amounts to more than three-quarters of the sentence's bulk. We could lessen the reader's burden significantly by attending to this one problem.

However, there is another structural problem that also calls for attention: The arrival of the backward-linking old information in (9a) is delayed until the end of the sentence. We can recognize that piece of information even without having before us the sentence that preceded it: The backward link is "would also require the School Board's permission." The word "also" flags us that the text has recently been discussing something else that required the School Board's permission. "Also" now informs us that this sentence is about something that *also* requires such permission. As readers, we would have been delighted to know this up front in the new sentence. How much easier it then would have been to process all the rest of the sentence's information.

Which should we work on first -- the subject-verb separation or the old information problem? It does not matter. Any sentence that displays one structural flaw may well contain several. If X is where Y ought to be, then Y may be floating around somewhere else, perhaps displacing Z. Since a resolution of either problem affects the structure of the whole, altering one structural feature might well in turn alter others and possibly provide a remedy for the second problem, too. It does not matter with which problem we begin. At the moment, we are working on the backward link.

If we get the requirement of School Board permission up front in the Topic position, where it will do the reader the most good as a backward link, the rest of the sentence creates far less of a burden for the reader. Here is one possible revision:

9b. The School Board's permission would also be required before teachers would be allowed to assign supplemental readings -- even if those readings were referred to in works already approved by the official curriculum, were clearly germane to the subject in general, and could be demonstrated to be related to the core assignments.

This revision actually turns out to be longer than the original it replaces -- 51 words to the previous 47; yet most readers would find it easier to follow and interpret. The original sentence made us hold in mind a great deal of complicated material about "readings" while we were still waiting for two crucial things to arrive: (1) the verb (without which the strenuously retained subject would make no sense); and (2) some indication of how in the world all this material relates to material in the previous sentence.

Another way of saying the same thing: The reader was too burdened by considerations of the *structure* of the sentence to be able to pay a sufficient amount of attention to the unveiling of its *substance.* Those structural considerations concerned both the present sentence (the subject-verb separation problem) and the relationship of this sentence to its predecessor (the misplaced backward-linking old information problem).

Note that the revision (9b) brings with it a passive that did not exist in the original: "The School Board's permission *would also be required. . . ."* This, I would argue, exemplifies one of the strongest and most advantageous uses of the passive. The passive is to be preferred to the active when it is the only way to accomplish either of the following:

1) It is the only way the backward-linking old information can be moved to the Topic position; or

2) It is the only way to move the person or thing whose story it is to the Topic position.

An active construction here would sacrifice those structural gains in favor of obeying a "no passive" rule that has its origin more in convention than in logic or practicality.

We have now seen that two major questions represent a reader's major concerns at the start of a new sentence:

1. Whose story is this?

2. How does this sentence link backward to its predecessor?

The answers to those two questions, taken together, form the *context* for the rest of the sentence. Context controls meaning. If you firmly establish that context before announcing what is going on (which happens in the verb) and well in advance of the arrival of the most important information (in the Stress position), then your reader will be ready for everything *at the time of its arrival.* Example (9a) seems long not because of the number of words but because we as readers have to carry around so many words with which we as yet know not what to do.

The reader's need for this contextualizing information is so pressing that the reader will tend to use *whatever* is available up front to answer these questions. As we have seen with the "whose story" question, the reader will always be able to find some answer to that question, right or wrong, since something or someone has to occupy that up-front subject position. It therefore behooves the writer to get the right answer where it will be most likely to be discovered.

The search for the identity of the backward-linking old information is slightly different from the "whose story" problem, since it is entirely possible to supply nothing up front that can logically be connected backward. Let us say your previous sentence contained seven bits of information, represented here by these seven letters:

A B C D E F G.

If you start your next sentence with

Q,

your reader will not be able to link that backward. As a result, the reader has to hold on to "Q" while continuing the search for the backward link. Should your sentence continue with

(Q) R S,

by the time the "S" arrives, the reader has to forget about linking anything backward. There is too much new material to deal with; the primary reading effort now will be to make sense of this new sentence, in isolation. We are left to hope that once that is accomplished, the linkage between the two sentences will somehow become apparent.

But offering *no* old information, bad as it is for your reader, is not nearly as bad as offering the *wrong* piece of old information. Let us say that the sentence following your ABCDEFG sentence is meant to be connected to the previous sentence by the "G" piece of information. Should you start a new sentence with "B," you have not only blown an opportunity but also have seriously misled your reader. Your reader, with great confidence, will make this "B" connection, even if "G" shows up later on. The damage has already been done.

Here is an example with real words, instead of mere letters, to demonstrate both of these problems.

ABCDEFG: 10a.   *Hamlet*, like so many of Shakespeare's plays, but much more noticeably than most, focuses on the question of perceiving the difference between illusion and reality.

Q: 10b.   Queen Gertrude . . .

Even though we know or assume that Queen Gertrude is a character in the play of *Hamlet*, we have no idea how she relates backward to the previous sentence.

QRS: 10c.   Queen Gertrude, both widow and bride, but continuously queen, . . .

We still have no clue as to how this sentence connects logically to its predecessor; but by this time we have to expend all our sentence-reading effort on figuring out what this new sentence is saying by itself. We'll have to put off worrying about how to make it fit into a continuous flow of thought.

Let us call "Shakespeare's plays" the "B" element of (10a) and "the difference between illusion and reality" the "G" element. If the next sentence starts with "B" but was meant to continue to talk about "G," we are in trouble.

10d.   *Hamlet*, like so many of Shakespeare's plays, but much more noticeably than most, focuses on the question of perceiving the difference between illusion and reality. Shakespeare's plays often. . . .

We do not know why "illusion and reality" were given the Stress position before, since we are now back to talking about "Shakespeare's plays" in general. We accept that "Shakespeare's plays" is the story being told in the present sentence. That remains the case, at least for a while, even if the "G" element shows up later on.

10e. Shakespeare's plays often set up important characters, like Queen Gertrude, for example, who blur the distinction between reality and illusion because we cannot tell what they are thinking, even by the end of the play.

See how much more digestible -- and how much less energy-consuming -- the same information can be if the logical backward link appears at the beginning:

10f. *Hamlet*, like so many of Shakespeare's plays, but much more notice-ably than most, focuses on the question of perceiving the difference between illusion and reality. That distinction is often blurred by the presentation of characters like Queen Gertrude, whose motivations remain unfathomable by us, even at the end of the play.

Most readers have understood more and expended far less reader energy at the end of (10f) than they have at the end of (10e). If that is the case at the end of a two-sentence example, think by how much the effect is multiplied if sentence after sentence after sentence and paragraph after paragraph after paragraph exhibit the same un-reader-friendly habit.

From this, we can generate two more statements about Reader Expectations:

....
Readers expect the material at the beginning of a sentence to contextualize them for the new and important material to be presented later in the sentence.
....

and

....
Readers form that context by answering two questions:
(1) Whose story is this? and (2) How does this sentence link backward to the sentence before it?
....

·· EXERCISE L

For each of the following sentences, create two alternative new sentences that could logically *precede* it. Make the difference between your two new sentences the way in which they connect with the given sentence: Make one connect through the information in its Topic position and the other through the information in its Stress position.

Example:

Given sentence:

> Hurricanes cannot be predicted with any sense of surety, despite the great leaps forward we have made in meteorology.

First new sentence in front of the original, linking the information in its Stress position:

> Those who have the job of telling us about the weather on our TV news stations look cheerful and confident on a daily basis when they deal with normal weather but tense and crisis-ridden when they warn us about *hurricanes. Hurricanes* cannot be predicted with any sense of surety, despite the great leaps forward we have made in meteorology.

Second new sentence in front of the original, linking the information in its Topic position:

> *Hurricanes* fascinate us, acting like willful, self-indulgent, and irrational characters in a high-intensity television drama. *Hurricanes* cannot be predicted with any sense of surety, despite the great leaps forward we have made in meteorology.

Note: The connection does not have to repeat the exact word, as in this example. Any lexical reference will do -- for example, ". . . warn us about *hurricanes. These storms* cannot be. . . ."

Here are the sentences with which you can work:

1. No matter how hard I tried, I could not seem to shake the feeling that something strange was about to happen.

2. Perhaps all elections that end with the candidates separated by less than one-half a percentage point should be declared a tie, with the office remaining unfilled for the duration of the next term.

3. If we turned left, we would circle back to the beginning; but if we turned right, we hit a dead end.

The Various Functions of the Stress Position

In Chapter 2 we looked at the reasons why a Stress position (any moment of full syntactic closure) exists in English. When everything comes to a full stop in the structure of a sentence -- either at a period, a colon, or a semicolon -- then a significant amount of emphasis is created by the psychology of the reading process, especially as it relates to our great need for closure. But just as there are no rules that hold true all the time for the writing process, so there is not just one effect produced by the arrival at a Stress position. In fact, there are at least three major varieties of Stress position effects -- and a good many more special effects as well. Let us take a look at those three, through which we will see what kinds of thought patterns they tend to produce.

The Herald Stress Position: The Forward Lean

First, there is the Stress position that produces a forward lean. It acts as a trumpet call, heralding the arrival of something new and important. If that new, important Stress position occupant does not explain itself fully at the moment of its arrival, then its position in the Stress position seems to announce, "That which is here, emphasized though it has been by arriving at this moment of closure, has not told enough of its story. You will hear more of it in the next sentence." So we lean forward in expectation that we will soon -- very soon -- learn more. The occupant of that Stress position will often become the "whose story" of the next Topic position. When the new sentence actually brings us that news, our expectation is satisfied. However, if we fail to get what we were promised, we are disappointed or confused; we will be expending a good deal of reader energy to keep alive the expectation that more on this important topic will shortly be forthcoming. It all makes for a bad read. In such a case, here is what seems to be happening:

1. Let us say the first sentence ends in "apricots," about which we have not yet learned enough. We expect the next sentence to tell us more about them.

2. The second sentence starts out with pears -- which is to us something of a disappointment.

3. It continues with apples, tomatoes -- (I want more apricots, please) -- cucumbers, felt-tipped pens, and purple loose-leaf binders -- (*where* are my apricots??) -- and ends with kumquats.

4. We've gone through a whole, long, confusing sentence; and yet we are still anxious to read more about that which the previous sentence had promised us -- some news about apricots.

If the writer has no conscious understanding of the power of the Stress position, then the writer may have no idea whatever about the nature of the reader's anxiety. Any writer who knows all about structural promises and expectations has only to check out the occupant of the Stress position and see if its promise had been fulfilled.

Do not fear that your reader will have some kind of anxiety attack if the promise of the Herald Stress position is not fulfilled by the very first word in the next sentence. As long as it appears relatively soon, the connection can be made with ease and assurance. Here is an example of this from that smoothest of essayists, Virginia Woolf:

11. The windows look out upon a few cultivated fields and a dozen hovels, and beyond them there is the sea on one side, on the other a vast

fen. A single road crosses the fen, but there is a hole in it, which, one of the farm hands reports, is large enough to swallow a carriage.

(Virginia Woolf. "The Pastons and Chaucer," *The Common Reader*. New York: Harcourt Brace, 1958, p. 15.)

The first sentence ends with "a vast fen." The second sentence begins with "A single road," which, we hope, has *something* to do with that fen. We are relieved to find it does: "A single road crosses the fen, . . ." Note Ms. Woolf's subtle camera work: We look out of "windows" and see "fields" and then, more specifically, "hovels"; then our eye travels farther and sees a sea on one side and, on the other, a "vast fen"; then, within that fen, a "single road" catches our attention, focusing our gaze suddenly on a single, unusual detail -- the gaping hole in the road.

When you use the Stress position to herald the arrival and promise the continuance of something interesting -- and then you fulfill the promise and make that herald the "whose story" of the next sentence -- you create a structural movement we will call *Topic Changing*.

Topic Changing

In the pattern called Topic Changing, the key word in the Topic position repeats or refers back to a word in the previous sentence. At its clearest, that backward link points to the occupant of the previous Stress position. If this happens several sentences in a row, we would get the following kind of schematic connection.

Topic	*Stress*
Old^1....................................	New_1
Old^2 (=New^1)...................	New_2
Old^3 (=New^2)...................	New_3
Old^4 (=New^3)...................	New_4

In this progression, the writer never settles on a particular topic for more than a sentence. Instead, the writer focuses our attention on the way in which each new arrival connects backward and moves on into new territory in the next sentence. It produces a kind of domino effect. Therefore, each statement must be comprehensible in and of itself; the intent of the whole passage is to focus on the *connections* between these various statements and the forward-moving quality of the progression as a whole. Topic Changing, therefore, is a technique that highlights cohesion: It makes any two neighboring sentences stick together. As a result, it is the most effective technique to use in writing certain kinds of narrative or descriptive passages -- stories that concentrate on "what happens next." When do you want to use it? -- when your material requires exactly that kind of domino effect.

Here is an example of Topic Changing being used well:

12a. Up to the time of Darwin, Lamarck was the only biologist to develop a theory of organic evolution in extensive fashion. Its failure as a scientific theory was discussed in the last chapter. The writings that will be taken up here as a background to the development of Darwin's theory will be those of such popularizers as Erasmus Darwin and Robert Chambers, whose work was read by Darwin. He apparently knew nothing of the development of evolutionary theory by the philosophers.

(Url Lanham, *Origins of Modern Biology*. New York: Columbia University Press, 1968, p. 155.)

Here is the same example again, with the Herald Stress position occupants and the Topic position's backward link both italicized.

12b. Up to the time of Darwin, Lamarck was the only biologist to develop *a theory of organic evolution* in extensive fashion. *Its failure* as a scientific theory was discussed *in the last chapter*. The writings that will be taken up *here* as a background to the development of Darwin's theory will be those of such popularizers as Erasmus Darwin and Robert Chambers, whose work was read by *Darwin*. He apparently knew nothing of *the development of evolutionary theory by the philosophers*.

Topic	Stress	
Old[1] (Lamarck)......................New[1]		(a theory of organic evolution)
Old[2] (=New[1]) (Its failure).....New[2]		(in the last chapter)
Old[3] (=New[2]) (here).............New[3]		(Darwin)
Old[4] (=New[3]) (He)................New[4]		(the development of evolutionary theory by the philosophers)

The prose moves with relative ease from sentence to sentence, establishing the connections by lighthanded lexical references and leaving us at the end with an introduction to "the development of evolutionary theory by the philosophers," which then becomes the focus of the succeeding paragraph. The whole paragraph then becomes a kind of herald for the paragraph that follows.

If we dewrite this paragraph, destroying the smooth cohesive links by putting the crucial pieces of information in the wrong structural locations, we get a relative mess:

12c. Up to the time of Darwin, the only biologist to develop a theory of organic evolution in extensive fashion was Lamarck. The last chapter demonstrated how much a failure was this scientific theory. Darwin had read as background the writings that will be taken up here, those of such popularizers as Erasmus Darwin and Robert Chambers. The development of evolutionary theory by the philosophers was apparently unknown to Darwin.

Every individual sentence sounds reasonably respectable here; but the lack of fulfillment of *any* promise made by a Herald Stress position severely damages both cohesion and coherence. The first sentence promises us we will hear more about Lamarck. We do not. Toward the end of the next sentence we hear something about Lamarck's theory; but it is too little too late. "This scientific theory" leads us to expect more about it in the Topic position of the next sentence; but instead we get "Darwin." (Where did *he* come from? we wonder.) Then we expect to hear more about Erasmus Darwin and Robert Chambers; but the mysterious and seemingly unconnected "development of evolutionary theory" takes over instead. As advertised -- it is a mess.

Topic Changing is *not* to be used as some kind of template or paradigm. You cannot preconceive a structure for your paragraph that will land every Stress position occupant in the next Topic position and expect to get lucky every time. Topic Changing often works well for a sentence or two, or even three -- in domino narrative situations; it is rather rare for it to hold sway for an entire paragraph longer than three sentences. Here is an unhappy example of the first page of a term paper written by a student who had fallen under the spell of constant Topic Changing.

13.   Over the last several years, much doubt has been raised as to the future of the US space program. The space program received a major setback on January 28, 1986, when the space shuttle *Challenger* exploded. The explosion of the *Challenger* was more than simply the tragic death of seven brave Americans, it represented the death of a dream. This dream of the conquering of space is crucial to our continued growth as a nation. Our nation needs space exploration and development in order to maintain the worldwide balance of power, to provide new sources of raw materials, and also to establish a new frontier, against which another generation of Americans may be able to grow and rediscover the values that made our country great. This greatness has been diminishing of late, and today's space program is now a prime target of both governmental and nongovernmental critics. These critics argue that we must radically cut back on, we have a number of different ways of we have a number of different ways of if not eliminate entirely, our space program because it has allowed itself to be dominated by the Defense Department (DOD) and has been unable to define a specific set of goals necessary for future progress. Progress must be made by designing new projects like the space plane and reorganizing NASA into a joint, Cabinet-level agency. This agency would be the sole directional institution for space-related activities within the country. Our country's future is, despite the complaints of critics, inexorably linked to the future of the space program; our space program must go forward.

After a while, a reader will stop attending to what this writer is trying to say and concentrate instead on seeing whether the Topic Change will happen yet again. Do you notice there are two extra-long sentences in this paragraph? (They are the ones beginning "Our nation needs space exploration" and "These critics argue.") Why so long? Because the poor fellow could not afford to stop until he had arrived at a piece of information that was capable of taking up the "whose story" position in the next sentence. And this was just the first page of a 12-page paper in which *every* sentence was Topic Changed to connect to its neighbors, just like circus elephants walking around in a ring, each trunk curled around the tail of the animal in front of it. It may have been a stunning achievement in one sense; but it was completely unreadable.

Topic Changing is neither a good thing nor a bad thing by itself. It certainly does not tell you how to produce paragraphs. It is highly effective when the business at hand moves from one statement to another without need of further development. It can be a disaster, sometimes even comically so, when the intellectual need is just the opposite -- that is, when the writer/reader needs to concentrate on one topic for a number of sentences in order to develop it fully.

The Cumulative Stress Position: Increasing Thickness

If the sole function of the Stress position were to herald the arrival of the next Topic position occupant, then every paragraph would produce consistent Topic Changing. Fortunately, that is not the case. Sometimes, the occupant of the Stress position offers a new piece of information that forms part of a continuing story. In order for the story to continue, the occupant of a number of consecutive Topic positions would have to remain the same. Look at the Topic and Stress positions in the following paragraph.

14a. If we want to surprise them with their anniversary present, we have a number of different ways of doing it. We could leave it on the doorstep, so they would find it when they return from dinner. We could leave it in their bedroom, so they will find it just before the go to sleep. We could, if you think they would be in the mood for some fun, leave a letter taped to the front door with a clue where they should look next -- and leave at that place another clue -- and so forth, until they finally find it as a result of a long scavenger hunt.

Here it is again, this time with the occupants of the Stress positions and the "whose story" part of the Topic positions italicized.

14a. If *we* want to surprise them with their anniversary present, we have *a number of different ways of doing it. We* could leave it on the doorstep, so they would find it *when they return from dinner. We* could leave it in their bedroom, so they will find it *just before the go to sleep. We* could, if you think they would be in the mood for some fun, leave a letter taped to the front door with a clue where they should look next -- and leave at that place another clue -- and so forth, until they finally find it *as a result of a long scavenger hunt.*

The first sentence is the story of "we"; it highlights that there are "a number of different ways" of surprising these lucky parents with their anniversary present. That Stress position occupant leans forward in a heralding way -- but not just to the next Topic position. It leans forward to the whole rest of the paragraph. From then on, every sentence is the story of "we," and every sentence's Stress position emphasizes one more bright idea for "a way to do it." Each new Stress position adds another idea in a cumulative process of completing the idea of the paragraph as a whole.

You can see how this would work smoothly and well in business situations or grant proposals or legal briefs: "The defendants are guilty for a number of reasons. They did X. They did Y. Furthermore, they did Z."

When this pattern asserts itself for two or more sentences in a row, we call it *Topic Stringing*: A string of the same thing appears in consecutive Topic positions, with the new additions to this cumulative story appearing in the Stress Positions.[3]

Topic Stringing

In Chapter 2, I argued that the old English-teacher advice to "vary the way you begin your sentences to keep your reader interested" was fine advice for grade-school students but bad advice for mature writers. We now proceed even further in that direction by offering the advice to keep the same person, thing, or idea up front in the "whose story" position as long as that story is being told. You may well wonder whether that is going to produce prose that could only be described as "boring." Here is the answer to that concern: Prose is boring not because of its structure but because of its content. If the occupant of your Stress position is not *worthy* of that Stress position, then of course you run the risk of boring your readers. But if a story grows continually more rich and complex, boredom will not be a problem. Here is half a paragraph that is Topic Strung throughout. Is boredom a problem?

15a. The wilderness masters the colonist. It finds him a European in dress, industries, tools, modes of travel and thought. It takes him from the railroad car and puts him in the birch canoe. It strips off the garments of civilization and arrays him in the hunting shirt and the moccasin. It puts him in the log cabin of the Cherokee and the Iroquois and runs an Indian palisade around him. In short, the frontier is at first too strong for the man.

(By the way, this example was written almost a century ago, by professor Frederick Jackson Turner, when the general pronoun was always "he." Today we would work our way around that problem. To keep Turner's prose intact, the "he" has been left as it was. The "wilderness" refers to the great unsettled areas of eighteenth- and nineteenth-century America. The "colonist" refers to those brave souls who ventured here from Europe, bringing with them their own culture but finding a new set of challenges in trying to carve out a stable existence from a hostile environment.)

Every sentence begins with "the wilderness" or some other term that refers to it. Professor Turner has therefore constructed a "wilderness" Topic String. Each new Stress position adds something relevant to the growing portrait of the wilderness as an entity, making the whole description fuller and richer. By doing so, he has focused our attention as readers on a single, developing story:

Wilderness ⟶ masters colonist.

Wilderness ⟶ finds him European in all things.

Wilderness ⟶ changes his transportation.

Wilderness ⟶ changes his clothing.

Wilderness ⟶ changes his housing.

Wilderness ⟶ is too strong for the colonist.

Like Topic Changing, however, Topic Stringing is neither good nor bad by itself. You will not do well merely by using it; you will only do well by using it well. "Using it well" means using it when it fits the needs of the development of your thought. Both Topic Changing and Topic Stringing are ways of controlling the reader's movement through the paragraph. Controlling that movement, to a great extent, is equivalent to controlling the reader's thought process.

Controlling Movement ⟶ Controlling Thought

Let us enlarge this Turner example by doubling the size of the paragraph, keeping the Topic String going almost to the end:[4]

15b. The wilderness masters the colonist. It finds him a European in dress, industries, tools, modes of travel and thought. It takes him from the railroad car and puts him in the birch canoe. It strips off the garments of civilization and arrays him in the hunting shirt and the moccasin. It puts him in the log cabin of the Cherokee and the Iroquois and runs an Indian palisade around him. In short, the frontier is at first too strong for the man. It imposes on him conditions which it furnishes or it destroys him, and so the Indian clearings come to fit him and the Indian trails lead him. Little by little, the wilderness changes because of him, but the outcome is not the old Europe. . . . The fact is, that here is a new product that is American.

Here is a continuing story of the wilderness, rooted in a Topic String. That story is a dramatic one: For the first half of the paragraph, the American wilderness is dominating the early colonists from Europe, forcing them to adapt to new circumstances. About halfway through, the domination of the wilderness diminishes as the colonist begins to adapt to the new surroundings. By the end, the wilderness is the one having to do the changing. The story is recognizably American, the subject of any number of films from the mid-twentieth century: The powerful figure holds sway until at first chastened and then eventually humbled and humanized by forces less powerful than it. But at the end of this paragraph/story, the result is not the defeat of the wilderness but its amalgamation, with the colonist, into a new hybrid called "America."

Now let us change the structure of each of the sentences (except for the last one), thereby changing the nature of the paragraph's continuing story:

15c. The colonist must submit to the wilderness. He comes to it a European in dress, industries, tools, modes of travel and thought. Because of it, he leaves the railroad car for the birch canoe. He must strip off the garments of civilization and array himself in the hunting shirt and the moccasin. He must adopt the log cabin of the Cherokee and the Iroquois and run an Indian palisade around himself. In short, the colonist is at first too weak for the wilderness. He must accept the conditions which it furnishes or perish, and so he fits himself to the Indian clearings and follows the Indian trails. Little by little, he transforms the wilderness, but the outcome is not the old Europe. . . . The fact is, that here is a new product that is American.

In this revision, the technique of Topic Stringing has been retained, but the occupant of the Topic position has changed. Now the story focuses on the colonist throughout. The colonist is dominated by the wilderness for the first half, after which he adapts and eventually takes over. It is once again a recognizably American story, also from midcentury films: The skinny fellow gets sand kicked in his face by the bully but then builds himself up and perseveres until he has overcome his adversary, after which they become great friends and make each other better people. Both (15b) and (15c) end with the same insistence that neither party has been vanquished. The great strength of this "new product that is American" lies in the hybrid nature of this new country. It is neither a former wilderness made European nor a society of Europeans transformed into frontiersmen.

Try now yet another permutation. See if you can spot the change:

15d. The wilderness masters the colonist. It finds him a European in dress, industries, tools, modes of travel and thought. It takes him from the railroad car and puts him in the birch canoe. It strips off the garments of civilization and arrays him in the hunting shirt and the moccasin. It puts him in the log cabin of the Cherokee and the Iroquois and runs an Indian palisade around him. In short, the frontier is at first too strong for the man. He must accept the conditions which it furnishes or perish, and so he fits himself to the Indian clearings and follows the Indian trails. Little by little, he transforms the wilderness, but the outcome is not the old Europe. . . . The fact is, that here is a new product that is American.

In this revision, the Topic String of the wilderness dominates the first half of the paragraph; but then it cedes the Topic position to the colonist, who is Topic Strung for the second half. The transition is neatly accomplished by a Topic Change in the middle: "In short, *the frontier* is at first too strong for *the man. He* must accept the conditions. . . ."

This is the original paragraph by Frederick Jackson Turner -- the central point of his influential work articulating the frontier thesis of American history. Version (15d) serves Professor Turner's needs far better than either of the preceding versions. Whose story is (15b), all the way through? -- that of the wilderness. Whose story is (15c), all the way through? -- that of the colonist. Whose story is (15d), all the way through? -- that of *America.* How is that the case, when there are two different Topic Strings? Because in Professor Turner's paragraph (15d), the "whose story" occupant of the Topic position is always the one who is stronger -- the one who is "winning." As long as the wilderness is winning, it gets to keep control of the Topic position; but as soon as the colonist turns the tide, the colonist takes over the Topic position. As a result, by the end, the paragraph has throughout been the story of winners: America is created from the hybridization of winners. It is made of the best each of the combatants has to offer. That, says Professor Turner, is what gives America its special character. His work, although almost a century old, is still read and still used in the teaching of American history.

With apologies for disturbing Professor Turner in his grave, here is the paragraph revised again, with the Topic Strings reversed -- the colonist's story dominating the first half and the story of the wilderness dominating the second:

15e. The colonist must submit to the wilderness. He comes to it a European in dress, industries, tools, modes of travel and thought. Because of it, he leaves the railroad car for the birch canoe. He must strip off the garments of civilization and array himself in the hunting shirt and the moccasin. He must adopt the log cabin of the Cherokee and the Iroquois and run an Indian palisade around himself. In short, the man is at first too weak for the frontier. It imposes on him conditions which it furnishes or it destroys him, and so the Indian clearings come to fit him and the Indian trails lead him. Little by little, the wilderness changes because of him, but the outcome is not the old Europe. . . . The fact is, here is a new product that is American.

In this strange version, America turns out to be an amalgamation of losers. It is made up of what is left over after the stuffing has been kicked out of both combatants. The facts have not changed; but their varied locations change the way in which the facts will most probably be perceived.

Turner's thesis is not an accumulation of facts; it is the particular intellectual synthesis he makes of those facts, thereby transforming information into ideas. He controls the reader's focus on whose story it is by Topic

Stringing first one and then the other. To control movement is to control thought. Context controls meaning.

To demonstrate further how important that structural control is -- especially when a great deal of information is concerned -- here is Professor Turner's paragraph dewritten (with *extreme* apologies to the dear man) with the Topic Strings destroyed. No two sentences continue a focus on the same story. None of the facts have been deleted; but do you think this paragraph would be remembered and read a century after its creation?

15f. Mastery was achieved by the wilderness over the colonist. European industries and tools mark his appearance, along with European dress, modes of travel, and thought. The birch canoe replaces the railroad car. The moccasin and the hunting shirt are worn by the colonist when he strips off the garments of civilization. The log cabin of the Cherokee and the Iroquois house him; he is surrounded by the Indian palisade. The strength of the frontier exceeds that of the man, in short. Acceptance must be afforded the conditions it furnishes, or he must die, and so the Indian clearings are accommodated, and he follows the Indian trails. Little by little a new product called America -- not the old Europe -- emerges from this transformed wilderness.

It *sounds*, for all the world, like there is a lot of "thinking" going on in this paragraph; but Professor Turner's famous frontier thesis of American history is now almost impossible to find.

The Final Stress Position: Bring It All to an End

The Stress position can also be used at the end of things to bring everything to a final end. It can sew everything up, bring it to a close, finish it off. Here is an example from the well-known essayist Joan Didion. It brings her essay called "Quiet Days in Malibu" to a resting place. She and her family had taken a trip to revisit a home in which they had once lived and which had almost been destroyed by a California forest fire. The 14-page essay ends like this:

16. After I said goodbye to Amando Vazquez, my husband and daughter and I went to look at the house on the Pacific Coast Highway in which we had lived for seven years. The fire had come to within 125 feet of the property, then stopped or turned or been beaten back, it was hard to tell which. In any case, it was no longer our house.
     (Joan Didion. *The White Album*. New York: Noonday Press, 1979, p. 223.)

This is not only the last sentence of the essay but also the last essay in the book. It was an eerie but effective way to end both the 14-page essay and the 223-page book.

Once you recognize the power of endings, you can use them for all sorts of special effects. Here is the end of a book by Dennis E. Baron about the history of grammar and spelling reform in the United States. He is discussing the "martyrs" of the English language -- people who have struggled to maintain the language in the condition in which they found it, despite the attempts by language reformers to make it into something new.

17. . . . [T]he martyrs in the struggle for good grammar and good taste are not the reformers, either the cranks and quacks on the fringes of English philology or the more linguistically sophisticated language planners, but the reformed, those speakers and writers of English who, out of an abiding sense of their own linguistic inadequacy, must "be correct or die"; those who, from internal or external pressure, seek to conform their spelling, grammar, and usage to the elusive norms of a mythical Standard English. These martyrs become confused in their usage. Aiming at correctness they produce language that the language guardians still judge to be inappropriate. Or they become bitter, or mute. In some cases . . . they join the ranks of language critics, and the cycle of linguistic reform begins again."

> (Dennis E. Baron. *Grammar and Good Taste: Reforming the American Language*. New Haven: Yale University Press, 1982, p. 241.)

By ending the whole book with "the cycle of linguistic reform begins again," Baron is effectively sending us all the way back to the beginning of his book -- where our reading/understanding process can "begin again." What goes around comes around.

Of most importance is the recognition that you, as a writer, are the one in control of the structural placement of any and all of your information. By organizing that structure, you transform information into ideas. A professional is someone who is paid to articulate the connections.

The Shape of Thought and the Variety of Structure

There are no set patterns you should follow. Learn what certain patterns do to and for readers; then use them when that is what you want your reader to do. Know the signals that Topic positions and Stress positions send to readers, and take advantage of that. Topic Change when necessary; Topic String when necessary. Control your reader's focus within sentences and from sentence to sentence. If you are consistent, your readers will come to trust you, to rely on your structural signals.

By this time, you should have a good sense of how the backward link must come up front in a sentence, that a one-clause sentence is the story of whoever shows up first, and that a multiclause sentence is the story of whoever shows up first in the main clause. (See Chapter 2 for a review of the latter.) Now we have to complicate life just a bit. Sometimes the backward link and the "whose story" element are one and the same piece of information; sometimes they are not. Here is an example, with the sentences listed vertically for greater ease in comparing the Topic positions:

18. Chris and Pat discussed the matter for three solid hours, after which both tempers flared.

    They shouted at each other, at increased decibel levels.

They banged on the table and overturned the chairs.

As a result of all the commotion, Jan came running down from upstairs to find out what was going on.

For the first three sentences, "Chris and Pat" are whose story is being told. In the second and third sentences, they are also the backward link. But in the fourth sentence, the backward link is "all the commotion," while the sentence becomes the story of Jan. Sometimes these two structural indicators are the same; sometimes they are not.

Look carefully at the following paragraph, also from the book by Baron that produced the previous example. What kinds of backward linkages and forward leans can you perceive in the Topic and Stress positions?

19a. Language was an important concern from early on in the New World. In New England, an area with an unusually high proportion of educated inhabitants, the Puritan emphasis on reading the Bible in the vernacular assured there would be a literate population, aware of the benefits of schooling. Compulsory education was established in the Massachusetts Bay Colony in 1647. The study of English was seen as a preparation for the study of the classics, which in turn was considered a necessary part of leadership training up to the time of the Revolution. Speech was as important as literacy, and there was a tendency in Puritan New England to equate speech with morality. Physical punishments were meted out to those considered guilty of various linguistic infractions, including swearing, anger, scolding, and gossiping. (p. 125)

Baron uses a variety of movement controls. When he needs to move on, he uses Topic Changing. When he needs to sit down on something for a while, he uses Topic Stringing. Sometimes the backward link and the "whose story" are the same; sometime they are not. Here is the paragraph again, with these structural controls indicated as they appear.

19b. Language was an important concern from early on in the New World.

Whose story:	Language
Backward link:	(None: It is the first sentence in the example.)
Stress position:	New World (a Herald Stress position)

19c. In New England, an area with an unusually high proportion of educated inhabitants, the Puritan emphasis on reading the Bible in the vernacular assured there would be a literate population, aware of the benefits of schooling.

Topic Changing

Whose story:	the puritan emphasis
Backward link:	New England
Stress position:	schooling (a Herald Stress position)

19d. Compulsory education was established in the Massachusetts Bay Colony in 1647.

Topic Changing

Whose story:	compulsory education (refers to "schooling")
Backward link:	compulsory education
Stress position:	Massachusetts Bay Colony in 1647 (a cumulative information Stress position)

19e. The study of English was seen as a preparation for the study of the classics, which in turn was considered a necessary part of leadership training up to the time of the Revolution.

Topic Stringing   (refers to "compulsory education")

Whose story:	The study of English
Backward link:	The study of English
Stress position:	leadership training ──────► the Revolution (a cumulative information Stress position)

19f. Speech was as important as literacy, and there was a tendency in Puritan New England to equate speech with morality.

Topic Stringing   (refers again to "compulsory education")

Whose story:	Speech
Backward link:	literacy
Stress position:	morality (a Herald Stress position)

19g. Physical punishments were meted out to those considered guilty of various linguistic infractions, including swearing, anger, scolding, and gossiping.

Topic Changing

Whose story:	Physical punishments
Backward link:	Physical punishments (refers back to "morality")
Stress position:	swearing, anger, scolding, and gossiping

We learn to trust a good writer. When we see the same thing in the Topic position of this sentence as we saw in the last one, we presume we are *intended* to keep the story going. When we see something different there, we presume we are *intended* to switch our focus. If the writer does not mislead us by misplacing pieces of information so they send the wrong instructions to the reader, then we ebb and flow with the thought just as we were *intended* to do. The greatest part of all these instructions concerning intention come from the structural placement of information.

··| EXERCISE **M** |···

For each of the following sentences, create two alternative new sentences that could logically *follow* it. Make one of your new sentences link backward to the given sentence's Topic position and the other link backward to the given sentence's Stress position.

Example:

Given sentence:

When a paragraph violated the English teacher's strict rules concerning structure, harsh penalties were handed out.

First new sentence, linking back to the given sentence's Topic position:

When *a paragraph* violated the English teacher's strict rules concerning structure, harsh penalties were handed out. When *a paragraph* demonstrated that teacher's teachings had been adhered to without missing a beat, there would be high grades and enthusiastic comments in the margin.

Second new sentence, linking back to the given sentence's Stress position:

When a paragraph violated the English teacher's strict rules concerning structure, *harsh penalties were handed out. Those penalties* ranged from low grades to scathing comments to a stern demand that the whole paper be rewritten.

Here are the sentences with which you can work:

1. No matter how hard I tried, I could not seem to shake the feeling that something strange was about to happen.

2. Perhaps all elections that end with the candidates separated by less than one-half a percentage point should be declared a tie, with the office remaining unfilled for the duration of the next term.

3. If we turned left, we would circle back to the beginning; but if we turned right, we hit a dead end.

This sentence-to-sentence connection is perhaps the single most important control you have over your reader's perception of the development of your thought. It is also perhaps the single most important tool you have to keep your own thought ordered. It can help you, as a result, to build your own thought -- to push it further, to strengthen the logical connections, so that everything you need to cover will eventually be covered. It is not nearly enough to produce many individual sentences that sound good and that suffer from no grammatical or syntactical errors; you must also control the way your thought connects and develops. The best way to control your thought is to control the occupants of your Topic positions and Stress positions.

The Flow of Thought from Sentence to Sentence

When information is distributed throughout a sentence with no sense of where the reader needs to encounter it, the result is a shapeless product we could call *splat prose.*

Splat prose results from writers not understanding the structural needs of readers. The reader presents an empty plate to the writer, with a keen interest in how the writer will fill it up. The writer drops one sentence onto the plate -- splat -- and then another, fully formed but not clearly connected -- splat -- and then another one, equally unconnected -- splat. With this delivery comes the implicit instruction, "*You* figure out what to do with these." Each sentence by itself may be grammatically and even substantively respectable; but together they fail to suggest specific ways in which the reader should connect them to form a whole, developing train of thought.

I will use as an example a paragraph that might seem rather tame, almost pedestrian; but it is probably one of the most important examples in this whole volume. It requires some patience to attend to all its details.

20a.   A disease that progresses with few or no symptoms to indicate its gravity is an "insidious" disease, under this definition. Asbestosis, neoplasia, mesothelioma, and bronchogenic carcinoma are all examples of insidious diseases. Asbestos insulation installers who have inhaled asbestos fibers over a period of many years regularly contract these diseases.

If we limit ourselves to the kinds of responses writing teachers have traditionally relied upon, we can find little to say that will help the writer revise this paragraph and do a better job in creating future paragraphs. We can cite no grammatical errors, no diction problems, no lack of research, and no lack of effort. We can hardly offer an "unclear" or an "awk."

Despite that, serious problems pervade this paragraph. The individual sentences may sound relatively unobjectionable; but the writer has failed to provide the reader with sufficient instructions for connecting the second sentence to the first or the third to the second. As a result, the intended shape of the whole paragraph's thought has not been made evident to the reader. It is also possible that those connections are not completely clear to the writer.

Let us start with a question: The frightening-sounding diseases of the second sentence exemplify the general definition of "insidious disease" offered in the first sentence; but do they also refer to the specific diseases contracted by the unfortunate workers in the third sentence? We cannot be sure how these three sentences are to be connected; and yet those connections turn out to be the essential part of what this paragraph was trying to communicate.

If we revise these three sentences based solely on the Topic/Stress principles, we can begin to perceive some of the writer's intentions and realize how far we are from perceiving others. Sentence by sentence, we will ask which piece of new information deserves the most emphasis; then we will find a way to move it where it belongs, to the Stress position. We will ask whose story each sentence is and which pieces of old information connect the sentence backward to previous discourse; then we will find a way to move them where they belong, to the Topic position. After we do that for each of three sentences, we will take a look at the new paragraph we have fashioned.

The first sentence:

20b. A disease that progresses with few or no symptoms to indicate its gravity is an "insidious" disease, under this definition.

The old information announces itself: "under *this* definition." The "this" indicates that a definition had been the subject of discussion prior to this sentence. At the moment, this old information occupies the Stress position, which for the reader is *doubly* unhelpful: (1) The information is not up front in the sentence, where it can make the appropriate backward link; and (2) it is usurping the Stress position from the new, more important information. It can be moved to the Topic position with ease:

20c. Under this definition, a disease that progresses with few or no symptoms to indicate its gravity is an "insidious" disease.

Note that this new sentence, (20c), does not *sound better* than sentence (20b). Topic/Stress revision cannot be judged by the ear but rather by the eye and the mind. This kind of revision helps forge intellectual connections between sentences that allow the writer to control the progression of the thought. Final value judgments concerning Topic/Stress revisions cannot therefore be made on a sentence-by-sentence basis but will have to be postponed until the whole paragraph has been transformed.

Now we turn to sentence (20c)'s newly created Stress position. Is "insidious diseases" the proper occupant? Or should we rather favor ending with "... to indicate its gravity"? Most people rely on the ear to make that decision; but once again the ear will not be a sufficient guide. Instead we should ask which of these two candidates was the one intended by the writer for us to emphasize. With the question put that way, we realize we have no way, at the moment, of knowing its answer -- at least not within the confines of this single sentence. If the paragraph continues to focus on the *continuing story* of "insidious diseases," then "insidious diseases" deserves the spotlight of this Stress position. Having called attention to the term in this way, "insidious diseases" could switch to the "whose story" location in the next sentence's Topic position, and we would be on our way. If, on the other hand, the paragraph proceeds to refine the *definition* of "insidious diseases," showing in more detail how it "progresses with few or no symptoms to indicate its gravity," then that material deserves the Stress position; then it could effectively take over the "whose story" position in the next sentence. Since we have not enough information in the first sentence to make this decision, let us, for the moment, leave revision (20c) as it is. We shall return to it when we have revised the other two sentences.

The second sentence:

20d. Asbestosis, neoplasia, mesothelioma, and bronchogenic carcinoma are all examples of insidious diseases.

Once again the old information is distinctly recognizable: We have heard about "insidious diseases" before. But it comes too late -- especially on a first reading. This old information is once again doubly unhelpfully located in the Stress position. Again we can easily move it to the Topic position:

20e. Examples of insidious diseases are asbestosis, neoplasia, mesothelioma, and bronchogenic carcinoma.

Since the four intimidating diseases are all that is left in the sentence, they stake a reasonable claim to the Stress position. Their presence there would be justified if their names need to be remembered for further use later in the text. But if they are more or less incidental information, not to be recalled later, their presence in a Stress position would lead us to value them too highly, thus wasting valuable reader energy. If this were the case, we would be left with nothing in sentence (20e) worthy of a Stress position. The four names then should be exported to the middle of some other sentence:

-- These diseases, such as asbestosis, neoplasia, mesothelioma, and bronchogenic carcinoma, are. . . .

In judging between (20d) and (20e), once again the ear will fail us as a guide. We shall be able to judge whether (20e) turns out to be an improvement over (20d) once we can view the whole of the resulting new paragraph.
The third sentence:

20f. Asbestos insulation installers who have inhaled asbestos fibers over a period of many years regularly contract these diseases.

Yet once again the old information arrives too late. We have heard about "insidious diseases" before. Once again, they are usurping the Stress position and can be moved to the Topic position:

20g. These diseases are regularly contracted by asbestos insulation installers who have inhaled asbestos fibers over a period of many years.

Now that we are attuned to this structural concern, we might ask, with some annoyance, "Can't the author *hear* that every sentence is ending with old information?" The answer, of course, is no. Until one understands the importance of these structural locations, one tends to be unaware of one's own structural patterns.

In trying to select the right piece of new information for this Stress position, we can identify the following candidates:

a) "installers";

b) "asbestos fibers";

c) "asbestos insulation"; and

d) "over a period of many years."

Not being the author, we have no way of determining which of these four was intended to prevail; the structure gives us no clue. Any one of the four *could* be appropriate -- as long as it is the one that takes over the story at the beginning of the next paragraph. At this moment of our revision, the Stress position is occupied by "over a period of many years." If it is indeed the best choice for the Stress position, then we as readers should expect the ensuing discussion to have something to do with "a period of many years" -- perhaps a consideration of prolonged exposure to asbestos. How long can a worker sniff this stuff before it becomes a health hazard? If that turns out to be the case, then sentence (20g) above is an effective revision of the original.

If, on the other hand, the next paragraph goes on instead to explore the nasty qualities of asbestos fibers, then those fibers deserve the Stress position. Because the substance is movable, we can reengineer the sentence to get those fibers where the reader will notice them the most.

20h. These diseases are regularly contracted by asbestos insulation installers who, over a period of many years, have [constantly] inhaled asbestos fibers.

If, in yet a third possibility, the next paragraph proceeds instead to discuss the plight of the people who are exposed to these fibers, then we should rearrange things to have the Stress position occupied by those people:

20i. These diseases are regularly contracted when asbestos fibers are inhaled over a period of many years by asbestos insulation installers.

It is also possible that the next paragraph might instead concentrate on asbestos insulation. If so, we know what to do:

20j. These diseases are regularly contracted when asbestos fibers are inhaled over a period of many years by installers of asbestos insulation.

Since the original text actually did continue in the next paragraph to discuss the effects of prolonged exposure, we will leave "over a period of many years" in the Stress position. Here, then, is the new paragraph that has resulted from our Topic/Stress revisions to this point:

20k. Under this definition, a disease that progresses with few or no symptoms to indicate its gravity is an "insidious" disease. Examples of insidious diseases are asbestosis, neoplasia, mesothelioma, and bronchogenic carcinoma. These diseases are regularly contracted by asbestos insulation installers who have inhaled asbestos fibers over a period of many years.

Although this may not yet be the ultimate version, it already does a great deal that its original failed to do. We can now return to our initial question: Do the diseases named in the second sentence form any meaningful connection between the two sentences that suround them? With the Topic and Stress positions now occupied by helpfully placed information, we perceive that diseases of the second sentence lean both backward and forward: They exemplify the general definition of the first sentence *and* then they specify the diseases caught by the people in the third sentence. That also turns out to be the medical reality.

Notice how the revised paragraph no longer suffers from the equally insidious disease of splat prose. The paragraph now has a helpful and discernible shape -- specifically, a funnel shape. It begins with the broad sweep of a definition producing a term of art, "insidious diseases"; it then narrows to producing examples of that first sentence's Stress position; and those examples further narrow the focus upon some people who do a particular act "over a period of many years." We now have three short sentences that form a continuum funneling us into the next paragraph, which will explore why "a period of many years" was the paragraph's final destination.

Under this definition, a disease that does x, y, & z is an insidious disease
Examples of insidious diseases include A, B, C, and D.
These diseases are regularly contracted
by asbestos insulation installers
who have inhaled asbestos fibers
over a period of many years.

Please understand: I am not suggesting that "funnel shapes are good" and that you should try to fashion a certain percentage of your paragraphs like funnels. A funnel-shaped paragraph is good only when the thought development in that paragraph is shaped like a funnel. You need not choose shapes for your paragraphs first and then fill them up. (See the next chapter for a detailed discussion of this concept.) You do need to take care of the flow of your thought from sentence to sentence by filling the Topic and Stress positions with the kinds of information readers expect to find there. Then the shape of the paragraph will, more often than not, take care of itself. It will be shaped like your thought.

There are yet three points of interest we should note before leaving this example -- one per sentence:

1. Returning to the first sentence, we can now settle the question we raised earlier: Which piece of information deserved the Stress position -- the term "insidious disease," or its definition, that ended with "with few

or no symptoms to indicate its gravity"? In our final revision (20k), the story of the whole paragraph has become that of "insidious diseases," because that term now occupies the "whose story" position in both the second and third sentences. Given that, the term "insidious diseases" well deserves the spotlight of the first sentence's Stress position, where it announces its own importance and makes possible its future "whose story" appearances in Topic positions.

[herald]	Please pay attention to INSIDIOUS DISEASES.
[topic change]	Four INSIDIOUS DISEASES are . . .
[topic string]	INSIDIOUS DISEASES are regularly contracted by . . .

2. The third sentence of the final revision (20k) contains a passive construction:

20m. These diseases *are regularly contracted by* asbestos insulation installers who have inhaled asbestos fibers over a period of many years.

I have argued before that the passive should be preferred to the active either when (1) it transports the backward-linking old information to the Topic position, or (2) it transports the person or thing or idea whose story it is to the Topic position. Those who argue for active over passive at all costs might protest that sentence (20m) could retain "these diseases" in the Topic position and still manage to support an active verb:

20n. These diseases regularly *afflict* asbestos insulation installers who have inhaled asbestos fibers over a period of many years.

I would argue that neither construction is superior to the other in and of itself; once again, it depends on the context in which the sentence appears and what the sentence was intended to do. The distinction between the two is subtle but potentially powerful:

a) If the original three sentences were only the first half of a six-sentence paragraph that continued to tell the story of "these diseases," the active voice of (20n) would do the better job. It would keep the focus on the continuing activity of the diseases:
"... a disease that progresses ... is an "insidious disease."
"Examples of these diseases are. . . .
These diseases regularly afflict. . . .
These diseases also afflict. . . .
They make it impossible to. . . .
They pose a serious threat to. . . ."
The story remains throughout that of insidious diseases and what they actively do.

b) If, on the other hand, our three sentences are the complete paragraph, followed by a new paragraph that shifts to the story of "prolonged exposure," then the passive construction of (20m) does the better job. It subtly but powerfully dilutes the focus on "these diseases" (which will soon no longer be active or aggressive as the agent) and thus transports the reader's attention further into the sentence to the "installers" and the "over a period of many years." The passive may sometimes be "weaker"; but sometimes weaker is better. This passive is an intentional weakener:

"These diseases are regularly contracted by
those people, who do this
over a period of many years."

Because of the passive here, yet more attention is focused on that which arrives at the end of the sentence.

3. Concerning the second sentence, we had been wondering whether anything in it deserved a Stress position. It turns out that the text never returns to discuss any of those four diseases individually. Since that is the case, we can undercut their importance by disallowing them a Stress position and transporting them into a neighboring sentence, where they can occupy a nonemphatic middle location.

20o. Under this definition, a disease that progresses with few or no symptoms to indicate its gravity is an "insidious" disease. Several of these diseases -- namely asbestosis, neoplasia, mesothelioma, and bronchogenic carcinoma -- are regularly contracted by asbestos insulation installers who have inhaled asbestos fibers over a period of many years.

Good prose -- on the sentence level, the paragraph level, and most often on the document level as well -- tends to demonstrate three consistent characteristics:

1. Nothing arrives that the reader cannot handle at the moment of its arrival.
2. Everything leans forward.
3. Everything actually goes in one of the directions it had been leaning.

With these three characteristics in mind, reread (20a) (on page 85) and (20o) above. Can you sense the difference better now?

·· EXERCISE N

The following paragraphs are the first seven of Lewis Thomas's *The Lives of a Cell: Notes of a Biology Watcher*. The material is sophisticated and not uncomplicated; but the flow of the prose could be called effortless. Read all seven paragraphs. Then choose two or three paragraphs to investigate the individual sentences in terms of the occupants of their Topic and Stress positions. For each sentence, determine the following: What is the backward link? Whose story is it? What kind of Stress position occupant does it have? Is there anything that deserves a Stress position but does not have one? Is there any Topic Changing or Topic Stringing going on?

A. We are told that the trouble with Modern Man is that he has been trying to detach himself from nature. He sits in the topmost tiers of polymer, glass, and steel, dangling his pulsing legs, surveying at a distance the writhing life of the planet. In this scenario, Man comes on as a stupendous lethal force, and the earth is pictured as something delicate, like rising bubbles at the surface of a country pond, or flights of fragile birds.*

B. But it is illusion to think that there is anything fragile about the life of the earth; surely this is the toughest membrane imaginable in the universe, opaque to probability, impermeable to death. We are the delicate part, transient and vulnerable as cilia. Nor is it a new thing for man to invent an existence that he imagines to be above the rest of life; this has been his most consistent intellectual exertion down the millennia. As illusion, it has never worked out to his satisfaction in the past, any more than it does today. Man is embedded in nature.

C. The biologic science of recent years has been making this a more urgent fact of life. The new, hard problem will be to cope with the dawning, intensifying realization of just how interlocked we are. The old, clung-to notions most of us have held about our special lordship are being deeply undermined.

D. *Item.* A good case can be made for our nonexistence as entities. We are not made up, as we had always supposed, of successively enriched packets of our own parts. We are shared, rented, occupied. At the interior of our cells, driving them, providing the oxidative energy that sends us out for the improvement of each shining day, are the mitochondria, and in a strict sense they are not ours. They turn out to be little separate creatures, the colonial posterity of migrant prokaryocytes, probably primitive bacteria that swam into ancestral precursors of our eukaryotic cells and stayed there. Ever since, they have maintained themselves and their ways, replicating in their own fashion, privately, with their own DNA and RNA quite different from ours. They are as much symbionts as the rhizobial bacteria in the roots of beans. Without them, we would not move a muscle, drum a finger, think a thought.

E. Mitochondria are stable and responsible lodgers, and I choose to trust them. But what of the other little animals, similarly established in my cells, sorting and balancing me, clustering me together? My centrioles, basal bodies, and probably a good many other more obscure tiny beings at work inside my cells, each with its own special genome, are as foreign, and as essential, as aphids in anthills. My cells are no longer the pure line entities I was raised with; they are ecosystems more complex than Jamaica Bay.

F. I like to think that they work in my interest, that each breath they draw for me; but perhaps it is they who walk through the local park in the early morning, sensing my senses, listening to my music, thinking my thoughts.

G. I am consoled, somewhat, by the thought that the green plants are in the same fix. They could not be plants, or green, without their chloroplasts, which run the photosynthetic enterprise and generate oxygen for the rest of us. As it turns out, chloroplasts are also separate creatures with their own genomes, speaking their own language.

Endnotes

1. In using these terms, I am following the example of my colleague Joseph Williams.
2. To judge the work of Rudolph Flesch for yourself, see any of the following: *The Art of Clear Thinking* (New York: Harper's, 1951), *The Art of Plain Talk* (New York: Macmillan, 1962), *The Art of Readable Writing* (New York: Harper & Row, 1974), *How to Write Plain English: A Book for Lawyers and Consumers* (New York: Harper & Row, 1979), *How to Write, Speak, and Think More Effectively* (New York: New American Library, 1964).
3. Joseph Williams uses the terms *Topic Chaining* and *Topic Stringing*. *Topic Changing* seems to me just a touch more evocative of what is happening to the structure.
4. I borrow this example, and its first three alternate revisions, from Joseph Williams.

4

"Whose Paragraph Is It, Anyway?": The Shapes of the English Paragraph

Procrustean Problems in Constructing a Paragraph

What have most of us been taught as the proper method of constructing a paragraph? Since the beginning of composition instruction in this country, most high school textbooks have suggested that if we know how to produce correct sentences, then combining several into a proper structure would produce a proper paragraph. That structure has most commonly required that the opening sentence should be a "topic sentence," which, by definition, states the issue and point of the paragraph. The topic sentence is to be followed by "support" (examples, proofs, or reasons) -- usually three of them -- each encapsulated in its own sentence. Then the final, fifth sentence should restate the claim of the first sentence. This produces a form we could call the "Wizard of Oz" paragraph -- with its middle three sentences singing "because, because, because. . . ."

For students in grammar school and middle school, this structure accomplishes a great deal of good:

-- It provides a place to start. Once you have the topic sentence nailed down, paragraph construction seems all downhill from there.

-- It makes young students feel secure, grounded, founded, found.

-- It teaches the helpful lesson that good writing demands good structure.

But this rigid regulation of paragraph construction produces serious problems: Although well suited to the needs of eighth-graders, it fails to describe the actual shape of paragraphs created by professional adults. If you took any published book down from the shelf, selected a paragraph at random, and inspected the next 99 consecutive paragraphs, how many of them would be likely to contain precisely five sentences, the first of which is recognizable as a topic sentence, the next three as support, and the fifth as the conclusion which restates the topic sentence? Perhaps zero. Perhaps one. The odds are low that you will find two. To understand how real paragraphs are formed, we have to recognize how varied and complex those paragraphs really are.

Greek mythology tells us that in the days of Theseus, there was a villain known as Procrustes who ran a macabre bed-and-breakfast place just off the road somewhere between Corinth and Thebes. Knowing that travelers would be unable to complete the journey in a single day, he would wait on the road at sunset, ready to persuade a weary pedestrian to spend the night at his place. "You'll need a good meal and a good night's rest to finish the journey. Why not stay with me tonight?" It sounded like the kindest of invitations. But although the unsuspecting houseguest might well have enjoyed the fine dinner, he could take little pleasure in the sleeping accommodations; for Procrustes suffered from a murderous compulsion that all visitors should fit the length of his guestroom bed -- precisely. Those who were too tall had their feet amputated or their legs shortened and died from loss of blood. Those who were too short were stretched on the rack and died from the resulting complications. Only occasionally were travelers just the right shape for the predetermined structure. Those lucky few escaped unharmed and thought all was right with the world.

The Topic Sentence paragraph structure is just such a Procrustean bed. One size fits all. It matters not what size or shape the bulk of your thought might be: To fit this prescribed resting place, it must be foreshortened or (more often, in the sixth grade) unnaturally extended to satisfy the requirements of your host, the teacher. Somehow we know, when we become adults, that we cannot function with such restraints; but too few of us have received any guidance in understanding the structure(s) readers expect to experience when making their way through an adult paragraph. It should come as no surprise, when we stop to think about it, that no single structure could possibly accommodate the wide variety of shapes human thought can take.

The five-part Topic Sentence paragraph model fails for many reasons, three of which are paramount:

(1) It assumes that the issue of the paragraph can always be stated in a single sentence.

(2) It assumes that the issue of a paragraph is always the same as its point.

(4) It limits our perspective on the paragraph; it looks inward, treating the paragraph as a unit that exists all by itself. That distorts a reader's normal experience. Readers rarely read isolated paragraphs; most paragraphs proceed from a previous one and lead to a following one. Nor do readers usually stop at the end of each paragraph to analyze its contents in retrospect.

To understand paragraphs better, we have to take into account the realities of how adult paragraphs function:

-- Readers do not assume that once they have read the first sentence of the paragraph, nothing new will happen to them until the next paragraph begins.

-- Readers do not assume that a paragraph's *issue* is always the same as its *point*. The issue is the ground the paragraph may cover; the point is the intellectual claim it wants to make.

-- Readers experience a paragraph as discourse that is constantly unfolding. Their interpretation of a paragraph therefore shifts and changes with the appearance of each additional word.

Let us therefore take a closer look at the relationship between the issue of a paragraph and the point it tries to make. From that, we can begin to see how varied the shapes and movements of paragraphs really are.

The Issue

The Topic Sentence approach was right about one important reality of reading: It is generally the case that readers expect a paragraph will be about whatever appears up front. In this sense, a paragraph resembles a sentence: Whatever comes first provides a context for all that follows.

Paragraphs written by grade-school students are essentially over by the end of the first sentence. The rest is merely support -- examples that demonstrate they were justified in saying what they said in the topic sentence. Here is a real example from grade 6:

1a. I like the Spring because of the pretty flowers. I like the Spring because of the tulips. I like the Spring because of the roses. I like the Spring because of the daffodils. I like the Spring because of the pretty flowers.

By the end of the first sentence, the *thinking* is complete. A more mature mind would recognize that there is only one sentence's worth of thought in the entire paragraph:

1b. I like the Spring because of the pretty flowers -- the tulips, the roses, and the daffodils.

Mature paragraphs *start* from the first sentence but continue to develop from there, allowing the thought to unfold. *Unfold* is the important word here. We read each succeeding sentence of a paragraph to see how that issue develops. Let us look at a paragraph unfolding in slow motion.

2a. Much has happened since the Apollo program and the Mercury and Gemini missions that paved the way for it in the early 1960s.

If the rest of the paragraph is about this initial sentence, what is the rest of the paragraph likely to be about? Most (but not all) readers expect either that we will hear more about what has happened in the development of the space program or that we will hear why the 1960s was such an important time. (The former information occupies the Topic position in (2a); the latter occupies the Stress position.)
Here is the second sentence:

2b. Numerous scientific and communications satellites have been launched into Earth orbit.

Does this begin to fulfill the promise of (2a)? It could: It might be the first of several examples of the "much that has happened" in the space program. On the other hand, it might not: The paragraph may settle down to talk exclusively about Earth orbit experiments -- in which case it would have taken two sentences, not one, to state the issue. We will not know until we read at least one more sentence.
Here is the next sentence:

2c. Unmanned deep-space probes have been sent to the sun, the moon, and the planets, where they gathered a wealth of information about our solar system.

Apparently we are not going to linger over the Earth orbit experiments. Because we are hearing about yet more of the "much that has happened" in the space program, it now looks like the whole paragraph will be devoted to this continuing effort -- the one that was presented to us in the first sentence. The next two sentences confirm this suspicion:

2d. Skylab demonstrated that American astronauts could live and work in space for months at a time.

2e. And a dramatically different launch vehicle entered service: the space shuttle.

Here is the final sentence of the paragraph.

2f. The winged reusable craft was supposed to make space flight routine and cheap.

The "winged reusable craft" refers backward to "the space shuttle." Thus, for the paragraph as a whole, it took only one sentence to get on the table the issue that would be discussed. We could not be *sure* of that until the paragraph had progressed for more than one sentence.
Here is the paragraph in its entirety:

2. Much has happened since the Apollo program and the Mercury and Gemini missions that paved the way for it in the early 1960s. Numerous scientific and communications satellites have been launched into Earth orbit. Unmanned deep-space probes have been sent to the sun, the moon, and the planets, where they gathered a wealth of information about our solar system. Skylab demonstrated that American astronauts could live and work in space for months at a time. And a dramatically different launch vehicle entered service: the space shuttle. The winged reusable craft was supposed to make space flight routine and cheap.

Often, however, a mature paragraph requires more than a single sentence to state its issue. Readers have to be aware -- and actually are naturally aware -- of that possibility. Since we do not print big numbers at the beginning of the paragraph to indicate how many sentences will be necessary to state the issue, readers have to figure it out for themselves. Once again, it is a process of watching the paragraph *unfold*. Let us watch another paragraph appear in slow motion.

3a. I did not allow blindness to intimidate me.

This sounds like a good candidate for being a regulation high school essay topic sentence -- a one-sentence issue if there ever was one. If it is indeed a one-sentence issue, then we should be ready to hear about a number of ways in which blindness did not prevail over the human spirit:

I did not allow blindness to intimidate me.
It didn't stop me from X.
It didn't stop me from Y.
It didn't stop me from Z.

Let us see if that is what happens in this particular paragraph. Here is the second sentence:

3b. I set about memorizing the number of stairs in each staircase of the new house, searching for ways to keep them all straight.

This does not have the ring of "It didn't stop me from X." It is not, in itself, an example of how blindness did not intimidate her. It is not in any clear way a fully self-explanatory statement. It sounds like it is leaning forward to a sentence that will either explain or begin to explain why this memorizing was a strong, self-reliant act.

Here is the third sentence:

3c. The fourteen steps of the front hall staircase summoned the word "fortunate" -- the way I felt about being able to have a new and better place in which to live: "*Fourt*een"; "*fort*unate."

This partially explains the second sentence. We might now be developing a suspicion that we will soon hear about other staircases. If that is indeed the case, then what we have here is a *two*-sentence issue. The next sentence should solve the puzzle for us. Here is the third sentence:

3d. The seven steps to the upper level, where my CD player and all that wonderful music resided were my "seven" steps to "heaven."

Now we are more or less convinced. The first two sentences, put together, announced the issue of the paragraph: So as not to be intimidated by blindness, she memorized the number of stairs in the various staircases. The third and fourth sentences are developing that issue. We might expect that development to continue.

Here is the rest of the paragraph:

3e. The ten stairs to the basement recalled the "ten steps" of St. John of the Cross, who tells us that "the way down," through denial and self-cleansing, is a good way to find God. And the three steps of the front doorstoop could be distinguished from the two steps of the back doorstoop because to ascend in life is always a step more difficult than to descend.

The structure of the paragraph now seems clear: The two-sentence issue is followed by a number of examples.

I was not going to be beaten by blindness.

I figured out mnemonic devices for dealing with the various staircases.

Staircase #1

Staircase #2

Staircase #3

Staircases 4 and 5.

Here is the whole paragraph:

3. I did not allow blindness to intimidate me. I set about memorizing the number of stairs in each staircase of the new house, creating a device

for keeping them all straight. The fourteen steps of the front hall stair-case summoned the word "fortunate" -- the way I felt about being able to have a new and better place to live: *"Fourteen"*; *"fortunate."* The seven steps to the upper level, where my CD player and all that wonderful music resided were my "seven" steps to "heaven." The ten stairs to the basement recalled the "ten steps" of St. John of the Cross, who tells us that "the way down," through denial and self-cleansing, are the best way to God. And the three steps of the front doorstoop could be distinguished from the two steps of the back doorstoop because to ascend in life is always a step more difficult than to descend.

Let us do this once more, looking at a paragraph that has yet a different shape.

4a. All through the 1950s and well into the 1960s, his published articles glowed with patriotic zeal and communal self-satisfaction.

If the rest of the paragraph goes on to tell us all about those glowing articles, or the zeal and the self-satisfaction, then what we have here is a one-sentence issue, much resembling the old-style topic sentence. Here is the second sentence:

4b. They praised the country's stability, our national sense of progress, our international status on the rise, and the political resiliency that allowed us to survive the McCarthy Era and the Korean War effort.

It seems our expectation is being fulfilled. This sentence might be the beginning of the kind of discussion that (4a) promised. By the end of the third sentence, we will be convinced, one way or another. Here is the third sentence:

4c. But in the late 1960s, everything changed, and his prose grew sour and darker.

The "But" changes our mind. The discussion of the glowing articles of the 1950s and early 1960s is over. The "But" signals that we are turning in a new direction. The Stress position occupant in this sentence, "sour and darker," seems to herald a new discussion -- one that will have little space for more "glowing" articles. Here is the fourth sentence:

4d. The Vietnam War depressed him.

We seem to be descending into the "sour and darker" side. Will it continue?

4e. The widening "generation gap" made communication seem increasingly difficult, if not impossible. The assassinations of Bobby

Kennedy and Martin Luther King seemed to promise that the assassination of John F. Kennedy had not been an isolated event, but rather had been the implanting of a national poison that was spreading and conquering. And with the Watergate scandal in the early 1970s, he seemed to give up hope altogether. He stopped writing.

It continued. This paragraph set us up with two sentences of "glowing" only for the purpose of emphasizing by contrast the descent into the "sour and darker." Thus, we have a *three*-sentence issue:

In the 1950s and early 1960s, everything was great.

Boy, was everything great.

But, after that things went downhill.

> Bad thing.
> Bad thing.
> Bad thing. . . .

Here is the whole paragraph:

4. All through the 1950s and well into the 1960s, his published articles glowed with patriotic zeal and communal self-satisfaction. They praised the country's stability, our national sense of progress, our international status on the rise, and the political resiliency that allowed us to survive the McCarthy Era and the Korean War effort. But in the late 1960s, everything changed, and his prose grew sour and darker. The Vietnam War depressed him. The widening "generation gap" made communication seem increasingly difficult, if not impossible. The assassinations of Bobby Kennedy and Martin Luther King seemed to promise that the assassination of John F. Kennedy had not been an isolated event, but rather had been the implanting of a national poison that was spreading and conquering. And with the Watergate scandal in the early 1970s, he seemed to give up hope altogether. He stopped writing.

I have noted twice that by the end of the third sentence, we should know what is really going on with the development of the paragraph's structure. That is a curiously common expectation among native readers of English. Three is perfection. Three is complete. The arrival of three suggests the beginning and the end of things -- "ready, set, GO!" . . . "and *so* we *come* to an *end*" -- or the perfection of things -- "the red, white, and blue." Three is mystical, magical, and melodic. If we are handed more than three -- even if the number is only four -- we tend to feel overburdened. If three is perfection, four is a crowd. Can you imagine Goldilocks and the *four* bears?

"Somebody's been sleeping in *my* bed," said the Papa Bear.

"Somebody's been sleeping in *my* bed," said the Mama Bear.

"Somebody's been sleeping in *my* bed," said the Baby Bear.

"Somebody's been sleeping in -- -- " [Oh shut up already!]

This limit of three applies to our reading endurance when trying to determine how many sentences make up the issue of a paragraph. Any first sentence *could* be a one-sentence issue of a paragraph. We therefore keep (subconsciously) aware of that possibility as we proceed to the second sentence. At the end of that sentence, we are able to maintain our sense that "the jury is still out": The second sentence could be (1) the beginning of the discussion of a one-sentence issue, or (2) the second half of a two-sentence issue, or (3) the setup for the arrival of another sentence that will complete a three-sentence issue. That is a complicated state of affairs to hold in mind -- too complicated for us to be able to absorb any more complications. The puzzle will have to be solved by the end of the third sentence. By then, we should know how many sentences it took to state the paragraph's issue -- one, two, or three sentences. If by the end of the third sentence we are still muddled, we tend to give up on the question and proceed to absorb the rest of the information as best we can. Alternatively, once readers have wandered three sentences into the paragraph, they might seize upon whatever material they can in those first one, two, or three sentences and make it *their* issue, regardless of whether the rest of the paragraph discusses it or not. Experience has demonstrated that when this is the case, ten readers are likely to make anywhere from five to ten different decisions as to what the issue was supposed to have been.

Under the old topic sentence model, we were taught that issues should always be easy to spot. The first sentence should always translate, "This paragraph will be about X."

5. I like the Spring because of the pretty birds. I like the Spring because of the robins. I like the Spring because of the blue jays. I like the Spring because of the cardinals. I like the Spring because of the pretty birds.

In sophisticated prose, however, the two-sentence issue is not only quite common but also quite necessary. Here are a few of the many recognizable two-steps that have to be danced before some issues are completely stated:

6a. "So you see where we've come from. Well, here's where we're going...."

6b. "Here is a general statement. From that generalization, I'm going to focus on this more specific development...."

6c. "You may think that things are X. Well, they're really Y...."

Even three-sentence issues are possible, and not unfamiliar:

7a. "So you see where we've come to. It's not been much help. Let's take a look at X instead...."

7b. "Here is X. Here is Y. The important thing to consider here is the relationship between X and Y. . . ."

7c. "X is intriguing. Just look at how intriguing X can be. But that is the case only when you ignore Y. . . ."

7d. "X looks convincing. Y looks convincing. But neither does the job very well when you consider Z. . . ."

7e. "We began with X. Then we moved on to Y. Only when we had experienced X and Y could we turn our full attention to Z."

Our middle school and high school composition texts have urged students to become proficient at forming correct sentences, to learn how to make a comprehensive topic sentence, and to learn how to support it with examples. Even those more sophisticated college texts that stress what they call development of thought tend to talk about the "construction" of paragraphs, suggesting a process of concrete accumulation. It would be like constructing a paragraph-building out of brick-sentences. It might be visually represented like this.

We create sentence #1. It is a visible entity, whole unto itself, like a brick. Call it brick #1. Then we create the second sentence, brick #2. If we are "good" writers, we might provide the reader with some sort of mortarlike connecting material that cements the two together. Then we create brick #3, perhaps with more mortar -- and then bricks #4 and #5 and so forth, until we have "finished" our paragraph. A six-brick paragraph might look like this:

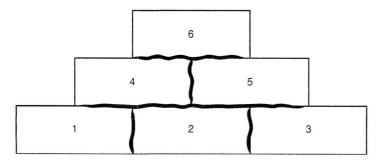

As we gaze at this paragraph-building, we can still see clearly the definition of each individual brick. The unit as a whole remains the sum of its individual, still perceivable parts.

I submit that this image provides a false representation of what actually happens to readers in their linear journey through a paragraph. It even more greatly falsifies the nonlinear experience the reader has of perceiving the paragraph as a whole.

Let us not think of paragraphs as essentially linear:

$\longrightarrow$

nor as brick buildings,

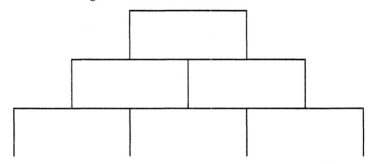

but rather as having a liquid, fluid shape that continually changes as we progress into it.

In the figure below, consider the dotted line a moment of time -- the moment when the reading eye encounters the information flowing to it from the sentence. Sentence #1 of the paragraph is pictured as a wavy line, approaching that eye-moment from the left. On the right, the brain is forming a concept of the thought of the sentence as the eye encounters its words. Once the eye has taken in the totality of the sentence, the totality of its thought is pictured as a liquid pool.

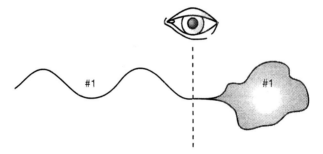

At that moment, sentence #2 starts to flow past the eye. As the brain processes sentence #2, it *adds* that information/experience/thought to the pool generated by sentence #1. The result is not a bricklike juxtaposition of two distinct thoughts but rather a new, conglomerate pool that is shaped differently from the sentence #1 pool. The former pool is no longer perceivable as the unit it once was, absorbed as it now is in a two-sentence pool.

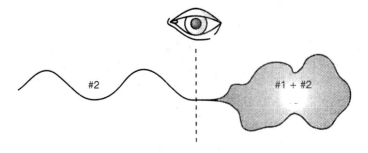

Then sentence #3 flows by the eye, is processed by the brain, and further changes the shape of the pool, making it now a three-sentence pool. Some parts of the pool may be enlarged; some may be constricted; some old shapes may have disappeared; and some new ones may have been generated.

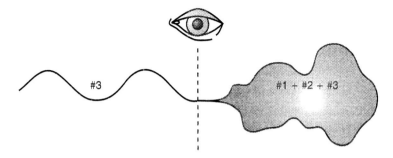

By the end of sentence #3, the pool often tends to have expanded to what will more or less be its final shape. That is, by the end of the third sentence, we as readers should know what the *issue* is and be prepared for further strengthening and weakening of the shape that is now before us. Fourth, fifth, and other succeeding sentences may continue to fill up the pool. Whether that happens after sentence #3 or not, by the end of the paragraph the pool will have attained a shape; but it will no longer be possible to recognize sentence #1 -- or any other of the individual sentences -- as a discrete unit. How different this is from the brick metaphor, where brick #1 -- and each of the others -- is *always* recognizable and re-recognizable in its original shape.

I would argue that one can *never* see sentence #1 again in the way one experienced it the first time around. Even when we reread the paragraph, the experiencing of sentence #1 will be influenced and contextualized by our having read the paragraph before. One can never step one's toe into precisely the same textual pool twice.

The reading of a paragraph is indeed a liquid experience: It constantly flows in a forward motion; every moment is new and different in itself, but it also *changes* the "meaning" of what has already been experienced; everything that has already arrived contextualizes and controls that which will arrive thereafter. In order for a writer to control -- *insofar as possible* -- the continual and continuing interpretive process of the reader, the writer must understand what kinds of expectations a reader is likely to have concerning what will come next. *Placement* of information highly influences what the reader will have perceived as the paragraph's meaning.

It seems Procrustes was the wrong mythical model; let us substitute for him another mythological creature: Proteus, the shape-changer. Whenever his freedom was threatened, he could turn into whatever shape he felt best suited the situation -- animal, vegetable, or mineral. Paragraphs should be Protean, not Procrustean. Their shapes should not be crushed to fit a pre-ordained, rule-dominated shape; instead, they should adapt their shape to the needs and nature of the thought they represent.

Every paragraph is constructed to accomplish some or all of the following:

It offers cohesion;

it presents unity;

it indicates purpose;

it raises an issue;

it makes a point;

it tells a story;

it generates development;

it provides coherence; and

it creates shape.

The last is of special importance. Paragraphs must not be crammed into a preexisting shape rather but must help create structural shapes that in turn help communicate their substance. A change of shape produces a change in meaning; a change of meaning requires a change of shape. And if we ask, "Whose paragraph is it, anyway?" we must assuredly answer, "It is the reader's." Since paragraphs should be judged by how well they show themselves to their readers and not by how well they conform to previously established academic regulations, we must avoid Procrustes and embrace Proteus.

All the paragraphs I used as examples above had a structural characteristic in common: They all stated an issue and then spent the rest of their time and energy exemplifying or supporting that issue statement. This kind of paragraph construction accounts for only a moderate percentage of professional and published paragraphs. More often than not, a well-written paragraph will grow continually and organically from beginning to end. There is no stopping point after which all the rest merely summons examples for what has already been said conclusively. Let us take a slow-motion look at just such a paragraph from an undergraduate essay. The first sentence:

8a. The office of the Vice President of the United States is often considered one of the most pointless positions in politics.

We might expect to hear why this office seems so dreary. If we do, this will have been a one-sentence issue. (Again, prose is fluid: We cannot tell whether or not this one sentence states the whole of the issue until we read further.) The second sentence:

8b. John Adams, the first vice president, referred to it as "the most insignificant office that ever the invention of man contrived or his imagination conceived."

That is an appealing and entertaining piece of support for what is now seeming quite distinctly to be a one-sentence issue paragraph. The third sentence:

8c. Daniel Webster refused to accept the job, saying, "I do not choose to be buried until I am really dead."

That is the same kind of support as was offered by the second sentence, but a touch funnier. Where from here? Sentence four:

8d. Because the vice president's only real duty is to preside over the Senate, the job is not very attractive, and vice presidents are not usually chosen because they are strong, experienced leaders.

This is something new. It does not merely *support* the first sentence but rather goes *beyond* it, developing a more sophisticated thought from the straightforwardly judgmental opening sentence. It speaks not only to the *nature* of the vice presidency but also to what *results* that nature generates. Nature: The office is silly. Results: The people who get the job are not necessarily among our best and brightest. Continuing:

8e. This is alarming because the vice president sits just a heartbeat away from the presidency.

This develops the thought yet further. Once you have these *results*, here are the *dangers* that naturally ensue. The final sentence:

8f. Since he could become the president of the United States at any time, his job should be regarded more seriously, and he should be an independently elected official.

Here, at the end of the paragraph, is the payoff *recommendation* toward which the writer had been working all along. After defining (sentence #1) and exemplifying (#2 and #3) the *nature* of the office, he demonstrated what *results* might follow (#4) and what *dangers* might arise (#5) thereafter. As a result of all this preparation, he was finally ready to offer us his *recommendation*. The paragraph has shape, flow, and purpose.

Here is the paragraph as a whole:

8. The office of the Vice President of the United States is often considered one of the most pointless positions in politics. John Adams, the first vice president, referred to it as "the most insignificant office that ever the invention of man contrived or his imagination conceived." Daniel Webster refused to accept the job, saying, "I do not choose to be buried until I am really dead." Because the vice president's only

real duty is to preside over the Senate, the job is not very attractive, and vice presidents are not usually chosen because they are strong, experienced leaders. This is alarming because the vice president sits just a heartbeat away from the presidency. Since he could become the president of the United States at any time, his job should be regarded more seriously, and he should be an independently elected official.

Readers have expectations concerning the beginnings of paragraphs that somewhat parallel their expectations concerning the beginnings of sentences. Just as readers tend to read a sentence as being the story of whoever or whatever shows up first, so they tend to assume that a paragraph will develop the issue stated at its beginning. The expectation is so strong that most readers will consider the first sentence or two or three the issue whether it was intended to be or not. In other words, what we can speak of as an expectation is perhaps more a habitual reading procedure. To demonstrate, let us revisit paragraph example (2) above, the one that announced in its first sentence that it would talk about the many things that have happened in the space program in the past few decades. Will the paragraph really become hopelessly muddled if that clear one-sentence issue appears someplace other than at the beginning, where readers need and expect to find it? Yes.

Let us transplant the first sentence (the one-sentence issue statement) to the end of the paragraph and see what happens. Again, we will take the slow-motion approach so we may see the paragraph revealing itself in the fluid way paragraphs appear to us when we read them for the first time. (Try to forget you have seen the paragraph before.) Our new first sentence, then, is that which was second sentence in the original.

9a. Numerous scientific and communications satellites have been launched into Earth orbit.

This opening sentence seems a reasonable candidate to be a one-sentence issue statement. If it is so, then the rest of the paragraph will probably go on to discuss earth orbit experiments. This paragraph's second sentence might clarify this matter for us.

9b. Unmanned deep-space probes have been sent to the sun, the moon, and the planets, where they gathered a wealth of information about our solar system.

Not only does this *not* launch us into an earth orbit discussion section, but there is no evident link that we can perceive between these two sentences. Since the promise of a one-sentence issue seems to have been undone, and we cannot see how the two go together to make up a two-sentence issue, our last hope for coherence is that the third sentence will show us clearly how this is the unfolding of a *three*-sentence issue. We would be pleased with a third sentence that began, "But whether in earth orbit or far beyond into outer space, our efforts. . . ." But here, alas, is what we actually get as a third sentence:

9c. Skylab demonstrated that American astronauts could live and work in space for months at a time.

Now we are in trouble. It is not absolutely impossible to figure out a way in which these three sentences could reasonable "talk" to each other; but we, as readers, would have to do all the work ourselves. That should have been the writer's job.

Since three sentences is our normal limit for recognizing issues, we are reduced to hoping we will be able to survive the rest of the paragraph and salvage whatever coherence we can. Here is the fourth sentence:

9d. And a dramatically different launch vehicle entered service: the space shuttle.

At this point we have four sentences that cover four different topics. All we are convinced of at the moment is that every new sentence will *not* be connected to its predecessor. Here, then, is the fifth sentence:

9e. The winged reusable craft was supposed to make space flight routine and cheap.

Oops. The one expectation in which we had confidence is now violated. For some odd reason, the shuttle seems to have deserved two sentences to everyone else's one. Now, thoroughly baffled, we stumble on to the final sentence:

9f. Much has happened since the Apollo program and the Mercury and Gemini missions that paved the way for it in the early 1960s.

We hardly know what to make of this. The paragraph as a whole is a disaster. And yet not a single sentence has been changed from the relatively clear and controlling prose of the original. Only a structural location -- a most significant one -- has been changed. The issue statement -- without a single word altered -- has simply arrived too late to *function* as an issue statement. The place for such a thing was up front. When it was not there, we presumed whatever *was* there had to be the issue. We tried for one, two, and three sentences and then gave up; by the time the real issue statement arrived, we were no longer looking for it, and therefore we could not recognize it.

Structure is 85% of the ballgame.

Context controls meaning.

For easy comparison, here again is the paragraph in its original form. Note how the contextualizing first sentence helps us make sense of all the other sentences as we encounter them.

9. Much has happened since the Apollo program and the Mercury and Gemini missions that paved the way for it in the early 1960s. Numerous scientific and communications satellites have been launched into Earth orbit. Unmanned deep-space probes have been sent to the sun, the moon, and the planets, where they gathered a wealth of information about our solar system. Skylab demonstrated that American astronauts could live and work in space for months at a time. And a dramatically different launch vehicle entered service: the space shuttle. The winged reusable craft was supposed to make space flight routine and cheap.

With paragraphs, as with sentences (and with most experiences in life), people wish to be contextualized before they have to deal with new and challenging material. Readers expect the issue to begin each paragraph, with the discussion of that issue usually filling the remainder of that unit. (There may or may not be a renegade kind of final sentence we will be calling a *coda*; but more on that later.)

Think of the upper part of the paragraph as a structural location -- a place where readers expect certain things to happen. That structural location is relatively fixed in terms of reader expectation and cannot be easily modified by any individual writer. The *substance*, on the other hand, is in the control of the writer. You can think up whatever you want and place it wherever you want. My advice here will be the same as the advice I offered at the sentence level: In general, place substance in the structural locations where readers tend to expect that substance to appear. And, once again, two major benefits will result: (1) That substance will be labeled and interpreted as you want it to be labeled and interpreted; and (2) the reader will spend a minimal amount of reader energy on unraveling the *structure* of the paragraph and have a great deal more energy left for contemplating its *substance*.[1]

STRCT	ISSUE	DISCUSSION (Coda)	FIXED
SUBS			MVBL

The above paragraph boxes are seriously flawed in one important way: The Issue is not always approximately the first third of a paragraph. Often it will consume only 10% of the space. On occasion it can extend to as much as two thirds of a paragraph; that is commonly the case for three-sentence opening paragraphs, especially in professional research articles:

Sentence 1: Experts have long said. . . .

Sentence 2: Experts have failed to realize. . . .

Sentence 3: This article sheds clearer light on the subject by demonstrating that. . . .

It is important to note that not all paragraphs present and discuss issues. Narrative paragraphs, for example, may simply tell a story in chronological (or otherwise logical) order. In such paragraphs, the Issue position should contain a clue for the reader *not* to expect an issue and a discussion but rather to expect a narrative. Here is an example:

10. The summer I was 16, I took a train from New York to Steamboat Springs, Colorado, where I was going to be assistant horse wrangler at a camp. The trip took three days, and since I was much too shy to talk to strangers, I had quite a lot of time for reading. I read all of *Gone with the Wind*. I read all the interesting articles in a couple of magazines I had, and then I went back and read all the dull stuff. I also took all the quizzes, a thing of which magazines were even fuller than now.

Here the emphasis on setting a time frame ("The summer I was 16") and the presentation of simple fact ("I took a train") may lead us to expect the ensuing travelogue. Whether or not you wish to think of this as an issue, there is no discussion. The Issue position is filled with the clue that raises the expectation of a narrative; the Discussion position is filled with the rest of that narration. Such paragraphs normally (but not always) present such a structural clue in the paragraph's first sentence and confirm it, at the latest, by the third sentence.

The traditional topic sentence paragraph model oversimplifies paragraphs. It takes no account of different paragraph functions; nor does it recognize the frequent need of sophisticated writers to take more than a single sentence to state the paragraph's issue. But if the latter were the only problem with the topic sentence approach, we could easily readjust the model instead of discarding it. We would need note only that sophisticated writers often take two or three sentences to create what for younger writers would be a single topic sentence. Far more problematic, however, is the assumption that the topic sentence must always state both the issue *and* the point. For sophisticated writers, issue and point are often not identical. After an exercise on Issue statements, we will turn our attention to the nature of the Point and the ways in which it can be distinct from the statement of the issue.

·· EXERCISE P ··

Here again are the opening seven paragraphs of Lewis Thomas's *The Lives of a Cell: Notes of a Biology Watcher*. You have seen them before, in the exercise at the end of the previous chapter. This time, go through all seven paragraphs to determine what you consider to be the issue statements. How many sentences does each paragraph's issue require? (Keep track of your responses. You will be able to use them again in a later exercise.)

A. We are told that the trouble with Modern Man is that he has been trying to detach himself from nature. He sits in the topmost tiers of polymer, glass, and steel, dangling his pulsing legs, surveying at a distance the writhing life of the planet. In this scenario, Man comes on as a stupendous lethal force, and the earth is pictured as something delicate, like rising bubbles at the surface of a country pond, or flights of fragile birds.

B. But it is illusion to think that there is anything fragile about the life of the earth; surely this is the toughest membrane imaginable in the universe, opaque to probability, impermeable to death. We are the delicate part, transient and vulnerable as cilia. Nor is it a new thing for man to invent an existence that he imagines to be above the rest of life; this has been his most consistent intellectual exertion down the millennia. As illusion, it has never worked out to his satisfaction in the past, any more than it does today. Man is embedded in nature.

C. The biologic science of recent years has been making this a more urgent fact of life. The new, hard problem will be to cope with the dawning, intensifying realization of just how interlocked we are. The old, clung-to notions most of us have held about our special lordship are being deeply undermined.

D. *Item.* A good case can be made for our nonexistence as entities. We are not made up, as we had always supposed, of successively enriched packets of our own parts. We are shared, rented, occupied. At the interior of our cells, driving them, providing the oxidative energy that sends us out for the improvement of each shining day, are the mitochondria, and in a strict sense they are not ours. They turn out to be little separate creatures, the colonial posterity of migrant prokaryocytes, probably primitive bacteria that swam into ancestral precursors of our eukaryotic cells and stayed there. Ever since, they have maintained themselves and their ways, replicating in their own fashion, privately, with their own DNA and RNA quite different from ours. They are as much symbionts as the rhizobial bacteria in the roots of beans. Without them, we would not move a muscle, drum a finger, think a thought.

E. Mitochondria are stable and responsible lodgers, and I choose to trust them. But what of the other little animals, similarly established in my cells, sorting and balancing me, clustering me together? My centrioles, basal bodies, and probably a good many other more obscure tiny beings at work inside my cells, each with its own special genome, are as foreign, and as essential, as aphids in anthills. My cells are no longer the pure line entities I was raised with; they are ecosystems more complex than Jamaica Bay.

F. I like to think that they work in my interest, that each breath they draw for me; but perhaps it is they who walk through the local park in the early morning, sensing my senses, listening to my music, thinking my thoughts.

G. I am consoled, somewhat, by the thought that the green plants are in the same fix. They could not be plants, or green, without their chloroplasts, which run the photosynthetic enterprise and generate oxygen for the rest of us. As it turns out, chloroplasts are also separate creatures with their own genomes, speaking their own language.

P *oint*

The Point and How to Find It

In the sixth grade, a paragraph's issue and the point the paragraph intended to make were almost always one and the same thing:

I like the Spring because of the pretty flowers.

The same continued to hold true throughout high school:

Capital punishment should be abolished because it is cruel and inhuman.

Violence on television should be eliminated because it influences people to go out and commit violent acts.

These statements were both the issue the paragraph would discuss and the point the paragraph intended to make. Summoning three examples and restating the Topic Sentence created a complete, cohesive, and coherent paragraph, and the job was done. It was a controllable task for the student and a reviewable task for the teacher.

But in sophisticated, professional prose, the *issue* the paragraph will discuss and the *point* the paragraph wishes to make are often distinct from each other. The *issue* refers to the intellectual geographic boundaries within which the discussion might wander; the *point* is the interesting place within those boundaries at which the reader is intended to arrive. It should come as no surprise that readers expect the point of a paragraph (with a lowercase *p*) to arrive in a particular structural location, which we will refer to as a Point position (with an uppercase *P*). The old Topic Sentence model taught us that the issue and the point are identical and should always be articulated at the start in a Topic Sentence; but in professional prose, this tends to happen only between 15% and 22% of the time. What happens the rest of the time?

Readers usually need to be told what the point of a paragraph is -- clearly and explicitly. They are grateful when that clear point is presented in a single sentence. They also want to *know* that sentence when they see it. An extensive investigation of thousands of professional paragraphs makes it evident that readers expect that point to appear at particular structural locations. To state this more compactly, readers hope the point will be stated in a Point sentence; and they know where in the paragraph to look for it.

Unlike any of the other reader expectations we have explored, however, there are *two* possible structural locations for the point to arrive in paragraphs. One is a fallback plan for the other: If the point did not show up in the first Point location, then we look for it in the other.

If we put together what we have already investigated about issues and what has just been claimed about points, notice what has happened to our conception of "the" paragraph: It no longer can be said to have "a" shape. It has many possible shapes, because the issue can be stated in one or two or three sentences, and the point can appear at one of two locations. And there are paragraphs that do not make points. And there are even paragraphs that explicitly announce their own variant structures. (We will return to those later.)

Let us revisit several of our example paragraphs to determine their points. Here are three ways of asking the appropriate question:

i)   "I am a busy and intolerant reader. I haven't the time to read your whole paragraph. I'll read only one sentence. Which do you choose?"

ii) Of all the sentences in this paragraph, which suffers least from the annoying question, "*So what?*"

iii) Which of the sentences in this paragraph explicitly articulates the point the paragraph is trying to make?

As a shorthand for all these combined, we will use the following question:

iv) In this paragraph, which is the point sentence?

(Note: It is possible to leave the paragraph's point unarticulated -- to allow it to hover over the surface of the prose, relying on the reader to figure out what you as writer see as obvious. That is possible to do, but risky.)

Here again is this chapter's example (2):

2.   Much has happened since the Apollo program and the Mercury and Gemini missions that paved the way for it in the early 1960s. Numerous scientific and communications satellites have been launched into Earth orbit. Unmanned deep-space probes have been sent to the sun, the moon, and the planets, where they gathered a wealth of information about our solar system. Skylab demonstrated that American astronauts could live and work in space for months at a time. And a dramatically different launch vehicle entered service: the space shuttle. The winged reusable craft was supposed to make space flight routine and cheap.

Which is the point sentence? The answer is hard to come by -- because we have this paragraph before us in isolation, out of its natural context. If we consider this paragraph only by itself, we could make a good case for the point being the first sentence: "Much has happened since the Apollo program and the Mercury and Gemini missions that paved the way for it in the early 1960s." The rest of the paragraph talks about this at all times; and no other single sentence seems to claim a superior importance compared to the others. As a result, we would say that this paragraph has a one-sentence issue, with the point being the first sentence.

But what if the next paragraph told us how although the space shuttle "was supposed to make space flight routine and cheap," it failed badly to do so? Then we might well make the argument that the point of its preceding paragraph had been the final sentence. Then we would have to say that paragraph (2) had a one-sentence issue with the point being the last sentence. The point a paragraph makes always depends on where we have come from and where we are going. The same paragraph, in two different contexts, could make two distinctly different points. Context controls meaning.

Now look once more at the paragraph from example (8):

8. The office of the Vice President of the United States is often considered one of the most pointless positions in politics. John Adams, the first vice president, referred to it as "the most insignificant office that ever the invention of man contrived or his imagination conceived." Daniel Webster refused to accept the job, saying, "I do not choose to be buried until I am really dead." Because the vice president's only real duty is to preside over the Senate, the job is not very attractive, and vice presidents are not usually chosen because they are strong, experienced leaders. This is alarming because the vice president sits just a heartbeat away from the presidency. Since he could become the president of the United States at any time, his job should be regarded more seriously, and he should be an independently elected official.

We noted that this paragraph had a one-sentence issue -- that announced the emptiness of the position of vice president. But was that the point of the paragraph as well? It certainly could be the point of *some* paragraph. Such a paragraph would develop examples and arguments until, in its totality, it would try to convince us that the vice presidency is *indeed* "the most pointless position in politics." But paragraph (8) does not do this. It progresses beyond that statement of definition to develop what the author sees as the problem that develops from it: "Since he could become the president of the United States at any time, his job should be regarded more seriously, and he should be an independently elected official." That final sentence, then, might well be considered the paragraph's point. Then we would have a paragraph with a one-sentence issue with the point in the last sentence.

Here is yet a differently shaped paragraph, example (3) from above:

3. I did not allow blindness to intimidate me. I set about memorizing the number of stairs in each staircase of the new house, creating a device for keeping them all straight. The fourteen steps of the front

hall staircase summoned the word "fortunate" -- the way I felt about being able to have a new and better place to live: *"Fourteen"*; *"fortunate."* The seven steps to the upper level, where my CD player and all that wonderful music resided were my "seven" steps to "heaven." The ten stairs to the basement recalled the "ten steps" of St. John of the Cross, who tells us that "the way down," through denial and self-cleansing, are the best way to God. And the three steps of the front doorstoop could be distinguished from the two steps of the back doorstoop because to ascend in life is always a step more difficult than to descend.

This was an example of a two-sentence issue: In order to maintain independence in the face of blindness, this person figured out how to memorize the number of steps in each of the house's staircases. Which sentence is the point sentence? The paragraph seems to be designed to show how this independence was achieved; if that is the case, then the point is the second sentence: "I set about memorizing the number of stairs in each staircase of the new house, creating a device for keeping them all straight." We thus would have a two-sentence issue with the point being the second sentence.

Here is yet one more paragraph, example (4) from above:

4. All through the 1950s and well into the 1960s, his published articles glowed with patriotic zeal and communal self-satisfaction. They praised the country's stability, our national sense of progress, our international status on the rise, and the political resiliency that allowed us to survive the McCarthy Era and the Korean War effort. But in the late 1960s, everything changed, and his prose grew sour and darker. The Vietnam War depressed him. The widening "generation gap" made communication seem increasingly difficult if not impossible. The assassinations of Bobby Kennedy and Martin Luther King seemed to promise that the assassination of John F. Kennedy had not been an isolated event, but rather was the implanting of a national poison that was spreading and conquering. And with the Watergate scandal in the early 1970s, he seemed to give up hope altogether. He stopped writing.

We had noted that it took three sentences in this paragraph to state the issue: While things looked bright in the 1950s and early 1960s, things looked darker thereafter. Which is the point sentence? One good candidate is the third sentence: "But in the late 1960s, everything changed, and his prose grew sour and darker." The rest of the paragraph certainly goes on to expand upon that statement. But there is another, equally strong candidate -- the last sentence: "He stopped writing." In other words, the point of the whole paragraph might have been to build up to the stark statement that "he stopped writing." How can we decide between two such equally convincing candidates? Once again, we would have to look to the context. If the next paragraph continues to talk about the depressing effect of events in the late 1960s and beyond, then the third sentence wins and contains the point; but if the next paragraph tells us more about why he stopped writing and the resulting effects, then the last sentence wins.

Let us see what the scoreboard looks like at this moment.

Example	Issue	Point
2	1	1 or last (depending on context)
8	1	last
3	2	2
4	3	3 or last (depending on context)

We can start to see a pattern:

Example	Issue	Point
2	1-sentence issue	point in the 1st
3	2-sentence issue	point in the 2nd
4	3-sentence issue	point in the 3rd

That turns out to be such a consistent mode of construction for mature paragraphs that we can call it another Reader Expectation:

Readers of English initially expect that the point of a paragraph will appear as the last sentence of the paragraph's issue."

That expectation, however, will not account for all the point placements in the examples we have been investigating. Another pattern exists on our scoreboard:

Example	Issue	Point
2	1-sentence issue	point in the last
8	1-sentence issue	point in the last
4	3-sentence issue	point in the last

To these we could easily add a paragraph example that would have a two-sentence issue with the point in the last sentence. It seems there is an alternate or fallback Reader Expectation concerning the location of the point sentence:

Readers of English expect that if the point of a paragraph is not the last sentence of the paragraph's issue, it will be the final sentence of the paragraph.

However, this statement is not quite accurate. There is yet one more paragraph-level structural location we must take into account. It is neither a common occurrence nor a scarce one; but it happens enough for us to take note of it. What would you consider the issue and point of the following paragraph?

11. Many residents in the several counties that surround the Perkins Nuclear Energy Plant have expressed concern over the potential dangers from the storage of nuclear waste in the Plant's four storage tanks. While it is true that we have not been successful in finding ways to eradicate the potential radiation altogether from the waste products, nuclear engineers have developed a storage system that is adequately monitored by a sophisticated system of safety gauges. The tanks are constructed of materials that will not deteriorate over time. They are filled with a liquid "bath" that renders the waste products completely harmless, as long as they are totally submerged in the liquid. And three backup systems of safety gauges, easily monitored by well-trained watch-personnel, make it virtually impossible for any leakage or spillage or bath evaporation to be a threat to the earth, the atmosphere, or human beings. The potential danger to the surrounding areas is therefore negligible, if there is no human error involved in the monitoring of the safety gages. That, of course, is a troublesome "if."

Let us follow the development of this paragraph sentence by sentence, as it would unfold for any first-time reader.

11a. Many residents in the several counties that surround the Perkins Nuclear Energy Plant have expressed concern over the potential dangers from the storage of nuclear waste in the Plant's four storage tanks.

This could presumably be a one-sentence issue. If it is, then the rest of the paragraph would go on to discuss any or several of its major component pieces of information: the residents' concerns; the potential dangers; or the storage of waste in the four tanks. Could this also be the point? It could, if the point of the paragraph were simply to make us aware that many residents were concerned. We await further developments.

11b. While it is true that we have not been successful in finding ways to eradicate the potential radiation altogether from the waste products, nuclear engineers have developed a storage system that is adequately monitored by a sophisticated system of safety gauges.

This sentence does not begin a discussion of any of the major components already stated in the first sentence. Rather, it takes one of those components -- the concerns -- and offers a counterbalancing point of comfort: Because a safe storage system has been created, there may be no reason for anyone to be concerned. At the moment, this sounds like a two-sentence issue. Is the second sentence the point? It certainly could be -- *if* no better point comes along later. Again, the reading experience is a *fluid* one, constantly offering the possibilities of change in its shape or its direction. As readers, we have to go with the flow. We continue:

11c. The tanks are constructed of materials that will not deteriorate over time.

This does not change direction. It sounds like the beginning of a discussion that will offer support to the second sentence's statement of comfort. At the moment, it sounds like we have here a two-sentence issue, with the point being either the second sentence or something yet more powerful that will arrive later in the paragraph. Now that we have left the Issue section and have launched into the Discussion section, our fallback expectation clicks into place: If there is a later, stronger statement that will state the point, it will appear at the end.

11d. They are filled with a liquid "bath" that renders the waste products completely harmless, as long as they are totally submerged in the liquid.

This continues the discussion. If it were the final sentence in the paragraph, we might consider it the point; but since there is yet more prose to encounter, we tend to continue to expect (if the paragraph is well written) that if the point is not the second sentence, it will appear at the end.

11e. And three backup systems of safety gauges, easily monitored by well-trained watch-personnel, make it virtually impossible for any leakage or spillage or bath evaporation to be a threat to the earth, the atmosphere, or human beings.

This sounds like more discussion. The "And" suggests we are hearing the last piece of evidence to be added to this move in the paragraph. It is quite possible that the next sentence, or one soon after that, will be the point at which we have been aimed throughout.

11f. The potential danger to the surrounding areas is therefore negligible, if there is no human error involved in the monitoring of the safety gauges.

That certainly has a pointlike ring to it. There is *no* danger -- as long as human beings do their job right. That point sentence, if that is what it is, answers all the concerns raised at the top of the paragraph. However, there is still one sentence remaining to be read. Will it supplant this one as the point sentence? Will it be even more conclusive, more comforting, more final? Here it is:

11g. That, of course, is a troublesome "if."

Oh dear. Just when we were getting comforted by the arrival of sentence (11f), along comes this last sentence to trouble us once again. But we cannot look at the development of thought in this paragraph and reasonably believe that it was all aimed at this last sentence. Most of the activity in this paragraph has expended energy in the service of telling us why the problem is not such a problem. That next-to-last sentence was the arrival place, the target, the end result of all that comfort-building development. What then is this last moment reversal? What could we call it?

Let us call it a "coda."[2] That is an Italian term, meaning "tail," used in music to describe a section at the end of a piece or a movement that is additional to the otherwise complete structural unity.

In a paragraph, the coda, when there is one, is always the last sentence. The Coda position functions as a wildcard spot. We can do all sorts of things there that we could not get away with elsewhere. It is used by good writers sparingly but to good effect. It is the safest place, for example, to insert a wisecrack, a witticism, or even a slight pun. It can be used to restate the point. It can be used as a repository for that additional example that, although unnecessary to the argument, is too delicious not to include. Or, as here, it can be used to blow the rest of the paragraph out of the water:

Issue . . .

Discuss . . .
Discuss . . .
Discuss . . .
Discuss . . .

Point!
[Coda]: OK, yes, but forget it!

Therefore in paragraph (11), the point appears not as the last sentence of the paragraph as a whole, but rather as *the last sentence of the discussion.* When there is a coda, the point will be expected to appear either as the last sentence of the issue or as the last sentence of the discussion. We should therefore make that adjustment to our last boxed statement of Reader Expectations:

Readers of English expect that if the point of a paragraph is not the last sentence of the issue, it will be the last sentence of the discussion.

Where there is no Coda, the last sentence of the Discussion will also be the last sentence of the paragraph. Visually, that can be expressed by our paragraph boxes:

STRCT	ISSUE	DISCUSSION (Coda)	FIXED
SUBS	POINT	POINT	MVBL

All the Reader Expectations that have preceded this one may well sound like common sense, available to you from your own experiences as readers. This one might sound a good deal more technical and a good deal less intuitive. Stated as it now is, it sounds like it must be memorized by rote. Here is a restatement of the same expectations that should make them sound much more recognizable from your own reading experience:

Readers expect the point of a paragraph to be made explicit either just before the discussion of it begins or just as the discussion of it ends.

The important relationship here is that of the point and the discussion: Either (1) "Here's the *issue,* which culminates in this *point,* which I will now *discuss*"; or, (2) "Here's the *issue,* which I continue to *discuss* until I am ready to make this comprehensive *point.*" Either make the point at the conclusion of the issue and then discuss it, or establish the issue and discuss it until you are ready to make a point.

A Note on Narrative Paragraphs

Not all paragraphs were born to make a point. Some were created just to tell a story, to put some facts on the table.

12. To prepare for the final project, the writing groups had to be formed by the third week of the semester. They were to meet during weeks four and five to choose a topic, establish its limitations, and divide the tasks equally among the group members. Sometime between week four and week six, the group had to submit a written prospectus and then meet with the instructor to discuss potential problems. By the end of week eight, the first working draft was due. That would be circulated to everyone in the group, with extensive written comments being due by the end of week ten. The final draft was to be handed in at the end of week twelve, bound in a single volume, with a communally produced three-page introduction.

There is no argument here, nor any development of thought; we therefore have no need for a point sentence. The job of this paragraph is to narrate the facts: We refer to it as a *narrative paragraph*.

Readers tend to expect a paragraph will have a point -- unless they are otherwise informed. It is up to the writer to make sure this contrary indication is somehow made clear. That has to occur up front in the paragraph, in the Issue position. Notice the way it happens as this example (12) unfolds:

12a. To prepare for the final project, the writing groups had to be formed by the third week of the semester.

This could be a one-sentence issue. It could even be the point. We stay tuned for further developments:

12b. They were to meet during weeks four and five to choose a topic, establish its limitations, and divide the tasks equally among the group members.

It seems quite possible -- even probable -- that what we have developing here is a chronology: "third week" . . . "weeks four and five." It is possible, of course, for this chronology to stop here, making this a two-sentence issue, with the discussion of that issue leading eventually to a point at the end. But if the next sentence continues with the chronology, or indicates the probability that the chronology will resume shortly, then what we probably have here is a narration. We continue:

12c. Sometime between week four and week six, the group had to submit a written prospectus and then meet with the instructor to discuss potential problems.

We are pretty much convinced by this point that the job of this paragraph is to take us through the process of the creation of this final project. We no longer expect to hear a point at the end but rather to continue with this string of "and then . . . ," "and then. . . ." And that is precisely what we get:

12d. *By the end of week eight*, the first working draft was due. That would be circulated to everyone in the group, with extensive written comments being due *by the end of week ten*. The final draft was to be handed in *at the end of week twelve*, bound in a single volume, with a communally produced three-page introduction. (Emphasis supplied)

Narrative paragraphs, like all other paragraphs, are in the service of making a point; but that point will appear sometime later in the document. We presume, as readers, that if we are handed all these facts without further comment on them at the moment, these facts will come into use someplace farther down the road. It is a bit like reading in a mystery novel: "Just as he closed the door, he heard the clock strike midnight." If that fact makes no sense by itself at this moment, we have a suspicion that eleven chapters later we will discover it was essential to know that the closing of the door happened precisely at midnight. (Of course, sometimes we are wrong.)

Reader Expectations are neither simple nor simplistic; but they do exist. Good writers take care of them either naturally or knowingly. The more you know about them, the better you can direct them, and the more natural it all will seem to your reader.

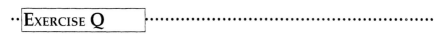

·· EXERCISE Q

Use one of the following sentences as the first sentence of a paragraph and write three different paragraphs based on it, as follows:

1) Make your chosen sentence a one-sentence issue and the point of your paragraph;

2) Make that sentence half of a two-sentence issue and make the last sentence of your paragraph the point; and

3) Make that sentence a one-sentence issue, make the next-to-last sentence of your paragraph the point, and add a coda.

Here are the sentences from which you should choose:

A) Violence depicted on television is a serious social problem because it leads people to be more likely to commit violent acts.

B) The first year of college study should be graded Pass/Fail only, to allow students to become accustomed to the higher level of sophistication college thought will demand.

C) All the freshmen should be housed on East Campus so they may be more safely and easily integrated into the college experience.

Point Placement and Paragraph Types

It may come as no surprise that readers have a pretty good idea ahead of time whether to expect the arrival of the point before the discussion begins (that is, at the end of the Issue) or just as the discussion is ending. It depends on what type of paragraph is being written -- which in turn depends to some extent on *where* the paragraph appears in the document as a whole. I list for you here five paragraph types that send these kinds of default value expectations. These five types do not by any means cover all the possible shapes of paragraphs nor all the expectations concerning the arrival of the point. They do, however, cover a great percentage of the paragraphs normally encountered.

First Paragraphs

Readers have a remarkably fixed expectation that the point of an opening paragraph will arrive at the end. As readers, we greatly desire to be led gradually into a new piece of prose, to be made as comfortable as possible with the new surroundings before we have to go to work. We do not appreciate being greeted in an opening paragraph with the following progression:

THIS IS THE POINT OF IT ALL.

And we'll be spending some time together.

This is what I sound like.

Did you know there was a problem?

Hello.

We much prefer the reverse order:

Hello.

Did you know there was a problem?

This is what I sound like.

And we'll be spending some time together.

So now that you have a sense of me and this document,

THIS IS THE POINT OF IT ALL.

There is the added expectation that in most pieces of expository or persuasive discourse the last sentence of the first paragraph will also state the thesis or contract for the discourse as a whole. Joseph Williams and Gregory Colomb constructed but never published a convincing piece of research that demonstrates this. They collected a number of essays by English graduate students, 20 to 25 pages each, all of which had received an A or A– at the University of Chicago. They made a second version of each essay by changing only one sentence -- the last sentence of the first paragraph -- so that it no longer promised what the essay would consider. They then made packets containing some original essays and some revised ones and sent them to several professors across the country, requesting them to grade the essays and to append a brief comment in support of the grade. The original essays came back with grades of A, A–, or B+, with complimentary comments; but many of the revised essays returned with substantially lower grades, some at the C and D level, with comments about poor development of thought, lack of focus, and fuzzy writing.

I had an occasion to describe this experiment to a dean at Duke University. It especially piqued his interest because on that very day he had learned that an article of his had been rejected by a journal -- the first such refusal he had suffered in some 20 years. They had apparently not understood the whole purpose of his text. The next time I met with him was some three months later. With a broad grin he told me he had indeed found that the last sentence of the opening paragraph -- the contract sentence -- had failed to inform his readers accurately what to expect from the article. He changed *only* that sentence and resubmitted the article to a much more discriminating journal; on this very day he received an acceptance from them, with glowing comments about the clarity and brilliance of his work.

This expectation -- that the last sentence of the opening paragraph will articulate the nature of the focus of the article as a whole -- may well be the single strongest of all the Reader Expectations in English. But even such a strong expectation as this cannot be rigidified into a rule for writers: "Always place your thesis statement at the end of your first paragraph" will not do. Just as some paragraphs take more than one sentence to state the issue of that unit of discourse, so some essays take more than one paragraph to get around to articulating their grand issue or thesis. If it does take (for example) three paragraphs to get that job done, readers will expect to discover the thesis statement -- I prefer the term *contract statement* -- in the last sentence of the third paragraph. In other words, just as with paragraphs, readers would like to know the issue of the discourse as a whole *just before it begins to be discussed*. Note that good writers usually give readers a clue that this is happening: After that third paragraph, there might be a quadruple space instead of a double space, or a horizontal line, or a Roman numeral, or a line of asterisks, or some other visual indication that the opening move had taken three paragraphs, not one.

Counterexamples of this expectation abound, but they all seem to have good explanations for why they function the way they do. Business memos, for instance, almost always begin with the contract statement, if any, in the very first sentence. The explanations: (1) In business, time is money; there is no money available to buy time to make readers comfortable; (2) the appearance of comfort contradicts the impression of hard work; (3) and, most importantly, there is usually a line preceding the first line of prose, headed by "re: ," in which the subject of the memo is announced. That line will establish a context for the reader far more quickly and directly than two or three sentences could manage. Like any other reader expectation, this one should be violated when there is a distinct purpose for doing so.

For an example of this, see the paragraph concerning the office of the vice president, on page 115 above.

Last Paragraphs

Readers have an equally fixed expectation that the point of a final paragraph will arrive at its end. We like our endings to bring with them a satisfying sense of closure. That closure can act as symphonic cymbals clashing or as a modest good-bye; it can produce a final thought not previously articulated or recapitulate material that has been thoroughly developed earlier; it can shock, or it can relax.

If the point were to appear at the beginning of a final paragraph, the progress of the sentences would produce a faltering sense of anticlimax rather than a fulfilling sense of closure:

SO YOU SEE I WIN

since I produced certain general theories

based on a number of individual details.

But when the point of a final paragraph appears at its end, climax and closure combine to create a far more satisfactory effect:

> So, having summoned a number of individual details,
> I created from them certain general theories,
> AS A RESULT OF WHICH
> I WIN.

Whatever form that closure takes, its nature, length, or impact should vary in proportion to the shape, size, and weight of the text as a whole. Long or complex documents may take several paragraphs to achieve a sense of final resolution. Again, no rule will be sufficient to handle all cases. The final paragraph(s) should reach out to the needs of the reader for closure rather than merely express the relief of the writer.

A great majority of students have been taught in school that the final paragraph of an essay should summarize everything the essay has presented. For some unknown reason, teachers rarely tell students how boring, unsatisfying, and sometimes downright annoying such formulaic closing paragraphs can be. Once a reader recognizes that nothing new will appear in such a final paragraph, she may be overcome by impatience. That is decidedly *not* the emotional state in which you wish to leave your reader. The document must not simply *end*; it must be brought to a state of *resolution*.

The final paragraph sometimes can end with a Coda -- a wry twist that opens up again that which had been closed:

> And so we come to an end.
> But where should we go from here?

For an example, see the final paragraph of Joan Didion's *The White Album*, quoted on page 80.

Most Medial Paragraphs

In most paragraphs between the first and the last ("medial" paragraphs), readers tend to appreciate being given the point up front. Many a reader will dip into a paragraph just long enough to decide whether it holds anything of promise for them. If it seems unlikely to engage their attention, they skip to the next paragraph. The writer who does not put the point up front in most of these paragraphs runs the risk of having the reader disappear before the point actually arrives.

One might wonder why readers expect the point to be at the end of first and last paragraphs but at the beginning of most others. There is a logical reason for this: You can afford to leave your point for the end -- and thereby make use of the dramatic crescendo effect -- *if* you can be fairly sure your reader will still be with you at that time. For most pieces of writing, readers tend to read *all* of the opening and closing paragraphs. At the beginning, they have a sense (intuitively and from long experience) that the most important message will arrive in that final sentence. Therefore, they stay around for it. And can you remember the last time you read just about all of a document or book but stopped halfway through the last paragraph? If you have read that far, by golly you want to stay for the great reward of getting all the way to the end. It brings with it a satisfying sense of accomplishment.

For an example, see the paragraph that begins "I did not allow blindness to intimidate me," on page 99.

Medial Paragraphs: Clear, With a Dramatic Point

A writer can effectively delay the point of a medial paragraph until the end if the paragraph will benefit from the drama of such a buildup. In order to maintain interest until that important moment, you should take care of the following:

1) Insofar as possible, the last sentence of the issue should *not* give the impression that it might be the point.

2) There should be a sense of urgency about the development of the discussion that hints that the paragraph has a goal not yet disclosed; readers should be able to feel something building -- enough to make them stay around for the end.

3) The reader should be able to understand everything during the paragraph's development without having had the point stated up front.

For an example of this, see my paragraph on page 126 that begins "One might wonder why readers expect. . . ."

Medial Paragraphs: Complex, With a Dramatic Point

What can you do if a point requires the dramatic emphasis of placement at the end but the development of the discussion is too complex to be understood without the point having been announced up front? In such cases, you would do well to state the point *both* at the beginning *and* at the end. When the point is first announced, the reader may be unconvinced or uncomprehending; but after the discussion has developed the supporting reasons, the second coming of the point can be greeted with a sense of new recognition -- "Ah, so *that's* what was meant before!" The point may be the same old point, but it will be comprehended in a new way.

Ironically, this somewhat scarce type of paragraph comes the closest to the old topic sentence model for writing paragraphs: State the issue and point; give your reasons; then state the point again. This second serving of the point works poorly in easily comprehended paragraphs, where the reader is annoyed to be burdened a second time with material already understood. It works well in paragraphs where the reader could not comprehend the point fully in advance of its being discussed.

In other respects, however, these paragraphs do not resemble the typical topic sentence style paragraph: These often have a two-sentence or three-sentence issue; they do not necessarily have precisely three examples between the two statements of the point; and the sophistication of the argument often connects the medial sentences in one long development rather than staking three separate claims as support for the point.

Here is an example, with a two-sentence issue and the point both in the second sentence and the last:

> Where readers are concerned, we cannot limit even such a small unit of discourse as a sentence to one perceivable interpretation. All units of discourse are infinitely interpretable. By "infinitely interpretable" I do not mean that for each unit of discourse an unthinkably large number of interpretations are simultaneously known or knowable. Instead, I am using the term in the following way: If the number of interpretations perceivable at a given moment for a unit of discourse is "N," then "N + 1" is always a possibility. Someone with a different frame of mind or semantic experience or cultural bias could come along and perceive in the unit of discourse something that no one yet had noticed -- and the number of interpretations increases yet again. All units of discourse are infinitely interpretable.

A Note on One-sentence Paragraphs

Can there be such a thing as a legitimate one-sentence paragraph? (Many of us were taught in high school that one-sentence paragraphs are strictly forbidden.) You can find one on almost any page of a newspaper; but they also show up in the scientific literature, often enough not to be considered scarce. One-sentence paragraphs are appropriate as long as they contain all the rhetorical elements necessary for the definition of a paragraph. For paragraphs that intend to make a point, we generally expect the following:

1. There must be a clearly stated issue.
2. There must be a clearly ascertainable point.
3. There must be sufficient discussion to establish that point.

To accomplish all of this in only one sentence, all of the following must happen:

1. The issue must be able to be stated in a single sentence. That is clearly a possibility.
2. The issue and the point must be the same. That also is clearly a possibility.
3. No discussion must be necessary. That can happen when all the necessary discussion happens just before or just after the one-sentence paragraph.

The best uses for a one-sentence paragraph, therefore, are either as a kind of punchline that summarizes a previous development or as a challenging claim statement that will require substantial future development to justify itself. Example:

-- No good will come of our spending $3,000,000 on the MXR project.

This will be a fine one-sentence paragraph if (1) The last five pages have been spent demonstrating why the MXR project is a disaster, or (2) the next five pages will be spent demonstrating why the MXR project will be a disaster.

P *ointless Paragraphs*

You run a real danger if you construct a paragraph that needs a point but has no point sentence. Sometimes, to be sure, many of your readers will figure out the point without further help from you: It may be relatively obvious to start with; or you may have led up to it so well that anyone could supply the next logical step accurately. Much more often, however, different readers will deduce different points from the material you have given them. That kind of multiple interpretation will get you in trouble sooner or later. There will come a time when it is crucial for some reason or other that you be as clear as possible, and you will have fallen short. But there is something even more troubling: When you fail to produce an explicit point statement in a paragraph, you may often fall short of completing your own thinking process. You may feel you know what you want to say; and you may be able to reread your paragraph intelligently, but the thinking process will not have been completed.

To explore these problems, let us look at example (13), which is a response to an assignment in a freshman writing course that required each student to write a real letter of comment or complaint to a real person. The final drafts were actually mailed, occasionally with interesting return results. Here is a letter to President Ronald Reagan in 1987 concerning the oppressive governing system in South Africa called apartheid.

13. Dear Mr. President,

As a concerned citizen of the United States, I am writing to you to express my disapproval of the current state of affairs in South Africa. Certainly you are aware of the system of apartheid, which has been in effect for some three hundred years. Apartheid is a system of racial segregation in housing, education, and commerce throughout the various provinces of South Africa. It is propagated by the government of South Africa, which is composed entirely of whites, in a nation with a large black majority. The government keeps the black majority in a state of disenfranchisement and denies all means of self determination to the country's majority.

Mr. President, this flagrant disregard for human rights and democratic principles flies in the face of all accepted principles of democracy and morality. Seeds of rebellion are being sown by black opposition leaders in South Africa. A liberated black majority in South Africa is a nation whose time has come. There will be no turning back.

Considering the geopolitical position that South Africa maintains, I urge you not to alienate the emerging black revolutionary forces that will inevitably claim power in South Africa. Please pledge the complete support of the United States to ending apartheid in South Africa and ensuring a healthy relationship with the new government that is to come.

Yours truly,

Let us take a slow-motion tour of this letter, this time asking two questions of each paragraph: (1) What is the issue? and (2) What is the point? Here is the first sentence:

13a. As a concerned citizen of the United States, I am writing to you to express my disapproval of the current state of affairs in South Africa.

If this first sentence is the entirety of the issue, then we probably expect to hear more about the author's disapproval of the state of affairs in South Africa. This sentence is hardly likely to be the paragraph's point: "I am writing to you" is an unlikely target for that kind of spotlight. Besides, we expect the point of an opening paragraph in such a letter to occupy the final sentence.

We continue:

13b. Certainly you are aware of the system of apartheid, which has been in effect for some three hundred years.

This conceivably might begin the discussion of the one-sentence issue of the first sentence. It is hardly likely, however, to be the point of the paragraph, since it does no more than note President Reagan's certain awareness of apartheid. Where are we likely to go from here?

13c. Apartheid is a system of racial segregation in housing, education, and commerce throughout the various provinces of South Africa.

This sentence is also unlikely to be the point. It is, however, a bit of an insult. After assuring the President that he knows all about apartheid, this student somehow feels the need to offer him a working definition of it.

13d. It is propagated by the government of South Africa, which is composed entirely of whites, in a nation with a large black majority.

Like its predecessor, this sentence further (and merely) defines apartheid and is therefore unlikely to be the point of the paragraph. However, we have finally arrived on the doorstep of the final sentence of the first paragraph -- a sentence we fully expect will articulate the paragraph's point.

13e. The government keeps the black majority in a state of disenfranchisement and denies all means of self determination to the country's majority.

This sentence makes exactly the same kind of move as its predecessor. It is yet a third sentence devoted to apartheid's definition and is therefore unlikely to be the point of the paragraph. But this sentence disturbs us more than the others, since we so strongly expected it would present us with that point. That expectation has been violated. We have here a paragraph that is pointless.

We begin the first sentence of the second paragraph expecting that it will announce or begin to announce the issue of the new paragraph.

13f. Mr. President, this flagrant disregard for human rights and democratic principles flies in the face of all accepted principles of democracy and morality.

This sentence suggests that the second paragraph will discuss questions of morality. This turns out *not* to be the case; but we cannot know that at this moment in time. The rest of the paragraph is going to concern itself not with general moral principles (which are the concern of this opening sentence) but rather with predicting a black victory in the unavoidable revolution.

What, then, is the real function of sentence (13f)? Since it asserts disapproval of apartheid on moral grounds, it turns out to be the point of the first paragraph. All the flailing about we witnessed in the first paragraph makes far more sense if it builds to the climax of this charge of immorality. To improve the first paragraph immeasurably, all we need do is surgically remove sentence (13f) from the second paragraph and suture it to the end of the first paragraph. Then not only does the point appear exactly where we expect it to appear but also it creates adequate closure for the paragraph as a whole.

Here now is the sentence that becomes the first of our new second paragraph:

13g. Seeds of rebellion are being sown by black opposition leaders in South Africa.

What is the function of this sentence? It turns out to be the real issue of the second paragraph, now placed where we expect to find it. It could be the point of *some* paragraph; but it turns out not to be the point of this one.

We continue:

13h. A liberated black majority in South Africa is a nation whose time has come.

Could this be the point? Again, it certainly could be the point of *some* paragraph; but it is neither the last sentence of this paragraph nor even the last sentence of the discussion here. We hope, therefore, that something yet more vital is yet to come.

The next sentence is indeed yet more vital:

13i. There will be no turning back.

Continuing to develop the issue announced by the issue sentence, this yet more dramatic sentence sounds like it could be the point of the paragraph; but if so, then what does the writer expect to gain by making this point to the president? We are still in hope that a yet more compelling point will arrive before the paragraph ends. We can hear the crescendo building.

That buildup seems to climax in the next sentence:

13j. Considering the geopolitical position that South Africa maintains, I urge you not to alienate the emerging black revolutionary forces that will inevitably claim power in South Africa.

This sentence seems a reasonable candidate -- indeed, an admirable candidate -- to be the paragraph's point. The issue was that the black population would eventually rebel and win out over the whites of South Africa. The author is now urging the president to make use of this certain knowledge. We are Americans, it argues. That means we like to be on the side of the winners. The South African blacks will eventually win. If we befriend them now, we will be able to say we supported them all along. We should get in while the getting is good. Machiavelli himself would have been impressed with this student's strategy.

There remains a problem here: Since sentence (13j) is the next-to-last sentence in the paragraph, it will not be located in one of the two places we expect the point to be announced -- unless, of course, the sentence that follows it acts as a coda.

We turn to that last sentence:

13k. Please pledge the complete support of the United States to ending apartheid in South Africa and ensuring a healthy relationship with the new government that is to come.

There is nothing about this sentence that suggests coda. Located as it is in this paragraph, it seems a lame way to end such a Machiavellian piece of political advice. If, however, this sentence were split off from this paragraph to form a paragraph of its own, the whole letter will function better: (1) It would allow the point of the second paragraph to be located in that unit's last sentence, where we expect to find it; and (2) It would transform the lame ending of the original second paragraph into a perfectly acceptable (and perhaps somewhat clever) one-sentence summation paragraph for the letter as a whole. Its first part ("Please pledge the complete support of the United States to ending apartheid") can be read as nodding backward to the moral statements of the first paragraph; its second part ("ensuring a healthy relationship with the new government") is a clear reference to the pragmatic advice offered in the second paragraph.

Note also that this final sentence is a fine example of a legitimate one-sentence paragraph: It requires no discussion, since the discussion has already taken place. Such marshmallowlike one-liners are quite acceptable just before a letter-writer says goodbye. A common example: "Please feel free to contact me if you have further questions."

This revised letter now becomes the product of a clever and insightful young man, aware of political and rhetorical realities. After articulating the mandatory moral principle in the first paragraph, he offers a sly and pragmatic reason for following what will seem a moral course of action.

The structural locations of the individual sentences now offer the reader instructions for interpreting the whole. Here is the entire revised version.

13k. As a concerned citizen of the United States, I am writing to you to express my disapproval of the current state of affairs in South Africa. Certainly you are aware of the system of apartheid, which has been in effect for some three hundred years. Apartheid is a system of racial segregation in housing, education, and commerce throughout the various provinces of South Africa. It is propagated by the government of South Africa, which is composed entirely of whites, in a nation with a large black majority. The government keeps the black majority in a state of disenfranchisement and denies all means of self determination to the country's majority. Mr. President, this flagrant disregard for human rights and democratic principles flies in the face of all accepted principles of democracy and morality.

Seeds of rebellion are being sown by black opposition leaders in South Africa. A liberated black majority in South Africa is a nation whose time has come. There will be no turning back. Considering the geopolitical position that South Africa maintains, I urge you not to alienate the emerging black revolutionary forces that will inevitably claim power in South Africa.

Please pledge the complete support of the United States to ending apartheid in South Africa and ensuring a healthy relationship with the new government that is to come.

Yours truly,

Before the revision, the first paragraph was pointless, the second paragraph raised a misleading issue, and the letter ended lamely. After the revision, the issues are clear, the points appear where expected, the development is surer, and the tone stronger. All this was accomplished by restructuring, without the alteration of a single word choice -- or even the reordering of a single sentence. We have just made sure that the sentences arrive in structural locations that send the right interpretive messages to the reader.

Could the author have discovered for himself the same things I discovered? Yes; he merely needed to ask himself *where he had located* the points he was trying to make in these paragraphs. He might well then have been led to exactly the revision we have here. In other words, the weakness of the *structure* could have led him to perceive the incompleteness of his *thought*.

Note the difference between his asking *where* the points are and *what* the points should be. The former is a relatively objective question with the relatively objective answers of "here," "there," or "nowhere." The latter is the more abstract inquiry into the thought process, all too easily answered by "I meant to say exactly what I said."

·· EXERCISE R

For each of the following two paragraphs, determine which you think are the point sentences. Compare your choices (and the reasons for your choosing them) with those of two or three classmates. What problems do you encounter?

A. Violence on television may offend people of highly moral beliefs. These people live cleanly and despise any corrupt acts. For example, if people worship the devil then this could greatly disturb their life. These scenes presented on television demoralize people of definite tenets. Besides providing a bad influence, this type of violence may affront people considerably.

B. The summer I was 16, I took a train from New York to Steamboat Springs, Colorado, where I was going to be assistant horse wrangler at a camp. The trip took three days, and since I was much too shy to talk to strangers, I had quite a lot of time for reading. I read all of *Gone with the Wind*. I read all the interesting articles in a couple of magazines I had, and then I went back and read all the dull stuff. I also took all the quizzes, a thing of which magazines were even fuller than now.

Connections Between Paragraphs

In some ways, connections between paragraphs resemble connections between sentences. In both cases, the reader is departing from a unit of discourse that has raised numerous possibilities for further development. In both cases, the reader wishes to know as soon as possible exactly which strands of the former discourse will be the connecting links to the present and ongoing discourse. The writer can furnish that information (1) by signaling forward at the end of the previous unit, (2) by motioning backward at the beginning of the new unit, or (3) by doing both of these.

One might think that since sentences are usually much shorter than paragraphs, they might offer far fewer possibilities for linkage to future sentences than paragraphs do for future paragraphs. This turns out not necessarily to be the case. Any of the contents of a sentence are available for future development. The occupants of the Topic position or the Stress position may often be the leading indicators of future linkage, but they are never the only possibilities. Any important word in a sentence can become old information in the next Topic position and take over the storyline. Paragraphs, on the other hand, usually work with much larger units of thought. Their structure and development often aim at limiting the likelihood of what can come next, sometimes far more than sentences tend to do.

Sentences offer a much larger number of future possible connections than one might think upon first reading them. I borrow an example from fiction -- the ironically argumentative opening sentence from Jane Austen's *Pride and Prejudice*:

14a. It is a truth universally acknowledged, that a single man in possession of a good fortune must be in want of a wife.

Consider the wealth of possibilities for development crammed into this one delightful sentence. Here is only a partial list:

truth	universally
acknowledged	universal truth
universally acknowledged	a single man
a man	possession
a good fortune	in possession of a good fortune
must be	must be in want
a wife	in want of a wife
must be in want of a wife	

Any or many of these stepping stones might be used to forge the connection to the next sentence. If you ask 20 people who have not read *Pride and Prejudice* to create a logical second sentence to follow Austen's first, the chances are high that no two people would come up with precisely the same sentence.

Here is the one Jane Austen provided:

14b. However little known the feelings or views of such a man may be on his first entering a neighborhood, this truth is so well fixed in the minds of the surrounding families that he is considered as the rightful property of some one or other of their daughters.

Note how many of the candidates on my list she managed to cram into this single sentence. The rest of the book can be read as a virtuosic development of precisely the information she has hurled at us, in ever so genteel a manner, in the book's opening sentence.

·· EXERCISE S ··

The following four sentences are each the first sentence of a paragraph of a well-known essay. Produce one or two reasonable sentences to follow each of them. Consider what the forward lean seems to be and fashion something both cohesive and coherent as the next sentence. After you have finished, you may be interested to see what actually was the author's second sentence. I have reprinted them in an endnote to this chapter.[3] Do not be surprised if you are surprised by what you find there. There is no reason you should have been able to guess precisely where the author was going. All the same, note what kind of backward link was created. Prose is fluid.

1. I remember one splendid morning, all blue and silver, in the summer holidays, when I reluctantly tore myself away from the task of doing nothing in particular, and put on a hat of some sort and picked up a walking-stick, and put six very bright-colored chalks in my pocket.

   (G. K. Chesterton, "A Piece of Chalk")

2. The acquisition of books is by no means a matter of money or expert knowledge alone.

   (Walter Benjamin, "Unpacking My Library")

3. Being blind has its advantages.

   (Jorge Luis Borges, "Blindness")

4. I remember once, one cold bright December evening in New York, suggesting to a friend who complained of having been around too long that he come with me to a party where there would be, I assured him with the bright resourcefulness of twenty-three, "new faces."

   (Joan Didion, "Goodbye to All That")

If you have just done the above exercises, you can see that the possibilities of where "the next sentence" may go in any piece of discourse are infinite. The possibilities for linking paragraphs are also infinite, but somewhat less surprising. I will not attempt to offer a detailed catalogue of the types of transitions that can be made from paragraph to paragraph; a brief discussion of just a few will have to suffice. I begin with the narrative paragraph.

Narratives take us from point A to point B in time and experience. As readers, we maintain a few dominating expectations for the beginning of the paragraph that follows:

1) It might continue the chronology of the previous paragraph, beginning from where the previous one left off.

2) It might choose a particular detail or moment from the previous paragraph upon which to dwell and expand.

3) It might shift dramatically to a topic that the reader has been given no cause to expect.

Readers are pleased and relieved when they are told as early as possible -- preferably in the first sentence -- which of these options will be realized. For an example, reconsider example (10) of this chapter, briefly encountered on page 111 above and which you may have worked on as the recent exercise on page 134:

10. The summer I was 16, I took a train from New York to Steamboat Springs, Colorado, where I was going to be assistant horse wrangler at a camp. The trip took three days, and since I was much too shy to talk to strangers, I had quite a lot of time for reading. I read all of *Gone with the Wind*. I read all the interesting articles in a couple of magazines I had, and then I went back and read all the dull stuff. I also took all the quizzes, a thing of which magazines were even fuller than now.

The paragraph that follows this one could continue the discourse in any number of ways, including innumerable variations on the three general directions suggested above.

1a) [continuing the chronology]: "After a nearly terminal case of boredom, I finally arrived in Steamboat Springs."

1b) [a different way of continuing the chronology]: "Having finished with the quizzes, three times each, I was heading toward reader's despair. In a last gasp effort, I resorted to studying the prose on the back of my ticket. 'The Railroad is not responsible for personal items lost or damaged during passage.' I started to wonder: What if I lost the. . . ?"

2a) [expanding on a particular detail]: "After all those quizzes, I started to appreciate the complexity of a sprawling novel like *Gone with the Wind*."

2b) [expanding on a different particular detail]: "The one that held my undivided attention was called 'How Masculine/Feminine Are You?'"

3) [an unexpected shift]: "Little did I know that the entire summer would pass by without my being allowed to read a single page."

Of particular help here is the nature of the paragraph's final sentence. Especially in narrative paragraphs (but somewhat in all paragraphs), it provides the surest of launching pads for the flight into the next sentence. Since example (10) is the opening paragraph of the essay from which it comes, the last sentence has particularly strong powers. Why should it end with those quizzes? If it is a well-written paragraph, with the quizzes prominently displayed in the final sentence, might we not expect that this essay will go on to tell us all about the author's opinions of them? Let us look at the paragraph again, this time in slow motion. If you can, pretend you have never seen the paragraph before.

10a. The summer I was 16, I took a train from New York to Steamboat Springs, Colorado, where I was going to be assistant horse wrangler at a camp.

Any of the pieces of information here -- summer, 16, train, took a train, New York, Steamboat Springs, Colorado, going to be, assistant, horse, horse wrangler, assistant horse wrangler, camp -- any of it is available as old information in the second sentence. Any one of them might be a reasonable candidate for taking over the Topic position of that sentence, as long as it turns out to be "whose story" the second sentence is all about. The leading candidates are probably the occupants of the Topic position (the sentence's first eight words or so) and the occupants of the Stress position (the sentence's last five or six words): Either we are going to hear more about the train trip or more about the horse-wrangling camp experience.

10b. The trip took three days, and since I was much too shy to talk to strangers, I had quite a lot of time for reading.

The Topic position here harkens back to the Topic position of the first sentence, forming a short topic string: We are to continue to hear about this train trip. The Stress position is filled with "a lot of time for reading," new information that is presumably stressworthy. While the third sentence could take off from anywhere, we rather expect it will tell us more about the reading, since it receives such special emphasis here and is not self-explanatory. It sounds like a herald Stress position. If the next sentence goes on to something else, we will be somewhat perplexed as to why "reading" had deserved its privileged location.

10c. I read all of *Gone with the Wind*.

A Topic Change: The occupant of the previous Stress position has taken over the new "whose story?" position. "A lot of time for reading" has more than adequately been filled up with the lengthy, sprawling novel, *Gone with the Wind*. Where will we go next? We might expect a topic change, importing *Gone with the Wind* into the Topic position of the fourth sentence in preparation for pages of analysis of Margaret Mitchell and the burning of Atlanta. We could just as reasonably expect a continuation of the "I read" topic string. Either would seem smooth, logical, compelling; anything else would be jarring, disconnected, unsettling. (None of those adjectives need carry any value judgment along with them. It might be effective to jar, disconcert, or unsettle a reader at times.)

10d. I read all the interesting articles in a couple of magazines I had, and then I went back and read all the dull stuff.

The "I read" topic string wins. Instead of being the announced topic for the rest of the article, *Gone with the Wind* has now become just the first of a number of things our narrator managed to read. We are even more impressed now, not only with how much time he had for reading but with how voracious and capable a reader he must have been. After all, *Gone with the Wind* is a long novel, and the trip was by train to Colorado, not by goat-cart to Peru.

Where do we expect to go from here? We might well expect the topic string to continue, leading us on to even more of what he read; or we might be prepared for a topic change to the occupant of the current Stress position, the "dull stuff."

10e. I also took all the quizzes, a thing of which magazines were even fuller than now.

Quite neatly, this Topic position reaches back to both the Topic and Stress positions of the former sentence: (a) It continues the Topic string, expanding the "I read" into an interactive reading experience (quiz-taking); and (b) it changes the topic by categorizing the quizzes as part of the "dull stuff" -- perhaps, by declination, even the dullest of the dull stuff.

The paragraph is over. Where do we expect the next paragraph to take us? We would not be at all surprised if the author launched into an analysis of magazine quizzes. He has taken us across the country, read up a storm, and landed us at the end of the paragraph in a subject that is of no importance whatsoever unless it turns out to be the main concern of the approaching discourse. In other words, if this article is *not* about magazine quizzes, then the magazine quizzes are annoyingly and misleadingly located at the ending moment of this paragraph's structure.

The article indeed proceeds to investigate the nature of magazine quizzes and their reflection of American popular culture.

Watch now what happens if we lift one chunk of information in this paragraph and transport it to a different structural location. Note how our expectations change, making us think differently about where the next paragraph will take us.

10f. The summer I was 16, I took a train from New York to Steamboat Springs, Colorado, where I was going to be assistant horse wrangler at a camp. The trip took three days, and since I was much too shy to talk to strangers, I had quite a lot of time for reading. I read all the interesting articles in a couple of magazines I had, and then I went back and read all the dull stuff. I also took all the quizzes, a thing of which magazines were even fuller than now. I read all of *Gone with the Wind*.

The first two sentences remain the same as in the original. However, the next three arrive in a different order, which changes the way we see the author. He reads the interesting short stuff; he reads the dull stuff; he takes the quizzes; and then, finally prepared for the plunge, he takes on *Gone with the Wind*. The last sentence, being last, and being so much shorter and blunter than the others, convinces us it is the true climax of this paragraph's development. We firmly expect the next paragraph to launch into either his experience of reading *Gone with the Wind* or something connected to the process he has mysteriously outlined. This might be, for instance, an article about his great struggle with procrastination -- always leaving the more daunting task for later. In any event, if this paragraph is "well written," the article is *not* going to be about quizzes.

Here is another dewriting of the original paragraph:

10g. The summer I was 16, I took a train from New York to Steamboat Springs, Colorado. The trip took three days, and since I was much too shy to talk to strangers, I had quite a lot of time for reading. I read all of *Gone with the Wind*. I read all the interesting articles in a couple of magazines I had, and then I went back and read all the dull stuff. I also took all the quizzes, a thing of which magazines were even fuller than now. I was going to be assistant horse wrangler at a camp.

In this version, only the horse wrangling has been moved; but that small change has made a significant difference. The trip passes before us in the form of reading and quiz-taking activities, at the end of which is the arrival in Colorado for horse-wrangling purposes. Why is horse wrangling the closure point for a paragraph that is otherwise about frantic reading? Could it be that this bookish sort is going to have a tough time in the wake-up-and-smell-the-coffee Wild West? Or will he discover "real" meanings of life once he gets his nose out of a book?

Here is yet one more dewriting of the original:

10h. The summer I was 16, I took a train from New York to Steamboat Springs, Colorado, where I was going to be assistant horse wrangler at a camp. Since the trip took three days, I had quite a lot of time for reading. I read all of *Gone with the Wind*. I read all the interesting articles in a couple of magazines I had, and then I went back and read all the dull stuff. I also took all the quizzes, a thing of which magazines were even fuller than now. I was much too shy to talk to strangers.

The only change from the original is the location of the "too shy to talk to strangers." That piece of information had been buried in the middle of a sentence in all the other versions, thereby perhaps escaping our attention. It seemed to have functioned only as a supportive reason to justify all the reading and quiz-taking upon which we were invited to concentrate. In this version, however, all that has changed. The reading and quiz-taking take on a kind of desperate quality as he goes to extreme lengths to entertain himself. We may not have noticed in the earlier version that both of these activities are decidedly solitary occupations; that fact is revealed to us by his resolving the paragraph with the admission of his shyness. The long delay in its arrival seems itself a manifestation of that shyness. Given the placement of "strangers" at the end of all this, what are we to expect of the next paragraph? Perhaps we might meet "her" -- the local version of Scarlet O'Hara.

There are no paradigms, no preset instructions that can help a writer decide where to take the reader next. That must be dictated by the writer's thought process. A writer can bend a narrative in any number of directions at any given moment. Readers tend to be willing to follow; but they must be given adequate warning where to turn next. As with sentences, beginnings and ends are the main places readers look for such help.

Non-narrative paragraphs also resemble sentences in the way they connect to each other. As we explored in some detail in Chapter 3, when forming a new sentence in a continuing discourse, there are two favored candidates for that new Topic position: Either (1) we can repeat the occupant of the previous Topic position -- thus continuing that occupant's story and forming a Topic String; or (2) we can repeat the occupant of the previous Stress position -- thus shifting stories and creating a Topic Change. Paragraphs are somewhat similar to sentences in this respect: They often benefit from linking backward either (1) to the occupant of the previous paragraph's Issue position, or (2) to its final sentence. Here are examples of both kinds of linkage, using once again the examples (3) and (4) we have seen before, this time augmented by the beginnings of their next paragraph:

3. I did not allow blindness to intimidate me. I set about memorizing the number of stairs in each staircase of the new house, creating a device for keeping them all straight. The fourteen steps of the front hall staircase summoned the word "fortunate" -- the way I felt about being able to have a new and better place to live: *"Fourteen"; "fortunate."* The seven steps to the upper level, where my CD player and all that wonderful music resided were my "seven" steps to "heaven." The ten stairs to the basement recalled the "ten steps" of St. John of the Cross, who tells us that "the way down," through denial and self-cleansing, are the best way to God. And the three steps of the front doorstoop could be distinguished from the two steps of the back doorstoop because to ascend in life is always a step more difficult than to descend.

   Knowing the steps of my house gave me the courage to gain control of many other parts of my daily life. I learned to organize -- everything. If I kept the silverware in exactly the same partitions of its holder, I could depend on finding what I needed without anxiety. If I had one drawer for brown socks and another for blue, I was on my way to daily color coordination. . . .

The backward link of "Knowing the steps of my house" allows the second paragraph to flow with ease from the first in a steady stream. Part of the purpose of the first paragraph was to establish an example in such detail that succeeding examples could be constructed more economically. The two paragraphs together read as easily as putting one foot in front of the other.

4.   All through the 1950s and well into the 1960s, his published articles glowed with patriotic zeal and communal self-satisfaction. They praised the country's stability, our national sense of progress, our international status on the rise, and the political resiliency that allowed us to survive the McCarthy Era and the Korean War effort. But in the late 1960s, everything changed, and his prose grew sour and darker. The Vietnam War depressed him. The widening "generation gap" made communication seem increasingly difficult, if not impossible. The assassinations of Bobby Kennedy and Martin Luther King seemed to promise that the assassination of John F. Kennedy had not been an isolated event, but rather was the implanting of a national poison that was spreading and conquering. And with the Watergate scandal in the early 1970s, he seemed to give up hope altogether. He stopped writing.

In the earlier, brighter period, writing had been for him a source of energy. Each day had begun with a sense of promise -- a sense that the new day could build on the old with the feeling of progress. . . .

This new paragraph leaps lightly over all the depressing part of its predecessor and revisits the 1950s, with all its energy and hope. It also might offer a clue for where we will be going next:

First paragraph: 1950s and early 1960s good; late 1960s and 1970s bad

Second paragraph: Let us look again at the good period

Third paragraph: Let us look again at the bad period

Beginnings and endings once again stand out in the reader's mind far more than anything in the middle. Of course you *can* begin a new paragraph with linkage back to the middle of the preceding paragraph, but when you do, the reader is (at least) momentarily jolted by the appearance of unexpected information. For example, what if the paragraph that follows example (4) began with "The Korean War had been a challenge, to be sure." Although we might remember the Korean War having made an appearance in the previous paragraph, its reemergence comes as a surprise. To make this linkage, we have to leap backward, passing over all the unpleasant memories of the late 1960s and early 1970s. Once we have left our mental feet in that leaping process, our expectation would lead us to believe we will land in the previous Issue position, where he was upbeat about good things happening. Instead, we stumbled onto the Korean War -- something he has supposedly overcome; but now it is presented as a lingering problem. We are lost. The writing has failed us. It raised expectations that were dashed, leaving us muddled.

How much explicit connection is needed at the beginning of a paragraph to link it to the previous paragraph? The answer is mildly annoying: You need as much connection as is necessary to make it clear to your reader how to proceed without insulting or delaying your reader by being unnecessarily explicit. It is always a judgment call, but the judgment should be made not in terms of what sounds good to the writer but rather in terms of what is needed by the reader. Readers need to be contextualized first, informed what action is taking place, and then presented with the stressworthy material. Readers expect stressworthy materials to arrive at the end of a sentence, at the beginning or end of a paragraph, and toward the beginning and/or end of a whole document.

I repeat the three characteristics of good prose, which apply as well to paragraphs as they do to sentences:

1. Nothing arrives that the reader cannot handle at the moment of its arrival.
2. Everything leans forward.
3. Everything actually goes in one of the directions it had been leaning.

S ummarizing Paragraph Structures

Your paragraphs should be shaped not to conform to some sort of Procrustean model but rather with a Protean need in mind. The shape of each of your paragraphs should reflect the shape of the development of its thought. We have encountered a fair number of paragraph shapes in this Chapter:

-- Narrative paragraphs (with a hint of that narration in the Issue position)
-- Non-narrative paragraphs with many possible organizations. Here is a table to bring the most common of these all together.

Issue	Point	Coda
1 sentence	first sentence	No
1 sentence	first sentence	Yes
1 sentence	last sentence	No
1 sentence	next-to-last sentence	Yes
2 sentences	second sentence	No
2 sentences	second sentence	Yes

Issue	Point	Coda
2 sentences	last sentence	No
2 sentences	next-to-last sentence	Yes
3 sentences	third sentence	No
3 sentences	third sentence	Yes
3 sentences	last sentence	No
3 sentences	next-to-last sentence	Yes

But we can add to these an infinite variety of paragraph shapes -- each of which is created specially for the occasion and is communicated to the reader right then and there. For example, we can put two points in the same paragraph -- as long as we say so right up front.

15. When we consider all the possibilities, we become convinced that there are only two plans of attack that make sense. (1) Either we do X. . . . That would lead us to prepare L and revise M and of course we would have to recondition N. (2) Or we could do Y, which entails. . . .

The paragraph is a long enough unit of discourse to allow us to send explicit instructions to our readers. As with anything having to do with writing, the primary piece of advice must be "Take your reader with you."

·· EXERCISE T

Here, once again, are the opening seven paragraphs of Lewis Thomas's *The Lives of a Cell: Notes of a Biology Watcher*. You have seen them before, in the exercises at the end of the previous chapter and earlier in this chapter. This time, go through all seven in search of what you consider to be the issue and point statements. How many sentences doe the issue require? (This is the task an earlier exercise in this chapter asked you to do.) Where is the point articulated? Compare your results for all seven paragraphs. Notice how many different paragraph shapes Thomas manages to create. The shape is always well suited to the function.

A. We are told that the trouble with Modern Man is that he has been trying to detach himself from nature. He sits in the topmost tiers of polymer, glass, and steel, dangling his pulsing legs, surveying at a distance the writhing life of the planet. In this scenario, Man comes on as a stupendous lethal force, and the earth is pictured as something delicate, like rising bubbles at the surface of a country pond, or flights of fragile birds.

B. But it is illusion to think that there is anything fragile about the life of the earth; surely this is the toughest membrane imaginable in the universe, opaque to probability, impermeable to death. We are the delicate part, transient and vulnerable as cilia. Nor is it a new thing for man to invent an existence that he imagines to be above the rest of life; this has been his most consistent intellectual exertion down the millennia. As illusion, it has never worked out to his satisfaction in the past, any more than it does today. Man is embedded in nature.

C. The biologic science of recent years has been making this a more urgent fact of life. The new, hard problem will be to cope with the dawning, intensifying realization of just how interlocked we are. The old, clung-to notions most of us have held about our special lordship are being deeply undermined.

D. *Item.* A good case can be made for our nonexistence as entities. We are not made up, as we had always supposed, of successively enriched packets of our own parts. We are shared, rented, occupied. At the interior of our cells, driving them, providing the oxidative energy that sends us out for the improvement of each shining day, are the mitochondria, and in a strict sense they are not ours. They turn out to be little separate creatures, the colonial posterity of migrant prokaryocytes, probably primitive bacteria that swam into ancestral precursors of our eukaryotic cells and stayed there. Ever since, they have maintained themselves and their ways, replicating in their own fashion, privately, with their own DNA and RNA quite different from ours. They are as much symbionts as the rhizobial bacteria in the roots of beans. Without them, we would not move a muscle, drum a finger, think a thought.

E. Mitochondria are stable and responsible lodgers, and I choose to trust them. But what of the other little animals, similarly established in my cells, sorting and balancing me, clustering me together? My centrioles, basal bodies, and probably a good many other more obscure tiny beings at work inside my cells, each with its own special genome, are as foreign, and as essential, as aphids in anthills. My cells are no longer the pure line entities I was raised with; they are ecosystems more complex than Jamaica Bay.

F. I like to think that they work in my interest, that each breath they draw for me; but perhaps it is they who walk through the local park in the early morning, sensing my senses, listening to my music, thinking my thoughts.

G. I am consoled, somewhat, by the thought that the green plants are in the same fix. They could not be plants, or green, without their chloroplasts, which run the photosynthetic enterprise and generate oxygen for the rest of us. As it turns out, chloroplasts are also separate creatures with their own genomes, speaking their own language.

A Note on Whole Documents

It may seem strange that in a book of this length I should spend only a few paragraphs on the question of reader expectations concerning whole documents. The reasons can be stated briefly.

(1) On the one hand, the possibilities for structuring and developing a whole document are geometrically more variable than those for structuring sentences or paragraphs. No two people would be at all likely to produce identical documents, even when they started with precisely the same materials. It is difficult, then, to talk in detail about how we as readers would expect whole documents to unfold on a regular basis.

(2) On the other hand, certain strong conventions for structuring and developing whole documents have been crisply communicated to writers by individual professional communities. There are great differences between the expected structures of a legal brief, article on literary criticism, and a federal grant proposal; but the courts, the academy, and the federal government each have let it be known what expectations they have of the gross structure of those documents. Composition courses at the college level need not steal their thunder. There will be plenty of time to learn these things later, on the job.

For example, medical journals in each separate subfield have well-articulated conventions for the submission of data and analysis. Those conventions may differ from subspecialty to subspecialty; but an individual cannot be accepted in that community -- that is, be published -- without demonstrating an ability to conform to those standards. Certain kinds of information belong in a section called the Abstract; other kinds are relegated to the Methods section; yet others appear in the sections on Findings; yet others belong to the Discussion sections. Tables and graphs have their place. The main point had better be announced up front and presented pictorially in a prominent location. Methods must not appear in places where argument should be taking place -- and vice versa. All this must be learned by the new scientific professional.

All that knowledge might be of no avail to the writer of a legal brief, a business memo, or an article for a journal of literary criticism. Each of those document types is founded on a similarly indigenous set of community expectations. Some are parallel to medical expectations; some seem parallel but are not; others could hardly be more different.

For example, a reader of a scientific article confidently expects that the main message of the article as a whole will be delivered at the outset; but a reader of an essay in literary criticism equally strongly expects that the punchline will appear somewhere between the two-thirds and three-quarters mark. Many a scientific article has been structured as follows:

Here is what we have found and why it is important.

Here is how we ran our experiments.

Here is the data we developed.

Here is what those data mean.

Here is a discussion about why we think what we found means what we say it means.

Many an article of literary criticism, however, has been structured as follows:

Critics have long said X.

Critics have been foolish to think that way.

Look at all the problems there are with what they have said.

Look what that leaves us yet to clarify and discover.

Now if you follow a different way of thinking, mine, here is what you would do.

If you do that, you will discover Y and Z.

Given this new way of thinking, you come to the following wonderful conclusions.

That was pretty good, wasn't it?

See you.

These conventions will be made clear to you early on in whatever career you choose. A professional company will quickly show you "how we do things here." Law school will teach you the component parts of a brief and a memo and a letter to a client. A government agency will show you what pieces of information have to be made apparent in which kinds of public documents. All of this is dependent on expectation; but the expectations will be local, not global.

Endnotes

1. I am borrowing this box arrangement, with a minor variation, from Joseph Williams.
2. Again I am borrowing a term from Joseph Williams.
3. Chesterton: I remember one splendid morning, all blue and silver, in the summer holidays, when I reluctantly tore myself away from the task of doing nothing in particular, and put on a hat of some sort and picked up a walking-stick, and put six very bright-colored chalks in my pocket. I then went into the kitchen (which, along with the rest of the house, belonged to a very square and sensible old woman in a Sussex village) and asked the owner and occupant of the kitchen if she had any brown paper.
Benjamin: The acquisition of books is by no means a matter of money or expert knowledge alone. Not even both factors together suffice for

the establishment of a real library, which is always somewhat impenetrable and at the same time uniquely itself.

Borges: Being blind has its advantages. I owe to the darkness some gifts: the gift of Anglo-Saxon, my limited knowledge of Icelandic, the joy of so many lines of poetry, of so many poems, and of having written another book, entitled, with a certain falsehood, with a certain arrogance, *In Praise of Darkness*.

Didion: I remember once, one cold bright December evening in New York, suggesting to a friend who complained of having been around too long that he come with me to a party where there would be, I assured him with the bright resourcefulness of twenty-three, "new faces." He laughed literally until he choked, and I had to roll down the taxi window and hit him on the back.

[All of these examples can be found in *The Art of the Personal Essay: An Anthology from the Classical Era to the Present*, selected by Phillip Lopate. New York: Anchor Books, 1994.]

5

"Write the Way You Speak" and Other Bad Pieces of Advice

O ur educational process does the best it can at every step of the way. Major parts of your college-level instruction are devoted to undoing much of what you have learned earlier. You may have been taught in high school that the main cause of the Civil War was the question of slavery and that Abraham Lincoln was a great man because he freed the slaves in his Emancipation Proclamation. In college you learn that the war had no single cause, that economic and political sovereignty counted more than anything else, and that Lincoln, great man though he was, never made it his agenda to free the slaves but rather to do whatever was necessary to keep the Union together. Remember that the Emancipation Proclamation was issued in 1863 -- halfway through the war. His timing, according to his own writings, was motivated not as much by the ethical issue of slavery but by the political necessity of the moment.

Does that mean that in high school you were misinformed? I think it means that in high school you were taught that which a high school student was likely to be able to process and use. The complex political issues of the retention of power would probably have been beyond your powers of intellectual synthesis. The same is true of much of what you might have been taught about writing. We need not blame anyone who might have given you any of the pieces of advice I attempt to unteach in this chapter. Most of this advice is based on something reasonable; most of it produces good effects -- in the context of a high school classroom.

But now you are older and more sophisticated. It is time to reassess some of the advice that was aimed at solving younger problems. I will not spend much time demonstrating what might have been the good intentions of these rules of thumb; learn what the other half of the story looks like and then decide for yourself how much of each pronouncement to maintain. I am not out to give you a new set of rules to replace the old ones but rather to make you think about any sort of rule with an independent mind.

B ad Advice, and Why Not to Take It

You may have heard the advice "Write the way you speak." Far more often than not, this is bad advice. When I talk to you, I have a great many ways of indicating which of my words I wish you to emphasize; I can wave my hand, each flourish directing your attention to one word at the expense of others; I can summon all sorts of body English -- eyebrows that question, facial lines that frown, a nose that can smirk, a head that can incline to call things into question, or shoulders that can indicate anything from increasing concern to total helplessness; and, most directly, I can use my voice, either by accentuation, to emphasize particular syllables, or by modulation -- louder or softer, faster or slower, higher or lower -- to differentiate by variation. When I speak, I can use all of these, and more, in varying combinations and permutations, in an attempt to control your attention and comprehension. But when I write, all of these visual and auditory aids disappear: Aside from a few flag words and an occasional typographical accent (italics, underlining, capitalization), the main way I can indicate intended emphasis is through structural location. Instead of writing the way you speak, write the way your readers read.

Of course, there are always exceptions. The advice to write the way you speak can help the writer who is so overly conscious of the formal requirements of written discourse that he or she litters the page with convoluted syntax and rented vocabulary, making it impossible for a reader to discover what is being communicated. "Write the way you speak" can help unstuff this particular shirt; but once that is accomplished, the advice ceases to be of help. To be clear and effective, writing must be more than unstuffy.

This piece of bad advice, long considered good advice, has a great many companions -- some of which appear earlier in this volume. It may do some good to bring them all together as Part I of this volume ends. Here they are, with a few sentences of reexplanation, if and as needed.

1. "Write the way you speak."
2. "To see if your writing is good, read it out loud."
   When you read your own writing aloud, you -- being the author -- know exactly which words to deemphasize and which to stress. You know when the pace should quicken and -- when -- it -- should -- slow -- down --- for ----- dramatic ----- effect. In short, you already know how to interpret it. Your readers do not come to this text with your prior knowledge. They need to take their clues for interpretation from the text itself and only from the text. Because you know what it is "supposed to

sound like," you can falsify -- albeit unintentionally -- the "reading experience." So reading aloud is highly likely to mislead you.

That does not mean that nothing good can come of reading your prose aloud. Any time you revisit your prose you may find ways to improve it. Reading aloud slows you down and makes you revisit each individual word. You can find typographical errors, spelling mistakes, unintended repetitions, grammatical errors, and awkward rhythms. The danger, however, is that by reading it aloud without encountering these kinds of *errors* or *inelegances*, you may fool yourself into thinking that a reader will experience it the way you do. That is a danger.

3. "To make it better, make it shorter."

Length, by itself, indicates nothing whatever about clarity or force. If the words are in places where readers do not expect them to be, the sentence, although ever so short, can be difficult or impossible to comprehend. Sometimes longer is better. Sometimes longer is necessary.

It may be true that a great deal of bad prose is also prose burdened by unnecessary length. The problem there, however, is not the length, but rather the rhetorical failures that produced the unneeded length. The length is a symptom, not a cause. The same is true for coughing and sneezing when you have a cold. We cannot cure the cold by telling people not to cough and sneeze. Nor can we cure people's problematic prose by telling them to make it shorter.

4. "A sentence is too long when it exceeds 29 words."

Nonsense. Professional sentences average 24 to 26 words. Therefore, there must be many sentences with 29+ words out there to balance all the sentences with 8, 10, 12, and 14 words. The longer a sentence is, the harder you must strive to control its structure; but long, complex structures are often necessary to express long, complex thoughts. Past 29 words, a sentence is reaching for a third clause; three clauses are more difficult to control than two. After 29 words, a sentence does not become harder to read; but it does become harder to write.

5. "Avoid the verb *to be* and other weak verbs."

No verb is weak or strong by itself, but only in context. A verb is "strong" if its meaning represents what is happening in that clause or sentence. The verb *to be* means "exists," or "equals," or "is labeled as." When any of those is the action of a clause or sentence, then *is* is a strong verb. No matter how impressive a verb may look, if its meaning is not what is going on in the sentence, it is a "weak" verb.

6. "Vary the way you begin your sentences to keep your reader interested."

In the professional world, your reader is paid to read you and need not necessarily be interested. The beginning of your sentence is too important a location to vary just for the sake of variety. Make sure it contains your backward link and the answer to the question "Whose story is this?" Keep the "whose story" element the same sentence after sentence until the answer to the question "Whose story is this?" changes.

When I suggest your reader is paid to read you, I am not being cynical. In the working world, your prose is a tool for getting things done. Getting them done is the key. It is an extra delight for any of us if we can be interested in our work as we do it. Those are the best jobs. But interest alone will not get the job done after graduation -- even though it accomplishes a great deal at school.

7. "Never start a sentence with the words *but* or *however*.

    These matters are native to the Latin language and need not concern us when we are dealing with the English language. *But* and *however*, properly used, clearly tell English readers that whatever was said just before its arrival is now to be qualified. Take care of your present readers and leave the ancient Romans to fend for themselves.

8. "Never use numbers or letters in formal prose."

    Anything that helps your reader understand your structure is a good thing -- unless it unnecessarily condescends to your reader by suggesting he is an uncomprehending dolt.

9. "Every paragraph should start with a topic sentence."

    True, every paragraph should begin with what is going to be at issue in that paragraph; but often that takes two or three sentences and cannot be accomplished in a single topic sentence. Moreover, sometimes the issue of a paragraph is not the same thing as its point. The old topic sentence was supposed to encapsulate both issue and point.

10. "Most paragraphs should contain five sentences."

    That is simply not true of professional writing. Open any book and check it out for yourself.

11. "Never create a one-sentence paragraph."

    One-sentence paragraphs are fine as long as (1) they state the issue, (2) they state the point, and (3) they need no further discussion.

12. "All essays should end with a summary paragraph that restates the main points."

    This is most often an annoying and unhelpful way to end an essay. If your text was clear, we do not need to be reminded of what you so clearly told us before. Make sure your ending has the sense of an ending -- a sense of comfortable and fulfilling closure. Lead us to rest; don't give us a review session for the exam.

13. "Always make a carefully numbered and lettered outline of your essay before writing it."

    (I have not talked about this before.) Have you been taught always to make such an outline before you write the essay? I would advise you to make such an outline if you cannot write without one; otherwise, don't. Once you are out of school, who cares? Will the National Science

Foundation let you know your grant proposal was terrible but your outline really made sense -- so here is $4,000,000? Not likely.

There are dangers in over-outlining. (1) How can you know exactly how all your thoughts will unfold before you actually try to write them out in detail? That outline might prohibit you from straying from it into richer pastures. (2) Too often students simply make full sentences out of all the outline fragments, erase the number and letters, and push everything to the left margin, indenting five spaces where necessary. That is one of the prime reasons so many bright students produce so many dull papers.

Organize; but do not overorganize. Use whatever form of categorization you feel is best to get the lay of your intellectual land at the start; but allow yourself roaming opportunities. How do you know what you mean until you see what you say?

14. "Avoid the passive."

Again, nonsense. If you always avoid the passive, you sacrifice one of the subtlest, most versatile tools the English language affords us. Know what the passive does; then use it when what it does is what you need done. We have encountered a number of excellent uses of the passive in previous chapters. Here they are, together for the first time.

-- to avoid saying who or what did the actions (e.g., stating agency)

-- to get the answer to the question "Whose story is this?" up front

-- to get the backward link up front

-- to get the most important information to the Stress position

-- to indicate passivity

-- to weaken the focus on the occupant of the "whose story" location.

Use the passive when it is the only way to get the right information into the right structural location.

And once more, for good effect --- "No Rules! No Rules!" Reader expectations are not a new set of rules for writers. Instead, they are a series of predictions of what most readers do, most of the time. Every reader expectation can be violated to good effect. Our best stylists often turn out to be our most skillful violators. But in order for such violations to have the right effect, you must fulfill reader expectations most of the time. Constant violation produces chaos.

The Toll Booth Syndrome

With all the education in this country -- and especially with all the higher education -- why do so many people still write so inadequately? Why is so much professional prose so hard to comprehend? The answer may lie in a metaphor we can call "The Toll Booth Syndrome."

Picture the following as vividly as you can. You are a lawyer. You live in southwest Connecticut and commute into Manhattan to work. One day you arrive at the office at 6:30 A.M. to work on the big case. Everything that could go wrong does go wrong. At 9:00 P.M. you give up trying and decide to go home. You redeem your car from the parking lot and fight both the traffic and the increasingly bad weather over to the West Side Highway. Because of great goings-on in town that night, this takes you 90 minutes. Finally, after more than two hours of rain and sleet, you are nearing the Connecticut border. Just before you get there, you see a sign that warns you of an approaching toll booth. The sign says "40¢ -- Exact Change Left Lane." You reach into in your pocket and pull out all the change you have -- a nickel, a dime, and a quarter, totaling 40¢. (This is the only thing that has gone right all day.) You enter the Exact Change Lane. In front of you is a shining red light, but no barrier; to the left of you is the hopper that will receive your change. You are tired and irritable as you roll down the window, the wind and sleet greeting you inhospitably. You heave the change at the hopper. The quarter drops in; the dime drops in; but the nickel hits the rim and bounces out. What do you do? Do you put the car in park, get out, and grovel in the gravel for your nickel? Do you put the car in reverse and maneuver into another lane, where a human being can make change for your dollar bill? No. You go through the red light.

If you go through the red light, I would argue, you are harboring a misconception of the purpose of tolls. At this anxious moment you are not feeling -- as is the case in reality -- that before you continue on that road the government must *receive delivery* from you of 40¢ of your accumulated wealth, with which it will keep the roads in good repair and pay the toll-booth operators. Instead, you believe that before continuing on that road you must be *dispossessed* of 40¢ -- and you have been. Your job is done; your suffering is complete. Now you can leave that effort behind and continue with the rest of life.

That is the misconception so many professionals have concerning the writing task. They have done so much work before they turn to the task of getting things down on paper or up on a screen: They may have interviewed a client, discussed the situation with associates, delegated tasks to assistants, done the research, conceived of the strategies, made the right phone calls, and organized the entire project. The thinking, they think, is now done; now they only have to *write* it. They cast all of their knowledge on the subject out of their mind onto the paper, not caring if their audience will actually receive their 40¢ worth of wisdom; they care only that they disburden themselves of it. All their 40¢ is out there -- on the paper, in the gravel -- and that is what matters. They no longer possess it. They have suffered enough. On they go with the rest of life.

Of course that is *not* the way we should be thinking of the relationship between the work we do and the written product we produce. The writing process is not to be separated from the thinking process; it *is* a thinking process. If a teacher is the only person who will ever read the document, we may do well enough by merely spilling all the appropriate keywords and dates and other essential information somewhere on the paper. The teacher, after all, seems already to know everything that needs to be known about the subject covered by this paper and will know what to do with the assorted fragments we have let drop. But when our readers are people in the working world, people who need to be informed or convinced or persuaded of the rightness of our perceptions, we need to send them persuasive instructions for how to put all this information together. Those instructions are sent mostly by depositing information in the structural locations where readers will most readily look for it.

These days we hear about something called the Information Highway. (We have not been informed as yet whether it will remain a freeway or eventually be turned into a toll road.) All the information in the world may eventually be available to anyone who has access to a computer. It sounds wonderful. It also sounds overwhelming. The information, by itself, is worth next to nothing. It only has meaning when it can be found and applied to a particular need or situation. Having loads of information but no ideas is like having huge piles of gold on a desert island -- with nothing to spend it on. Such wealth in such isolation "means" nothing. In order to be worth anything, that wealth has to exist in a context in which it can function. That should be reminiscent of much this book has to say. Words, like gold coins, "mean" nothing until they are put in a context that allows them to do the job they were created to do. Context controls meaning. Putting the right information in the structural location where it is expected to arrive will create the appropriate context for your communicating your thoughts.

CONTEXT

STRUCTURE

SUBSTANCE

EXPECTATION

Mark My Words: A Reader's Perspective on the World of Punctuation

From Fetters to Facilitators: Punctuation as Power

It seems quite simple: Punctuation marks tell you when to stop and when to start again. They tell you when to breathe, when to interrupt your main train of thought, and how severely to do so. They inform you when to raise a question and when to read with the power of an exclamation. They let you know when to lean forward and when to bring it all to a halt. They suggest differing relationships between different units of discourse.

Although they function in ways that are relatively distinct from one another, every mark of punctuation both unifies and divides, both joins and separates, both looks back and leans forward. The wonder of it all is how much work these little marks actually accomplish -- and how many distinctions they can make in the ways prose is interpreted by readers.

Punctuation has primarily been studied in school settings as a series of rules or social conventions. These rules, we are told, must be mastered if we are to be taken seriously some day as a producer of written discourse. The rules are articulated in some detail by a textbook or handbook; the student-writer can get them "right" or "wrong." It appears to be the most objective, the most knowable part of writing.

Why, then, do so many people -- even a majority of the most highly educated, highly literate people -- feel insecure about this supposedly objective and available knowledge? Part of the answer lies in the exaggeration of its own objectivity; the "rules" are not quite as firmly established as we are led to believe from the confidence exuded by the writers of handbooks. Here is a quick quiz:

1. You have three colors to chose from for the upholstery of your new car. Which of the following is the grammatically correct listing of those three colors?

   a) red, white, and blue

   or

   b) red, white and blue

   Answer: Even though (b) is the worse option (because it can produce ambiguity), either one is correct.

2. When a comma or period comes at the end of a quoted word or passage, is it placed before or after the closing quotation mark?

   Answer: Before, at all times, in the United States; and after, at all times, in Great Britain.

3. May a semi-colon be used between two independent clauses linked by a coordinating conjunction, whether or not the clauses contain internal punctuation?

   Responses: 1) It depends on which handbook you consult. Some say definitively no. Some hedge. Some say it is certainly allowed if there *is* internal punctuation, but if there isn't, well. . . .

2) How many of us can even understand this question? How many English teachers can understand this question unless they are currently professionally involved in reconsidering the semi-colon? Why is this a question that needs to be settled?

So the rules are not as clear as they might appear on first glance; but that alone cannot explain why so many people feel so insecure about their knowledge of punctuation. The greater part of the answer lies in the less than ideal approach we take to teaching and learning this subsystem of our communication process.

We do ourselves a disservice, I believe, when we think about punctuation as a set of social norms that pre-existed us and that is intended to regulate our written expression. I am not suggesting, by any means, that we discard or disregard punctuation and all the other seemingly mechanical aspects of writing. Written communication is hard enough without increasing the chaos by disregarding conventions. On the contrary, I am suggesting that we gain better control over punctuation by reconceiving our relationship to it. Let us stop seeing ourselves as permanent grade school students, forever in danger of having points deducted for nonconformation to rules; instead, let us recognize that punctuation is one of the means we as writers have for better controlling the interpretive acts of readers.

To do this, we have to adopt a new perspective on the issue. Instead of memorizing what the books say we must do as writers, let us look at how marks of punctuation actually affect us as readers. If we know consciously what readers *do* upon encountering a semi-colon, then we can better understand in what situations we as writers should put a semi-colon in the reader's path. We then become the empowered ones, using punctuation to help create and shape our readers' expectations and responses.

··Exercise U

The following five examples contain essentially the same pieces of information; however, the ideas they shape are distinct in important ways. Read them carefully to see what those differences are. Can you sense how variations in punctuation actually create distinctions in meaning? Do not be distressed if this exercise does not make perfect sense to you now. It should be much easier to understand when you finish reading this chapter.

1. Under the new set of governance rules developed by the Administration of the College, students have the right to be represented on committees making decisions not only on budget control, faculty hiring, and rules governing student life, but also on admissions policies.

2. Under the new set of governance rules developed by the Administration of the College, students have the right to be represented on committees making decisions on budget control, faculty hiring, and rules governing student life; most surprisingly, they now have a voice in the establishing of admissions policies.

3. Under the new set of governance rules developed by the Administration of the College, students have the right to be represented on a number of committees from which they have been traditionally excluded: budget control, faculty hiring, student life, and admissions.

4. Under the new set of governance rules developed by the Administration of the College, students have the right to be represented on a number of committees from which they have been traditionally excluded: They can now bring their opinions to bear on matters of budget control, faculty hiring, student life, and admissions policies.

5. Under the new set of governance rules developed by the Administration of the College, students have the right to be represented on committees making decisions on budget control, faculty hiring, and student life. They also can bring their opinions to bear on admissions policies.

T *he Semi-colon: A Hope for an Afterlife*

I begin with what is perhaps the least well-understood mark of punctuation because it may be the best example of the subtlety with which we can control readers' responses. Despite having been around for 1,400 years, it seems not to have achieved a user-friendly status.[1]

To be completely straightforward with you, for a very long time I harbored a suspicion that the semi-colon had something to do with sex. I remember the day -- I was 12 years old at the time -- when my English teacher reached the section of our textbook that dealt with the semi-colon. With a noticeable amount of emotional discomfort, he told our all-male class, "We won't go into the semi-colon. You don't need that now. You'll need that later." He was relieved not to have to tell us; we were relieved not to have to face the unveiling of the mystery. We were feeling that way about a number of concerns at that particular stage of life and had seen our fathers undergo the same discomfort and the same escape by avoidance.

My teacher was right, of course. I didn't need the semi-colon at age 12. Unfortunately, by the time I was grown up enough to need the semi-colon, there was no one around to explain it to me. By then, I was somehow supposed to know all about it. I went around for years thinking I was one of the few people who did not understood this mystery. I now know that most people are just as insecure about it as I was.

So let us approach the question from the perspective of a reader. What does a reader *do* when a semi-colon appears? What does a semi-colon inform a reader about at that particular moment in the development of thought? Immediately there seems to be a problem. If so few people have fully learned the rules for the semi-colon, can we even begin to talk in terms of what "readers do"? Yes, I think we can. A reader "does" something when he or she encounters *anything* on a page -- even if it is a coffee stain that has no integral part in the written discourse. As readers encounter more and more semi-colons, they learn to "do" similar things with each new reoccurrence. It does not matter that of the millions who process semi-colons on a regular basis, only a small percentage could articulate explicitly how it makes them respond to the text the way they do. If most of the semi-colons they have seen were "correctly" used, then their response will eventually become a "correct" response, whether conscious or not. It is simply a question of conditioning through constant problem solving.

What, then, do most people do when they see a semi-colon? They pause more than if they had seen a comma and less than if they had seen a period. However, it is the *nature* of the reader's stopping, not the mere extent of it, that makes the semi-colon so special and so useful. It is the subtlest and most supple of our punctuational signals to our readers. In a single instant, it is intended to convey to readers the following multiple messages:

1. "Please come to full syntactic closure here. What you have just finished is a independent clause, capable of standing by itself as a full sentence. You can let go of the reader energy you were just using to recognize a complete, full-fledged statement with beginning, middle, and end. In other words, you have reached a Stress position. However, . . .

2. "What you are now about to experience is another independent clause, also capable of standing by itself, and also with its own Stress position. However, . . .

3. "The relationship between these two thoughts is so intimate that they really deserve to be part and parcel of the same single sentence. So . . .

4. "Stop; but don't stop. Close; but keep open. Stress this; but expect more Stress at the sentence's end. You've heard something of interest; but what's to come makes it of even greater interest. These two clauses are two separate clauses, each with their own point to make; but together they make a point of even greater complexity or force."

That is a lot of work to be done by a dot and a squiggle.

What makes the use of a semi-colon different from the use of a period at that moment? To answer that question, let us ruin a wonderful paragraph of Lewis Thomas in which he discusses the delight and power of the semi-colon. Example (1a) is the original Thomas paragraph; example (1b) is a dewritten version, with all the semi-colons changed to periods.[2]

1a. I have grown fond of semi-colons in recent years. The semi-colon tells you that there is still some question about the preceding full sentence;

something needs to be added; it reminds you sometimes of the Greek usage.* It is almost always a greater pleasure to come across a semi-colon than a period. The period tells you that that is that; if you didn't get all the meaning you wanted or expected, anyway you got all the writer intended to parcel out and now you have to move along. But with a semi-colon there you get a pleasant little feeling of expectancy; there is more to come; read on; it will get clearer.

(Lewis Thomas: "Notes on Punctuation," from The Medusa and the Snail)

[*Note: The Greeks used the semi-colon to perform the function of our question mark.]

Now the dewritten version:

1b. I have grown fond of semi-colons in recent years. The semi-colon tells you that there is still some question about the preceding full sentence. Something needs to be added. It reminds you sometimes of the Greek usage. It is almost always a greater pleasure to come across a semi-colon than a period. The period tells you that that is that. If you didn't get all the meaning you wanted or expected, anyway you got all the writer intended to parcel out and now you have to move along. But with a semi-colon there you get a pleasant little feeling of expectancy. There is more to come. Read on. It will get clearer.

The comparative choppiness or clunky quality of the (1b) version is not only a matter of flow or style of elegance or even power; it is also a matter of how the reader is invited to weigh, balance, and connect various pieces of information or thought.

This can be articulated in reader expectation terms. Because a semi-colon comes at the end of an independent clause, it creates a moment of full syntactic closure -- enough to create a Stress position.[3] It also promises that another independent clause (with another Stress position) will follow immediately. Proper use of a semi-colon, then, can produce for a reader two Stress positions, two moments of major emphasis, in a single sentence. The unique product of the semi-colon, therefore, is the ability to suggest a relationship between two equally significant clauses more intimate than that between two neighboring sentences. "Here," it says to the reader, "are two separate statements, each with its own important information to stress; they then combine to make a single, more complex statement as a single unit."

As a result, the easiest way to decide if you should use a semi-colon at any given moment is to decide whether you need to create an additional Stress position in the middle of your sentence. If you do, *and* if the relationship between these two clauses merits their being part of a single syntactic unit, then a semi-colon will allow you to suggest all this to your reader without the utterance of a single extra word.

Here is a curious story that might help you keep this in mind. Edwin Muir (1887–1959) was a wonderful (but sadly underread) poet who relied heavily on his dreams for the production of his poetic images. His wife informs us that in his last week of his life he had a dream that consisted exclusively of a semi-colon. She made no claim as to what this might mean; but I am willing to suggest an interpretation. I think he was using the semi-colon as a metaphor for the moment of death.

<u>Independent clause</u> ; <u>independent clause</u> .

<u>life before death</u> ; <u>life after death</u> .

"All of life," the semi-colon seems to say, "is now finished. You have now experienced a unit of existence complete unto itself. This is a moment of completion, called death. However, what is to come hereafter," the semi-colon continues, "will also be a unit complete unto itself; but there is such an intimate relationship between the two units that they must be considered together as a single whole. That's death for you: One experience is over; but a different one is on the way. Together they make a whole." Death as a semi-colon; the semi-colon as death.

Let us look at the specific differences the resulting punctuational options can provide for a reader of a given sentence. Here is a quotation from a speech delivered by an alumna of a secondary school, celebrating her 30th reunion, to the students currently attending her alma mater. How do the three different punctuations of this alter its effect?

2a. I believe that I attended a school which differs from yours in significant ways; but then again, some things probably have not changed in the least.

2b. I believe that I attended a school which differs from yours in significant ways. Then again, some things probably have not changed in the least.

2c. I believe that I attended a school which differs from yours in significant ways but, then again, has probably not changed in the least.

Each of these sentences "means" in a great many ways, especially if multiple readers are consulted for their opinions. However, it may be safe to suggest ways in which they generally tend to differ.

[2a] Sentence (2a) establishes its first point ("school . . . differs"), but continues through the semi-colon to suggest more is to be considered ("things . . . have not changed"). Despite the syntactic closure of the first clause, the whole thought is not yet complete. The resulting progression may seem a kind of up-and-back journey.

Note that at the moment we encounter the semi-colon, we cannot predict precisely what the second clause will bring us. The sentence quite reasonably could have proceeded as follows: "I believe that I attended a school which differs from yours in significant ways; those differences have widened as the years have passed, to the point where you and I have nothing whatever in common." In other words, we have to stay tuned to find out what happens.

[2b] In (2b) we are perhaps taken in by the first sentence. The absolute full closure of the period suggests this thought is a complete one. It gets set in cerebral cement before the next one starts. The second sentence is therefore more of an annoying reversal than a circular balance. "Here is my first statement, and it's complete and finished. Well now, let's open up that closed topic for a new discussion and change our mind."

[2c] The lack of a medial Stress position for the first point in (2c) never allows that initial thought to get established with the same force created in either (2a) or (2b). Since its force is undercut by the lack of a Stress position, more emphasis is produced for the "not changed in the least" that occupies this sentence's single Stress position. "I'm in the process of saying something but am changing my mind before I finish."

Again, no one of these three is "right" or "wrong"; they all do different things and are likely to be perceived differently by a given reader. In deciding which to choose, the author would have found no help from consulting rules of usage. The decision can better be made by considering (1) what information needs a Stress position, and (2) what the relationship is between the contents of the two clauses. These are sophisticated matters: No wonder most 12-year-olds have not yet developed a need for the semi-colon.

EXERCISE V

Take any three sentences in this book that employ the semi-colon and dewrite them each in two different ways:

1. by replacing the semi-colon with a period, thus making two separate sentences; and

2. by replacing the semi-colon with a comma and supplying additional connecting words like *but* or *although* or *and* or *then*.

How do these dewritten variations "mean" differently?

There is a second, lesser use of the semi-colon: It separates examples of an immediately previous statement that has ended in a colon.

3. Imagine what existence-transforming changes a 90-year-old American has witnessed in her lifetime: the widespread use of electricity; the invention of the automobile; the advent of radio, television, stereophonic equipment, and now, most markedly, the computer; the movement toward human equality for some races and most genders;

the rises and falls of tyrants; the comings and goings of fads; and the lessening of the optimism that says to each generation that you can do better than the one before you.

Each of these semi-colons produces a Stress position, though perhaps of less individual force than if they had come at the end of a full independent clause. Some stress occurs at the end of each of these fragments because the reader is *expecting* them not to be completed clauses but instead to be mere fragments. At their end, therefore, we experience a sense of syntactic closure, which is the sole necessary condition for the production of a Stress position.

This catalogue-type use of the semi-colon is important; but the subtler use described earlier is far more important. The latter gives the writer a tool of control that is otherwise not easily available in our language. Lewis Thomas caught its magic nicely in a memorable metaphor:

> The things I like best in T. S. Eliot's poetry, especially in the *Four Quartets,* are the semicolons. You cannot hear them, but they are there, laying out the connections between the images and the ideas. Sometimes you get a glimpse of a semi-colon coming, a few lines farther on, and it is like climbing a steep path through woods and seeing a wooden bench just at a bend in the road ahead, a place where you can expect to sit for a moment, catching your breath.
>
> (Lewis Thomas: "Notes on Punctuation," from *The Medusa and the Snail*)

To "catching your breath" I would add "wondering what could possibly be coming around the bend that will make the trip even finer, even more complete."

·· EXERCISE **W**

Articulate in as much detail as possible how and why the semi-colons in these examples function. Then dewrite the examples by making whatever changes are necessary to eliminate the semi-colons. This will not necessarily improve the sentences; but what differences in meaning may have been wrought by these changes?

1. On the one hand, Dr. Birtwhistle could put you appropriately in awe of the subject matter; on the other hand, she could make you feel that all science was beyond mortal comprehension.

2. I had thought that she was telling us not to be bored with General Science; eventually I came to think that she was telling us not to be bored with living and thinking.

3. To understand metaphor and all its workings is a lifetime's struggle; to explain it to others is a full-time profession.

4. One of the great differences between the Democratic and Republican parties in this country is their attitude toward the use of rhetorical

figures. Democrats love them; Republicans avoid them. Democrats see figures of speech as a way of reaching the minds and hearts of real folk; Republicans see the same figures as a smoke screen that hides the important stuff -- straight talk, plain facts, bottom-line numbers.

A Brief Glimpse at the History of Punctuation

The semi-colon is a curious mark. It seems to be composed of a period piled on top of a comma, which is not a bad approximation of its function: Like a period, it tells you to affect syntactic closure; but, like a comma, it urges you to keep on going. It might well be called a comma-period instead.

Comma, period, and semi-colon are at the heart of the history of punctuation. It is helpful to keep in mind that all parts of language *have* history; they were not produced full-grown from the mind of some Zeus-like god of language, ages before you were born -- even if that seems the case when we have to do all that memorization in middle school English classes. Putting things in historic perspective often gives us greater control over our own situation and lessens our debilitating sense of mystery. Let us take a quick peek at the development of these dots and squiggles we call punctuation.[4]

Over two thousand years ago, Greek scribes were copying texts in what was called *scripta continua* -- a handwriting in which words were not separated from each other by spaces; and thus there was no way of indicating pauses. This last sentence, printed in *scripta continua*, would look like this:

overtwothousandyearsagogreekscribeswerecopyingtextsinwhatwascalledscriptacontinuaahandwritinginwhichwordswerenotseparatedfromeachotherbyspacesandthustherewasnowayofindicatingpauses

If you think you can make that out with relative ease, it could be that your eye was aided by the recent echo in your ear. Try the following, which you are seeing for the first time:

washistoryaneasytasktoundertakewhennospaceslepttot

heeyetoaidthemindinunderstandingthatnowanewthoughtisbeg

iningnottobeconfusedwiththepreviousonesohowdidyoudowit

hdecipheringthiseh

Latin scribes could continue this Greek tradition because the construction of the Latin language resembled that of Greek: Both indicated the grammatical relationships between words by varying their case endings. For example, the subject of a sentence was always in the nominative case -- often marked by the letter *s*; and the direct object of the verb was always in the accusative case -- often marked by the letter *m*. In addition, these endings had a grammatical gender: Every word was categorized as either masculine, feminine, or neuter, whether or not it possessed any gender-specific characteristics. The vowel *u* often indicated masculine, while the vowel *a* usually indicated feminine. To translate our much-investigated "Jack loves Jill" into Latin, then, we need to give Jack a masculine and nominative ending (*–us*) and Jill a feminine and accusative ending (*–am*). Supply the Latin verb (third person singular, present, active, indicative) for *loves* ("amat"), and we have the sentence.

Jackus amat Jillam.

Having these cases, Latin did not need to rely heavily on word order. Those three words in any order would have the same syntactic relationship, dictated by their word endings. So in Latin, "Jackus amat Jillam" and "Jillam amat Jackus" would have the same meaning. In English, "Jack loves Jill" and "Jill loves Jack" are often worlds apart in meaning, which is demonstrated daily by numerous television soap operas. By the way, Latin normally began with the subject but ended with the verb:

Jackus Jillam amat.

As a result, *scripta continua* would not have bothered readers of Latin as much as it would bother us. They would see the *–us* and the *–am* and the *–at* endings and know not only where the words stopped and started but also how they related to each other.

In addition, Latin employed interrogative pronouns and adjectives that warned the reader of the immediate presence of a question, thus obviating the need for the question mark.

There is yet another reason that *scripta continua* would not have bothered those ancient scribes: They were not copying out the extraordinary variety of texts we now might encounter in just a day's reading. Many of their documents (in the absence of photocopying machines) had to be reproduced over and over by the same scribes, who therefore had little need to separate words or even sentences.

Cicero, the great Roman orator and rhetorician, disdained punctuation because he was in the business of producing oral speech. He expected a reader to be able to "hear" the end of a sentence by its well-wrought rhythm. Much of the most important transference of prose in those days was managed from mouth to ear, not from eye to eye.

It makes sense that a system of punctuation eventually would need to be developed, if for no other reason than to help new readers know how to distinguish the shape and function of individual words, and then phrases, and then sentences. That seems indeed to have been the case with Latin. Punctuation marks began as the linguistic equivalent of the training wheels we put on kids' bicycles: They were there to help you get your bearing and your balance; but once you were accustomed to the ride, you were proud to be able to do without them.

Our closest contemporary linguistic equivalent is the cardboard template we put on our computer keyboards to teach us the various commands for our word processing system. Once we know that the simultaneous depression of the Control and the F2 keys will produce our Spell-Check program, we cease to use the cardboard chart for that.

So punctuation was invented *to help the reader*. That is still its purpose. It does *not* exist primarily to burden schoolchildren and intimidate adults.

Punctuation made various kinds of appearances about two thousand years ago; we cannot date its first appearance with any accuracy. Some credit Aristophanes of Byzantium (c. 257–180 B.C.E.) with the invention (or at least publication) of the first systematized punctuation, using marks that approach the nature of our period, comma, and colon. (He is not to be confused with the more famous playwright Aristophanes who lived two centuries earlier.) The grammarian Aristophanes was a Greek scholar who settled in Alexandria and became chief librarian of the museum there. As an editor of the works of others (Hesiod, Homer, Anacreon, Pindar, and the earlier Aristophanes), he must have approached text as a reader more than as a producer; he seems to have devised a system of helpful marks -- helpful to readers -- so they could access the significance of texts with more ease than had been his own experience. This care for the comprehension of others is perhaps equally evident in the lists he compiled of rare words and foreign expressions.

Both the promulgation and the study of punctuation were intensified in the fourth century by the eminent Roman grammarian Aelius Donatus, whose *Ars Grammatica* served as the main text on the subject through the Middle Ages in Western Europe. It discussed the parts of speech, firmly established the concept of error (featuring the terms *barbarism* and *solecism*[5]), and extensively listed figures of thought and figures of speech. His work was so universally adopted over such a long period of time that his name (in the form of "Donat" or "Donet") became synonymous both with grammar itself and with an elementary text in any field. He shared the grammatical spotlight with only one other, Priscianus Caesariensis, known as Priscian, whose greatly expanded Latin grammar *Institutionis Grammaticae* (c. 500 C.E.) was so widely used for so long that to violate a grammatical rule was "to break Priscian's head."

Donatus recommended a three-fold distinction of punctuation, marked by the height at which the mark of pause was written:

(1) A mark inscribed at the bottom of a letter (a "low" mark) was used to indicate a minor pause in the middle of a continuing syntactical unit, creating a unit of discourse the ancients called a *comma*; it signaled an interruption and is equivalent to some of the uses of our modern comma;

(2) A midheight mark, inscribed halfway from the bottom of the letter to the top, was used after the unit of discourse they called a *colon*, where the sense of the subunit was complete, but the meaning of the whole unit (the *sententia*) was not. It is equivalent in use to our modern semicolon and colon; and

(3) A highly placed mark at the top of a letter, *periodus*, was used to indicate the end of the unit, where the sense of the whole (the *sententia*) was complete. It is equivalent in use to our modern period.

Since it was the height at which the mark was placed that signified the distinction in its use, writers could use the same square dotlike mark for all three of these. Although we use a number of different marks now, and do not much use the height of their placement to indicate function, we have still maintained this three-fold distinction between types of pauses. We have not completely abandoned the height system: An apostrophe is just an airborne comma.

Although punctuation began as an aid to inexperienced readers, it took on a far greater function in the writings of St. Augustine (354–430 C.E.), who was trying to use written discourse to spread a relatively new Christian religion. He was critically aware of the dangers that would result from either the Bible or his commentary being misinterpreted. Despite case endings, ambiguity could arise if it was not clear whether a word were leaning backward or forward in its associations with other words.[6] Ambiguity could breed misinterpretation; misinterpretation could result in serious error that could threaten not only the spread of the new religion but also the well-being of immortal souls. The Christian message was itself a message of interpretation, so important he felt no risk of bad reading or misreading could be endured. He was not concerned with a few select individuals who were being trained to read; he was concerned with large numbers of people who were being trained in salvation. To make sure their interpretation of his text was the precise one he wished them to have, punctuation had to be standardized and regularly employed.

The first person vigorously to encourage a comprehension of punctuation was St. Jerome (340–420 C.E.), who perceived the same needs as St. Augustine. In translating the Vulgate Bible, he used a combination of commas and colons to indicate separations for interpretive purposes; these marks also indicated possible breathing spots for those who were reading out loud, the colon being more interruptive than the comma. (There was an entirely separate set of marks to coach the raising and lowering of the voice in oral delivery -- including the *punctus elevatus*, the *punctus interrogotivus*, and the *punctus circumflexus*.) When, in the sixth century, the influential writer Boethius gave great emphasis to the study of punctuation, there was no turning back; punctuation was here to stay.

It was not as popular with monks. Since they read and copied the same texts over and over, they knew them all by heart and had no need to remind themselves or their learned readers how to pause, separate, and combine words. But Pope Gregory (late sixth century), in broadly publishing a treatise on pastoral care, so wished to control every issue and every interpretation that he insisted on even minor punctuation marks being maintained with consistency throughout. We have inherited his concerns. Having recognized our honorable ancestors, let us return to our consideration of what punctuation does to and for readers.

T *he Colon: Play It Again, Sam*

In ancient Greek, *colon* referred to a recognizable subunit of prose that was smaller than a sentence. That subunit might be grammatically complete or might just be recognizable because of its rhythmic shape; in either case, both sound and sense were involved. To balance two of them was to create an *isocolon*:

["Ask not what your country can do for you"]

was balanced in President Kennedy's inaugural address by

["Ask what you can do for your country."]

Even though the modern term that denotes the punctuation mark [:] no longer requires this exact auditory balance, it manages to retain a good deal of the original reader/hearer sense of expectation. What comes after a colon is expected either to redefine or to exemplify that which came before it: Therein lies the ancient sense of balance.

At present, the presence of a colon says the following to a reader:

1. "Please come to a full stop here. What you have just finished is an independent clause, capable of standing by itself as a full sentence. You can now cease to pay attention to the way in which this clause is ending, because here is its end, and you may now rest for a moment. In other words, this is a Stress position. However, . . .

2. "What you are about to experience as the second part of this sentence will consist of one of the two following options:

   a. "What follows is another independent clause that will restate or redefine the ideas presented by the clause that preceded the colon, offering you a second opportunity for understanding; or,

   b. "What follows is a list of examples that, taken together, will give you a fuller way of understanding those previously stated ideas."

Those two uses of the colon are closely related in some ways and quite distinct in others. Let us look at them separately.

The first option looks like this:

Independent clause : Independent clause.

Full syntactic closure arrives at both punctuation marks, thus creating at those locations two separate Stress positions. To clue in a reader as quickly as possible that this is the kind of colon use in process, I would advise you always to begin the second independent clause with a capital letter. Both upper- and lowercase letters are considered acceptable here; but the capital letter succeeds in sending a signal to the reader to expect the unfolding of a second independent clause. Note, however, that using a single space after the colon (as opposed to the double space we use after periods) suggests that the two clauses form a more solid unity than would be formed by two separate sentences.

The reader is likely to expect a tamer, often a potentially less subtle or less complex relationship between two clauses if they are connected by a colon rather than a semi-colon. The semi-colon suggests a further expansion of thought, or a deeper development, or at least a significant and related addition. The colon suggests we will hear the essence of the first clause repeated, but stated differently, in some helpful way. Here are two examples from John Demos's article "The American Family Then and Now." He is comparing the larger family of the seventeenth century to the family of today.

4. Thus there was little privacy for the residents, and little chance to differentiate between various portions of living space. *Life in these households was much less segmented, in a formal sense, than it usually is for us: Individuals were more constantly together, and their activities meshed and overlapped at many points.*

5. The point becomes clearer when set in contrast to the situation that obtains in our own time. *No longer can one feel such an essential continuity between the various spheres of experience: The central threads in the invisible web have been broken.*

These examples demonstrate two ways (among many) of relating two independent clauses by the use of a colon. In example (4), the second clause restates the point of the first by adopting the opposite or the mirror image. Instead of "less segmented," we get "more constantly together," "meshed," and "overlapped." Considered from this perspective, example (4) seems closely related to the other colon use -- the one that produces a list of examples instead of a restatement. It could have been structured that way, too.

4a. Three terms are contrasted with the initial term "less segmented": "more constantly together"; "meshed"; and "overlapped."

In contrast, example (5) turns the clause after the colon into a metaphor of its predecessor. The lack of "essential continuity between the various spheres of experience" is an attempt to make the point in a straightforward although somewhat abstract way; "the central threads in the invisible web have been broken" is a metaphor chosen to bring the abstract into clearer relief. Sometimes a point is worth playing again from a different perspective or with an illuminating figure of speech. In either case, the presence of a colon followed by a capital letter warns the reader that an experience of revisitation is at hand.

Example (5) also makes use of another figure of speech that appears quite commonly in this use of the colon. That figure of speech is the *chiasmus*: It requires the statement and repetition of at least two elements, with the repetition proceeding in reverse order (xyyx). Again we can look at President Kennedy's famous inaugural plea:

[x]   [y]

Ask not what <u>your country</u> can do for <u>you</u>:

Ask what <u>you</u> can do for <u>your country</u>."

[y]   [x]

Kennedy's chiasmus repeats the key words but alters their grammatical functions: The subject and object switch places. The chiasmus in example (5) is somewhat more subtle, since the repeated elements are not specific words but rather parts of speech. The [x] elements are the verbs, which indicate negative ability: Something can no longer be felt; something is broken. The [y] elements are the objects of those actions -- the things which are not felt, or which are broken. Since the first clause is stated in the active voice and the second in the passive, the order of verb-object is reversed to object-verb.

[x]   [y]

No longer can one *feel* such an *essential continuity* between the various spheres of experience:

The *central threads* in the invisible web *have been broken.*

[y]   [x]

With examples (4) and (5) in mind, you can begin to imagine the large variety of ways in which the two independent clauses that surround a colon could relate to each other: direct opposition; parallel similarity; chiastic reversal; contradistinction; metaphor; substitution of key words; and many more.

·· EXERCISE X   ···

Here follow a number of sentences. For each, turn the period into a colon and create at least two independent clauses to complete the new sentence. Example:

X April is the cruelest month.

   a. April is the cruelest month: It breeds lilacs out of the dead land and mixes memory with desire.

   b. April is the cruelest month: That is when I suffer most from hay fever.

The following sentences are also taken from John Demos's article, "The American Family Then and Now," some slightly doctored to fit this occasion.

1. We cannot recover all of the innermost feelings of the colonists as they faced this prospect.

2. There is more that can be said -- but only in a speculative way, since the relevant evidence has not survived.

3. The failure to sustain a tight pattern of community organization may also have exerted some influence here.

4. Yet in the final analysis, we should be aware of attributing too much importance to these hints of decline and decay.

Often, this use of a colon eliminates potential ambiguities. Take for an example the two-sentence disclosure we have become used to seeing at the beginning of a videotape or DVD movie:

8a. This film has been modified from its original version. It has been formatted to fit your TV.

Can you see what a difference it would make if that first period were replaced with a colon?

8b. This film has been modified from its original version: It has been formatted to fit your TV.

In the (b) version, it is clear that the reformatting of the film is the only way it has been modified:

"modified" : "formatted"

"modified" = "formatted"

The (a) version is capable of being interpreted in the same way but has all sorts of other possibilities as well. Its first sentence could mean that many different modifications have been made (to control language, violence, or explicit sexuality); and its second sentence might be therefore be saying, "Oh yes, in addition to all those changes, the film has also been reformatted."

Now we can consider the far more common use of the colon -- when it introduces a list of examples that, taken together, offer a more specific, almost pictorial way of understanding the previous clause. The list can either be printed as a linear continuation of the sentence:

6a. <u>Independent clause</u> : <u>example</u> ; <u>example</u> ; <u>example</u> ; <u>example</u> ; and <u>example</u>

or it can be indented vertically, with each member starting on a fresh line of its own:

7a. <u>Independent clause</u> :

<u>example</u> ;

example ;

example ;

example ; and

example .

In either case, the items on the list should be separated by semi-colons. Most grammar books will tell you that the comma is the preferred mark, unless one of the examples itself contains a comma. That advice made a great deal of sense in the days before the double dash became accepted as a formal mark of punctuation. That acceptance allows us yet one more punctuation refinement with which we can help our readers. Using a double dash to introduce a list, and commas to separate the members of that list, signals the reader that this list is relatively lightweight:

9a. The long-sleeved V-necked sweater is available in three colors -- aqua, mauve, and turquoise.

Can you see how relatively heavy-handed the use of a colon and semi-colons would be here?

9b. The long-sleeved V-necked sweater is available in three colors: aqua; mauve; and turquoise.

When the examples have more weight to them, the colon advertises this; and the semi-colons allow the reader more easily to separate the examples from each other. Those semi-colons also provide Stress positions for each example, even though the examples are mere fragments and not independent clauses. This is due, once again, to reader expectations: Once a reader understands that a colon introduces a list, the expectation arises that each member of that list is likely to be only the fragment of a sentence. Each fragment, thus, comes to full closure at the semi-colon, since it marks the completion of the kind of unit expected by the reader.

7a. Independent clause : [Stress]

example ; [Stress]

example ; [Stress]

example ; [Stress]

example ; [Stress] and

example . [Stress]

The choice between the linear form (6a) and the indented list form (7a) should depend on how much space you think your reader needs in order to absorb the material involved. The linear form (6a) above is probably preferable when the list of examples includes mostly short members. Because no single member of the list requires a lengthy consideration, readers can experience the list as a horizontal continuation without an undue sense of burden.

6b. The prom committee had to decide between a number of suggestions for the all-important color scheme: blue and gold; purple and gold; purple and silver; gold and silver; or purple, gold, and silver.

As the members of such a list become longer, more syntactically complex, or more intellectually challenging, readers need "more space" in which to consider them. Such an need for individual attention is better attended to by a vertical than a horizontal presentation.

7b. The prom committee had a number of issues before it more serious than in any previous year:
   -- Should anything be done about the principal's edict that same-sex couples would not be allowed admission;
   -- Should the students attempt to maintain their choice of the Search and Destroy rock group, despite the PTA's complaints of excessive violence in the group's lyrics; and
   -- Should there be an organized resistance to the new "Dress for Decency" clothing restrictions.

Length is an important consideration here, but not necessarily a definitive one. If brevity is attended by weightiness, the vertical arrangement can still be the more effective choice.

9a. The prom committee found itself concerned with a number of issues far more important than color schemes and fantasy themes:
   -- sexual preference bias;
   -- objectionable song lyrics; and
   -- the new dress code.

The very brevity of these items, together with the isolated importance suggested by the vertical and indented listing, tends to promise the reader that a discussion of each will follow.

Readers may take different clues even from the manner in which the listed items are marked -- by dashes, bullets, numbers, or nothing at all. In general, dashes tend toward the egalitarian -- each item being of equal importance; bullets suggest a cool, businesslike demeanor; numbers suggest an agenda or a ranking or a cataloguing or a logical progression of some sort; and no mark at all indicates a lack of commitment to any of these directions. (These tendencies are only tendencies and should not be taken as rules or as exhaustively descriptive.)

··| EXERCISE **Y** | ··

Explain how the following differ in effect for you.

a. The prom committee found itself concerned with a number of issues far more important than color schemes and fantasy themes:
   -- sexual preference bias;
   -- objectionable song lyrics; and
   -- the new dress code.

b. The prom committee found itself concerned with a number of issues far more important than color schemes and fantasy themes:
   • sexual preference bias;
   • objectionable song lyrics; and
   • the new dress code.

c. The prom committee found itself concerned with a number of issues far more important than color schemes and fantasy themes:
   1) sexual preference bias;
   2) objectionable song lyrics; and
   3) the new dress code.

d. The prom committee found itself concerned with a number of issues far more important than color schemes and fantasy themes:
   sexual preference bias;
   objectionable song lyrics; and
   the new dress code.

Whether the colonated list be presented horizontally, vertically, dashed, bulleted, numbered, or plain, it remains important that the clause that precedes the colon always be a full independent clause. This is a long-standing rule of grammar that has recently begun to be ignored even in formal publications. Especially common now is the use of the colon after a verb *to be* or after a participle. (The use of an asterisk (*) before a sentence indicates that it is in some way grammatically flawed or otherwise erroneous.)

10a. *The four most important things to consider are:
   1. The reason for undertaking the project;
   2. the possibilities of finishing it in time;
   3. the probability of success; and
   4. the chance that someone else will get there before we do.

10b. *There are several things to keep in mind, including:

    1.   The reason for undertaking the project;

    2.   the possibilities of finishing it in time;

    3.   the probability of success; and

    4.   the chance that someone else will get there before we do.

These are troublesome structures -- *not* because they abandon an accepted practice of the past but because they place an extra burden on readers of the present. The difference, once again, is subtle but significant. If that which precedes the colon cannot stand by itself as a sentence, then no full syntactic closure can be experienced at the colon by the reader. As a result, the reader has to wait until the entire list is over before experiencing a Stress position. The individual members of the list are likely not to receive the emphasis that is probably their due. The reader has to hang on to the initial phrase all the way through the list. It reads something like this:

10c. *The four most important things to consider are:

               1. The reason for undertaking the project;

[and they are] 2. the possibilities of finishing it in time;

[and they are] 3. the probability of success; and

[and they are] 4. the chance that someone else <u>will get there before we do</u>.

            [The sole Stress position is underlined.]

Because the opening phrase is left incomplete, the reader is never given the opportunity to let each of the important examples vibrate with emphasis. Too much reader energy is wasted in the attempt to keep the entire syntactic structure in mind.

Notice the difference if the material preceding the colon is brought to the full syntactic closure created by the fulfilling of the independent clause.

10d. There are four issues <u>most important to consider</u>:

    1.   The reason for <u>undertaking the project</u>;

    2.   the possibilities of <u>finishing it in time</u>;

    3.   the probability of <u>success</u>; and

    4.   the chance that someone else <u>will get there before we do.</u>

[The Stress positions are underlined.]

Because readers are allowed to finish and dispense with the first clause, they can treat each of the four members of the list separately and have the leisure or freedom to experience a minor Stress position at the end of each.

Thus instead of having one Stress position, the sentence has five -- one at the colon, three at the semi-colons, and one at the period. So be kind to your readers: Always complete an independent clause before employing the colon. Even the rather pedestrian "The four most important things to consider are the following" will give your readers a better chance to concentrate on your listed examples as individual entities.

The colon and semi-colon were used almost promiscuously in earlier centuries; it was as if writers were afraid to come to a complete stop: that if they did so, there was no more to be said on the subject; and there was seemingly always more: more could always be added, and then more; and then more; seemingly without end; even when you thought it was coming to an end; just like this sentence has been doing. They were not "wrong" to do so; nor are we "wrong" in preferring a more selective usage for those marks. The change came about along with changes in the needs of readers. We cannot tell which influenced which -- whether readers were the causative factor, or the adjustable reactor, or both. It is possible, perhaps even likely, that our own expectations will change or be changed before another century has passed. We need neither protect our own expectations nor grieve when they fade away. Language changes, and we must change with it. We change, and language must change with us. Why do we no longer wish to encounter a colon *after* we have seen a semi-colon in a given sentence? Because we need to rely on our expectation that after a semi-colon we will usually find a single independent clause that will bond with the previous independent clause. We are prepared for only one more Stress position to arrive. The arrival of a colon after a semi-colon will destroy that equilibrium for which we have prepared ourselves by expectation.

D ashes -- (Parentheses), Commas, and [Brackets]: Pardon the Interruption

Readers expect that a sentence will move smoothly and inexorably from its beginning through its middle to its end -- unless they are otherwise informed. Hesitations, interruptions, brief digressions -- all these are possible; but readers wish to know without ambiguity whether they are continuing to travel forward or have been momentarily deflected from that road into some interesting but ancillary pathway. Look what happens to the reader of the first clause of the preceding sentence if the warning mark of the dash is removed:

Hesitations, interruptions, brief digressions all these are possible;

We have developed a relatively complex series of marks to indicate a great many kinds of interruptions. The categories they produce are not rigidly enough constructed for us to fashion for them clear rules of usage;

but understanding what readers tend to do when confronted by the various warning signs will give writers better control over the signs and, therefore, better influence over their readers.

Each of these interruptive marks is too slippery in its usage to be defined by itself. Fortunately, we almost never have to consider these marks in isolation but rather in competition with each other. We tend to know *when* we want the reader to be aware of some kind of interference in the forward-leaning motion of our sentences; the trick at that time is to use the best possible signal to let the reader know as precisely as possible how much of an interruption to experience. The differences stem from the relative importance or the qualitative nature of the interruptive material. Therefore, we can serve ourselves better by considering these interruptive marks not by themselves but in contrast to each other.

The Dash Versus the Colon

[Note: Although I refer to "*the* dash," I always use what might be called a "double dash" -- like this. I find the one-dash dash is too easy to confuse with a hyphen. Therefore, when I refer to the use of "a dash," I mean the use of a single punctuation mark that is a double dash; and when I refer to "two dashes" or "a pair of dashes," I mean the use of two separate marks of punctuation, each of which is a double dash.]

The colon is an ancient mark, at least 2,200 years old. The dash is a relative newcomer, having appeared only about 300 years ago. It did not achieve full respectability until this century. Being so new, it raises some anxiety both in the user and in the teacher. Many of us as schoolchildren were warned that the dash was permissible but "should not be overused." (The advise that it "should not be underused" is never offered, but it seems at least as prudent.)

We should distinguish between two different uses of the dash. (1) When it appears just once in a sentence, it is related to the colon. Each invites the reader simultaneously to separate and to join the two halves of the sentence. (2) When a pair of dashes appears in the same sentence, that pair functions more like a set of parentheses or a set of commas. All of these indicate an insertion of interruptive material into the middle of things. Let us look at the first of these first.

The solitary appearance of a dash confronts a reader. Its very informality signals an interruption of rhythm, sometimes sharp; but it also warns readers to heighten the intensity of their attention -- for something emphatic will surely arrive.

Although it is "correct" to use a word, a phrase, or a series of single words after a colon, you mislead your reader when you do it. The colon invites readers to maintain a constant level of intensity. It is the ultimately rational and decorous mark of punctuation: It keeps everything calm and organized.

The dash invites just the opposite reaction, even as it performs a curiously parallel logical function. It invites the reader to raise both the (silent) decibel level of reading and the pitch.

When it follows the independent clause, it adds a "dash" of spice and makes the reader "dash" forward for a bit.

11a. There was one main reason she succeeded so quickly -- incredibly good luck.

When it follows the examples or the definition and precedes the independent clause, it raises our curiosity concerning how the examples might logically fit together:

12a. Degradation, humiliation, misrepresentation -- all these are the daily products of our contemporary news media.

Notice how tame these two energetic sentences become if the honest, rational, and sober colon displaces the dash.

11b. There was one main reason she succeeded so quickly: incredibly good luck.

12b. Degradation, humiliation, misrepresentation: All these are the daily products of our contemporary news media.

(11b) and (12b) would work well for a writer (think perhaps of a supremely self-confident and somewhat condescending political commentator on a television news show) whose trademark is the delivery of a scathing comment in a tone that is more suggestive of "Would you care for more tea?"

Neither choice, colon nor dash, is "right" nor "wrong": They just produce different effects. Those effects, in turn, depend on who you are, what your readers tend to do, and how much they know about you as a writer.

·· EXERCISE Z ···

For the following pairs of sentences, explain the difference made by using the dash or the colon. If you prefer one to the other, explain why.

13a. He never thought to look in the one place he would have found it -- behind the computer terminal.

13b. He never thought to look in the one place he would have found it: behind the computer terminal.

14a. I prefer only three cities to San Francisco -- Boston, Santa Fe, and Waukeegan.

14b. I prefer only three cities to San Francisco: Boston, Santa Fe, and Waukeegan.

15a. You should keep one thing in mind when you visit that city: Never drink the water.

15b. You should keep one thing in mind when you visit that city -- never drink the water.

16a. He did the only thing he could, given the circumstances: He made his apologies and retired for the night.

16b. He did the only thing he could, given the circumstances -- he made his apologies and retired for the night.

The Dash Versus Parentheses

When two dashes appear in the same sentence as a pair, they mark a significant interruption of the flow of the syntax. The same can be said of parentheses. The difference between the two is in the nature of the way the interruptive material is read.

17a. Today the emotional role of the family receives most attention. Things that could be done by other institutions (like feeding, sheltering, and "socializing" the young) are said to be done by the family in such a distinctive way that not to grow up in a family is to be deprived of something vital to emotional health.

(Beatrice Gottleib, "The Emotional Role of the Family")

Parentheses interrupt and subdue. The voice or the tone descends, suddenly. The parentheses are equivalent in some ways to the musical direction *subito piano* -- "suddenly quiet." The opening of the parentheses in (17a) signals us that we should "lower our voice" and perhaps speed up a bit; we reverse those directions only when the parentheses close. The interruptive material in (17a) modifies "things" -- the subject of the sentence that appeared earlier. The three parenthetical examples are important -- without which we might be mystified by the identity of these "things" -- but at the same time, their exemplification is only a minor task of this sentence, the major task of which is to complete the subject-link ("things . . . are said to be done"). That link allows the stressworthy concept to enjoy its privileged location in the Stress position at the sentence's end. The parentheses convey to us exactly the (lower) status and value of the information they shelter.

Dashes, on the other hand, interrupt and heighten. The voice or the tone intensifies, suddenly. They are equivalent in some ways to another musical direction, *marcato*, which means "marked, accented, emphasized individually."

18a. In the case of a justified abortion -- if such could ever be the case -- the psychological damage to the prevented mother would potentially be massive and long-lasting.

The dashes tell us that this interruptive comment is no mere throw-away, no parenthetical aside. As "loud" as the message in the Stress position may be, this interruption attempts to shout loudly enough to be heard above the din. It suggests that an equally vociferous argument could be made on the subject of the interruptive material, even though that argument is not being supported in this particular sentence. Thus it allows the sentence to make one major argument while simultaneously indicating the existence of another. It argues simultaneously that (1) justified abortions cause great damage, and (2) there is no such thing as a justified abortion.[7]

Note what a significant difference is achieved when the interruptive punctuation of the last two examples is interchanged.

17b. Today the emotional role of the family receives most attention. Things that could be done by other institutions -- like feeding, sheltering, and "socializing" the young -- are said to be done by the family in such a distinctive way that not to grow up in a family is to be deprived of something vital to emotional health.

This sentence is too long and complex to be able to support the additional intensive member created by the dashes. Too much reader energy gets expended too early in the sentence; as a result, too little is available for the appropriate stressing of the sentence's end.

18b. In the case of a justified abortion (if such could ever be the case) the psychological damage to the prevented mother would potentially be massive and long-lasting.

Here the parentheses tell us to devalue their contents; that probably contradicts the intention of the author, who would probably read aloud the parenthetical material with a good deal of emphasis. The point suggested by this parenthetical aside is probably intended by the author to be heard with more fervor than the rather apologetic parentheses can supply.

Parentheses establish such a marked difference of tone that when they are used more than once in a paragraph the parenthetical remarks can seem to speak to each other across the welter of all the more prominent prose noise. Note how the second parenthetical remark in the following example echoes the first. Together they represent the voice of a markedly rational or even cynical commentator.

19. If we can believe Herodotus, Aesop was a storytelling slave who lived on Samos in the middle of the sixth century B.C.E. and was killed by the citizens of Delphos. Writers later than Herodotus identify Aesop as either Phrygian or Thracian by birth. Aristophanes and Plutarch both contend that he was hurled to his death from a cliff when the Delphians discovered in his baggage a golden cup stolen from the temple.

(The story, however, is a common one; Compare Joseph and Benjamin in Genesis, chapter 44.) By the Middle Ages these stories had gained acceptance as the truth and had bred a host of other episodes and details. Most accounts picture Aesop as a deformed hunchback, grotesquely ugly, partially crippled, and defective in his speech, whose lively wit and imagination in storytelling allowed him to escape disaster in the direst of circumstances. (This too, however, has been a commonplace in literature: Compare the story of Scheherezade.) Some sources even resurrect him after death and send him off to fight in the battle of Thermopylae, handicap and all.

The first parenthetical remark tells us to take this all with a grain of salt. The second parenthetical remark says the same thing -- and therefore reminds us of the earlier parenthetical comment. Now we are being told to take *all* of this with a grain of salt.

By the way, the rules governing the use of punctuation that can surround parentheses have not yet been written. It is almost the only punctuational free-for-all. Parentheses can take the place of commas or be used with commas. They can entertain dashes or supplant dashes. The mixture is up to the writer.

Dashes and Parentheses Versus Commas

Both dashes and parentheses warn the reader of an immediately impending interruption of tone *and* sense. With dashes, the tone goes up; with parentheses, the tone goes down. In both cases, the progression of the syntax and the main line of thought take a brief vacation.

When a pair of commas is used to signal interruption, on the other hand, it signals an interruption of the sense but *not* necessarily of the tone. Note what happens if we opt for commas in rewriting (17b):

17c. Today the emotional role of the family receives most attention. Things that could be done by other institutions, like feeding, sheltering, and "socializing" the young, are said to be done by the family in such a distinctive way that not to grow up in a family is to be deprived of something vital to emotional health.

Now the sentence feels extraordinarily long, even though the word count and word order have not changed. The lack of differentiation in tone makes the shape of this sentence all but disappear for the first-time reader.

Commas interrupt in the least interruptive of punctuational ways. When that is the desired effect, they will do the job well.

20a. Family values are said to be old-fashioned, even timeless, and are assumed to derive from what the family was like before industrialization and its attendant ills.

(Beatrice Gottlieb, "The Emotional Role of the Family")

The quiet, even-keeled sense of timelessness and old-fashioned values may best be served here by the calm, stabilizing influence of commas. Look how much noise about timelessness would have been produced had she used dashes instead:

20b. Family values are said to be old-fashioned -- even timeless -- and are assumed to derive from what the family was like before industrialization and its attendant ills.

If we insert parentheses for these dashes, note how undercutting, rather than noisy, the "timeless" comment becomes:

20c. Family values are said to be old-fashioned (even timeless) and are assumed to derive from what the family was like before industrialization and its attendant ills.

A Radical Suggestion Concerning the Printing of Dashes

Many grammatical handbooks announce rules for the printing of dashes:

-- If possible, the dash must be a single, continuous line, twice the length of a hyphen;

-- If that capability is not available, a double hyphen will suffice;

-- In any event, there must be no space between the dash and the words on either side of it.

From a reader's perspective, I personally rebel against these rules -- without remorse. It is difficult to be sensitive (in a split second's time) to how long a short horizontal line really is intended to be. Some dashes will therefore be mistaken, at least initially, for hyphens. More importantly, if the role of the dash is to shock and separate, then a lack of space surrounding it undercuts its primary function. The lack of space makes the dash seem not to shock and separate but rather to elide and join. For example,

From a reader's perspective, I personally rebel against these rules—without remorse.

How can a claustrophobia-producing mark instill a sense of space and separation? Radically, I urge you to abandon the long tradition of dashes that connect and opt instead for the airy, free-floating, space-producing dash, surrounding it on both sides with empty space. Your editors may grumble; but most of your readers will benefit -- whether they know it or not.

From a reader's perspective, I personally rebel against these rules—without remorse.

Brackets Versus Everything

Square brackets send a more clearly defined message to the reader than any of the other interruptive marks of punctuation. The practiced reader understands from the presence of brackets that there has been a change not so much in dynamics or pitch or intensity but rather in voice. The brackets indicate that the writer is introducing his or her own voice as author, momentarily supplanting the more distanced, more fictional voice of narrator. It is a kind of reality check -- a message from the voice that really knows the score. It also seems to be a voice talking directly to you as an audience of one. [The rest of the prose sounds intended for the entire audience; the bracketed material is just for you.]

Those brackets are also more apologetic of themselves than any of the other marks. They bring with them a conciliatory message of "sorry to interrupt -- but this detail was necessary to introduce in my real voice."

Sometimes brackets can interrupt for the duration of an entire comment:

21a. Before investigating the car or asking any pointed questions, the officer read her her legal rights. [This procedure became necessary as a result of the Supreme Court's ruling in the *Miranda* case.] He then began to question her, but still with great caution.

At other times, they can interrupt more briefly:

21b. Before investigating the car or asking any pointed questions, the officer read her her legal rights [as required by the *Miranda* case]. He then began to question her, but still with great caution.

There is an unusual exception: When brackets are used within a direct quotation, they indicate that the enclosed words have been altered from the original quote to fit the grammatical context in which they now find themselves:

22. According to the Spokesperson, "[The President] believed [the reduction] would benefit everyone involved."

The original quote from example (22) had been, "She believed it would benefit everyone involved." The "she" and the "it" were clear when the sentence existed in the comfortable context of its own paragraph. The pronouns referred backward with ease. In the quote used in example (22), however, that context is absent, thus necessitating the author's interruptive tactic of informing us (1) who is meant by these pronouns, and (2) that the quote is not quite word for word from the original text.

Occasionally, square brackets are used as parentheses within parentheses. Note that their modest, interruptive, factual function has not changed much:

23a. (Such a challenge has been undertaken years ago by the General Accounting Office [the GAO], without success.)

You can see how confusing it would be if we used parentheses within parentheses here instead of the square brackets:

23b. (Such a challenge has been undertaken years ago by the General Accounting Office (the GAO), without success.)

Had the same statement been made without parentheses, the square brackets would themselves have become parentheses:

23c. Such a challenge has been undertaken years ago by the General Accounting Office (the GAO) without success.

The Future of Punctuation May Be Now

All the above marks of punctuation have been with us at least since the eighteenth century, and some a great deal longer. Our discourse has changed since those times, but gradually, rationally, and often imperceptibly. Recently, however, we have undergone a transition in communication at a speed that has dizzied all but the youngest among us. That development -- a kind of whirlpool of a communication revolution -- was generated by the birth, growth, and ascendency of e-mail.

E-mail is the electronic (and therefore immediate) written communication between people who have access to the same computer processing systems. Through it, we can write swiftly composed, informal, and even haphazard messages to people who can and often do respond with equal swiftness. Because the tone is informal and the time for composition is short, we seem to have accepted a far lower standard of correctness and formality than we have previously demanded from hard copy. Spelling mistakes and typographical errors rarely elicit the kind of annoyance they have traditionally provoked. Punctuation has reached a new level of nonconformity that might almost be termed *free-style*. The rule seems to be, "Whatever works works" -- or, maybe, "Whatever works, works."

E-mail and other electronic communication capabilities have also begun to offer us newly accepted uses of old punctuation, like the multiply repeated exclamation point -- !!!!! -- or the comic book–style combination of otherwise solitary marks -- ?!?. In the 1990s, a new series of punctuation marks appeared, sporting the name *emoticons*. They are intended to communicate states of emotion. Here are some of the most widely used newcomers:

The smile: :-)
The frown: :-(
The laugh: :-|)
The wink: ;-)

This is not a new version of Morse code but rather a much older pictorial form of writing, harkening back to prehistoric cave drawings. If you are still puzzled, turn this page 90 degrees clockwise, and all will be revealed. Given our present and future graphic capabilities, the progress of nouveau punctuation must be considered boundless. On the other hand, given the transitory nature of fads, all these novelties may pass speedily away.

We could argue that these new marks are not really punctuation at all. Most of our standard marks of punctuation tell us how to continue to make our way through the prose at hand. Only the exclamation point lets us in on an emotion the writer wishes us to experience. Even that happens after we have already finished reading all the sentence's words. That distinction between the exclamation point and all the others lies at the heart of the warning to avoid the exclamation point altogether. These emoticons perform a function markedly different from most punctuation. Either (1) they tell us readers how we *should have been* reading the previous text; or (2) they tell us how we should be feeling and reacting *now*, much like the annoying "APPLAUSE" signs that cajole audiences in television studios and ballparks; or (3) they are a statement of the emotional status of the writer at that moment. Whichever may be the case, these new marks, and the electronic communication they serve, hint at a brave new world of communication we could not have foreseen only a brief time ago. It will be some time before we can judge whether a new punctuational path has been blazed.

T he Hyphen: In the Midst of Things

The Single Hyphenated Word: Joining While Separating

The hyphen (-) is another mark that also both joins and separates. It came along rather later than one might imagine -- in the twelfth century. It took another four hundred years before it became common. At that time, it appeared as a double line and was printed on a slant. It joins two concepts, but it separates two syllables. Often it makes a major difference for the reader.

Consider the difference between *recover* and *re-cover*. We are so used to the first word that we could not easily discover the meaning of the second without the presence of the hyphen. Of course, we might say, the syllable *re-* indicates a repetition. Whatever the verb is that follows, do it again. But when the *re-* becomes permanently bonded to its companion, the *re-* quality can fade over time, as it has with *recover*. *Recover* is something we do to our senses; *re-cover* is something we do to our furniture. The hyphen separates the syllables so it may more clearly join the concepts.

It is always difficult to note the particular moment when the hyphen disappears from a word. In our language, however, that process is continually on-going. Would it have been harder to read the last sentence if its final word had been printed "ongoing"? Wouldn't "ongoing" be likely to strike at least some readers as a really silly word composed of two silly syllables, "ong" and "oing"?

Commonly, a joinable pair of concepts begins its life together by being brought together as two separate words. Here are two examples from the seventeenth century:

bed room

to morrow

After a while, if the two words appear next to each other often enough to form a single unit, they become engaged by a hyphen. The eighteenth century saw this transformation:

bed-room

to-morrow

If they stay together long enough and get along well enough, the engagement progresses to marriage, and the hyphen is invited to disappear -- as it did in these two cases by the twentieth century:

bedroom

tomorrow

In order for the marriage to take place, however, there must no longer be any visual difficulty to trouble the reader's eye. Until the last part of the twentieth century, we always saw the word *co-operative* printed with a hyphen (or with two dots over the second *o*, which performed the same function). The hyphen was allowed to disappear when we were no longer bothered by seeing the letters *coop* as a subunit of the word. *Cooperative* looked and sounded strange, until we got used to using *coop* as a diminutive form of the longer word. Co-operative Societies, like those at Harvard and Berkeley, were known for long enough as The Coop for *coop* no longer to look strange to the eye, and grocery stores called Co-ops became plentiful. Once again punctuation marks functioned like a set of training wheels on a bicycle: When we no longer needed the extra help, they could be discarded.

Floppy disks were not important to enough of us for long enough even to become floppy-disks; they didn't come anywhere close to becoming floppydisks. Gad flies, however, with their longer staying power, became gadflies. Did chamber pots ever become chamberpots? (Do we care any more?) Who is it that makes the decision to opt for a vowel instead of a hyphen, giving us speedometers instead of speed-meters? It is all rather mysterious. In any event, it always feels like *someone* is looking out for the language.

The hyphen, thus, is one of the clearest examples of a punctuation mark performing its essential function -- to make life easier for the reader. That is the bottom line we can use when deciding whether or not to employ one. Sometimes that "we" refers to "society." Somebody in the society (usually people in the business of publishing text) eventually decides it is time to join two words into one by using a hyphen. Later, somebody else in the same business decides it is time to save both space and paper by eliminating the hyphen. We have seen this happen at an accelerated pace in the last few years as *life style* and *day care* briefly became *life-style* and *day-care* on their way to their present happily married life as *lifestyle* and *daycare*. (Actually, the process for the latter word is not yet complete: Some of us still tend to seek out day care in a daycare center.)

On the other hand, sometimes the "we" in question is the individual writer. Each of us has a limited power to coin new terms, as long as (1) both our authorship and the meaning of our new term remain clear, and (2) we are writing for an audience that will allow us that power. Have you an important decision that you will soon announce? Then you perhaps may be allowed to refer to your soon-to-be-announced decision. It is highly unlikely you will ever be sanctioned to refer to your soontobeannounced decision.

That seems to be the case now with English. German is another matter altogether. The German language has evolved in part by the combination of multiple nouns into a single noun. That is how they manage to produce those endless-looking words. For instance, if German-speaking peoples were to adopt the game of baseball, they might eventually perceive a need to refer to that particular kind of joyful emotion that comes from your team hitting a two-run homer with two outs in the last of the ninth inning to overcome a one-run deficit and win the game. It is, after all, a very particular kind of emotion, rarely produced by any other moment in life. Should Germans ever take baseball enough to heart, we should not be too surprised were they to coin the word Comingfrombehindwithahomerinthebottomoftheninthtowinjoy. (And then again, maybe we should be.) The English-speaking peoples of the world prefer hyphens.

Some hyphen developments are controlled not by logic but by consistency. For example, we seem to accept a hyphenated adjective when it precedes its noun, but not when it appears in a predicate position. We are content to refer to a "two-ton truck"; but we would not be as likely to write "I've got a new truck. It's a two-ton." And, of course, we would be disconcerted to encounter a "twoton truck." We are all acquainted with a particular person's "well-worn excuse;" but we will not accept anyone's excuse as being "well-worn"; it would simply be well worn.

The Line-ending Hyphen: Separating in Order to Join

The uses of the hyphen described above are reader-focused. They allow readers to recognize what otherwise might be unrecognizable. They separate syllables that might not be perceivable as themselves, and they join concepts that are intended to be perceived as units.

The other major use of the hyphen ignores the reader and serves instead the needs of the printer. That hyphen cuts a word in two, allowing the first half to remain at the end of one printed line while the second half is transported to the beginning of the following line. It is usually a pain in a number of parts of the anatomy. It strains the eye; it unduly exercises the neck; it can make the stomach grumble. Fortunately, writing texts warn against its use; unfortunately many printers do not follow the same warning. Disassembling words can only make it harder for a reader to discern what the word is supposed to be; it does even greater damage to the orderly flow of the recognition process, and there-fore to the orderly use of reader energy. Isn't it annoying?

The best advice, fortunately, is the advice most commonly given: Never opt voluntarily for the separation of one word onto two lines. If you follow this advice, then you cannot run into the dangers of breaking the rules that govern the line-ending hyphen. (Rule #1: Only hyphenate between syllables; Rule #2: Never hyphenate an already hyphenated word anywhere but at the hyphen; Rule #3: Always hyphenate a word with a prefix or a suffix after the prefix or before the suffix; Rule #4: Always leave at least two letters on a line after hyphenation; etc., etc.) You can forget all these rules if you remember your reader and thus forego the word-interrupting, line-ending hyphen altogether. Word processing programs commonly have an automatic hyphenation option. It is distressing to note how many times that option has ON as its default value. I suggest you value your reader instead and turn the ON to OFF.[8]

T he Question Mark: Is Anything Uncertain Here?

This mark does not raise expectations, since it comes at the end of the sentence experience. It confirms what has already been happening. More often than not there should have been something at the beginning to raise the question for the reader -- an interrogative pronoun or adverb or adjective like *who* or *why* or *how many*. The question mark itself actually should be superfluous; but we have become so accustomed to it that its absence (and the presence of a period) would suggest to us the wrong kind of closure for the experience of that interrogative sentence. So just as quotation marks open and close a quote, the interrogative word and the question mark raise and close the variant reading experience we know as the question.

Most of the difficulties caused by the improper use of the question mark are mechanical. While they may annoy a reader momentarily, they tend not to destroy the meaning of the sentence. If you simply lose track of the fact that you are composing a question and therefore forget to include the question mark at its end, your readers suffer a bumpy and inappropriate syntactic closure; but in most cases they soon realize what has happened, shake it off, and continue the journey.

24a. *What possibly could be the explanation for such a poorly conceived and irrationally developed plan of attack.

The mispunctuation in example (24a) is annoying, but no more than annoying. As readers, we knew all along that we were experiencing a question, since we had that signal given to us at the start by the interrogative phrase "what . . . could be."

Also annoying, but perhaps even less so, is the reverse of this error -- using a question mark instead of a period at the end of an indirect question:

24b. *He wondered what possibly could be the explanation for such a poorly conceived and irrationally developed plan of attack?

The problem here stems from the relative lengths of the clauses. The main clause is "He wondered [X]." Clearly, such a sentence does not require question mark. But when the long subordinate clause -- (the "what" clause) -- seems by itself to be a question, it may also seem to require a question mark. A fair percentage of readers do not recognize the error here and therefore do not even lose stride as they pass it by. They silently make the emendation for the writer, processing the sentence as if it had been delivered as direct rather than indirect discourse:

24c. He wondered, "What possibly could be the explanation for such a poorly conceived and irrationally developed plan of attack?".

Even less noticeable are the grammatical errors concerning the relationship of the question mark to other marks of punctuation. You might *know* which of the following is correct; but you might well not *notice* the errors if you are reading for content and not (like an English teacher) for correction. Which is the correct one here?

25a. He asked, "How could you possibly explain this?".
25b. *He asked, "How could you possibly explain this?"
25c. *He asked, "How could you possibly explain this"?

(For the explanatory material that will furnish you with the right answer, see the section below that deals with the use of punctuation with quotation marks.)

It is, of course, important to get the mechanical details of the question mark correct; but more important than knowing *how* to use it is knowing *when* to use it -- and when *not* to use it. When a reader encounters a question mark, the reader experiences a momentary change in the nature of the writer-reader relationship: For that brief moment, the writer is acknowledging the reader's presence.

It makes the communicative process one step more intimate, no matter what the writer-reader relationship has been up to that point. If the reader has not yet been included (by the use of the pronoun *you*), a question mark shifts the focus of the writer somewhat from the object of discussion to the perceiver of that discussion. If the prose has constantly acknowledged the presence of the reader as "you," the question mark then takes the already existing intimacy one step further and seems to invoke the reader's response. The monologue becomes a semi-dialogue or pseudo-dialogue.

The general principle (never a rule) is simple enough: Avoid the use of the question mark unless you wish to engage your reader in a more intimate relationship than would otherwise be the case. Here are the decisions I tend to make:

-- In highly formal, published, professional articles, I almost never use a question mark. This non-acknowledgment of the process of readers highlights the intellectual content, making it more important than "me" or "you." Any explicit recognition of the reader seems to lessen the seriousness of the intellectual undertaking. If I do use an occasional question mark, it usually occurs toward the beginning of the piece and is ejected into the air as much as possible, not directly toward a reader.

-- In a work such as the present volume, I tend to use many more questions. This book is written about readers and for readers. Its aim is not to proclaim or rehearse rules about the English sentence but rather to talk with you about your experience in reading the language. I acknowledge your presence in many ways -- by form, by style, by tone, and occasionally by direct questions, thrown not into the air but directly at you.

-- In a letter to someone I know well, the question is a continual rhetorical option. Not only is the dialogue already intimately engaged from the start, but I actually expect in response to receive answers to some of my specific questions.

-- In using e-mail, the question mark is even more in evidence than in the personal letter. The personal letter has its roots in public speeches and in the nonfiction essay -- both written forms at some point in the process. E-mail, to the contrary, is more closely related to the telephone call. There is a more immediate sense of give and take. In such an intimate and immediate context, it makes good sense that questions and question marks might abound. The question is often a real one, requesting a real answer.

There is yet another kind of question that deserves a moment of our attention. I urge you to pause every time you are tempted to use the special argumentative tactic known as the rhetorical question. A question is rhetorical if it fits both of these descriptions:

-- It presumes and demands a single, obvious, clearly indicated answer, often a definitive yes or no. Example: "Can there be any doubt that when the Constitution says that individuals have the right to bear arms, it means that every one of us can own and, in appropriate circumstances, use firearms?" (Expected answer: "No, of course not; no doubt whatever.")

-- It is asked in place of making an argument on the subject, thereby suggesting that no discussion is necessary.

A rhetorical question often turns out to cause more damage than the asker of it can imagine. All an opponent has to do to overcome that rhetorical ploy is emphatically to answer the question in exactly the opposite way the writer intended it to be answered. Example: "Yes, there can be doubt -- and great doubt at that. What the Constitution really means is . . . ." By asking a rhetorical question instead of constructing an argument, the question-asker has provided an all-too-easy opportunity for a hostile response. Since the only argument such a question makes is to invite an assent, the adversarial response removes *all* trace of an argument on your side. Thus, the very presence of a rhetorical question signals a weak spot in your own argument. You would do well to avoid its use altogether in serious arguments. It causes more problems than it is worth.

In sum, then -- to question, or not to question; that is the question. The answer should become readily apparent once you have decided precisely what kind of relationship you want to construct between yourself and your reader.

T he Exclamation Point and Other Forms of Artificial Emphasis: Look at Me!

The exclamation point has few friends. While some handbooks manage to tolerate its existence, most advise against its use. Word processor keyboards place it far from the center of activity; the majority of typewriter keyboards excluded it altogether. Writing teachers often grumble about it; but by far the greatest contingent of detractors tend never to mention their negative feelings. That contingent comprises the readers of the English language.

Why do exclamation points annoy readers? Well let me tell you! Listen! I need to catch your attention! I am really excited! I am really exciting! In case you hadn't recognized that I'm excited and exciting! I'm using this exclamation point to tell you! It's not only telling you, it's beating you over the head to get the job done! You're so dimwitted that you wouldn't even *know* all this excitement was going on if I didn't go out of my way to tell you by using an exclamation mark! Boy, are you dumb!!?!

Unlike most other marks of punctuation, the exclamation point goes beyond offering syntactic and rhetorical directions to the reader; instead, it commands the reader how to feel -- or at least to recognize how the author feels. There is nothing wrong with either of those objectives. Good prose makes every effort to let readers in on the writer's state of mind, both intellectually and emotionally. Good expository or argumentative prose also aims at controlling (to some degree) how the reader feels when it is all over. In order to accomplish those goals, good writers try in a number of ways -- mostly natural ways -- to indicate to readers where they should expend different kinds and amounts of emphasis. Therein lies the problem of the exclamation point: The exclamation point is an artificial form of emphasis.

Natural emphasis is usually to be preferred to artificial emphasis. The "natural" ways seem to come from within. They emanate from word choice, sentence structure, the length of material, and the placement of material. The "artificial" ways come from without. In general, they can be done to the text after the prose is written. They involve a number of tactics to attract the eye:

-- <u>Underlining;</u>

-- **Boldface;**

-- CAPITAL LETTERS;

-- *Italics;*

-- Any combination of the above, such as <u>UNDERLINED CAPITALS</u> or ***bold face italics*** or <u>***UNDERLINED BOLD FACE ITALIC CAPITALS***</u>; and last, but not least,

-- The exclamation point!

If we are reading warning signs ("**DANGER! KEEP OUT!**") or important instructions ("Enclose THREE [3] copies of your proposal" or "Your payment is due by <u>March 15</u>"), we usually consider it helpful if the perpetrators of the prose take every available means to make us aware of the most crucial bits of information. If, however, we are engaged with an unfolding text that presents a story or a thought or an argument, many of us have little patience with the writer who assumes we are too thick-headed to notice something of importance as it goes by. Markings of artificial emphasis often tend to send that message. The most direct of these was a nineteenth-century icon, long now abandoned by publishers of prose: It consisted of a hand with a pointing finger, aimed from the margin at the passage to which you were intended to pay careful attention.

"Do not condescend to your reader" is a good enough reason to avoid the exclamation point -- and most other artificial emphases -- at almost all times; but writers would do well to recognize the urge to use artificial emphasis as a warning sign that the sentence is otherwise unlikely to be read as the writer intended. For a fuller discussion of this, with examples, pleased see the first few pages of Chapter 3.

With the popularization of computers, boldface type has become a possibility no longer reserved for publishers. Now **anyone** can make a word jump out at you, just **anytime** they want. We even have created a new verb for this possibility: We now talk about whether or not "to bold" a particular passage. If you wish to use boldface just to make yourself feel better, you would do well to restrain yourself. If it is a real service to your reader, try it out. Some of your readers will be willing to let you know how well it worked; just ask them. The more formal the prose, the less likely it is that you ought to boldly go.[9]

In sum, the existence of artificial emphasis benefits writers in two main ways: (1) It allows them to make readers aware of emphasis when no natural way is available; and (2) The urge to use it in all other circumstances can function as a wake-up call for the writer that the sentence's structure needs to be revised. You can therefore do your readers a service both by using it and by refraining from using it.

The Use of Punctuation with Quotation Marks: Consistency, Logic, and Illogical Consistency

In the seventeenth century, France decided that its language should be placed in the control of a carefully chosen, centrally located, and infallibly omnipotent group of savants. They therefore created the National Academy, a group of (presumably) the best educated, most intellectually astute, and most sanely judicious keepers of the cultural flame. "Proper" French would not change without this group's explicit authorization. The Academy even created a police arm to try to enforce its policies. Even though such linguistic power politics did not always prevail, the result has been that the French language has changed at a much slower rate than has English in the past three hundred years.

There have been many calls for the formation of just such a National Academy in the United States -- all to no avail. Its proponents have argued that the language has long been hybrid in nature because it has been so fundamentally influenced by two markedly distinct linguistic traditions -- the Teutonic (German/Scandinavian) strain, which arrived in England with the Angle, Saxon, and Jute invaders as early as the fourth century, and the Romance (Greek/Latin/French) strain, which was brought by the Normans when they conquered the island in 1066. That hybrid nature, innately hospitable to a sense of acceptable variation, has been thrown (some argue) into total disarray by the multiple influences of worldwide immigration to America, the forces of advanced communication technologies, the influences of regionalism, and the shock effects of a widely disseminated and constantly changing popular culture.

Opponents of the establishment of an American National Academy have argued that the language of a democracy should not be ruled by an oligarchy. Central control of the language is by definition antithetical to all the forces that make a democracy function. As a result, if such a body should be empowered with the care and control of the language, it would be widely and energetically ignored.

The complaints about the alleged chaos of the English language usually stem from concerns at the level of words and sentences, centering mostly on spelling and punctuation. A detailed look at a grammatical handbook demonstrates how the combination of pure reason, historical exigency, and the lack of central language control can produce a set of rules that can be mastered only by rote memorization. Since we are unlikely at any time in the near future to witness a total overhaul of the language, the best we can do is to become aware of these various influences and muddle along as we always have. Truth to tell, the seemingly irrational factors of the language are relatively few in number and affect mostly superficial details. The more important concerns of language are more or less understandable without having to keep a textbook close at hand.

Here it is -- a concern so small it almost never affects comprehension; but occasionally it raises such an angry response from the purists among us that writers would do well not to waste their readers' energy by committing the grammatical faux pas. Question: When a mark of punctuation is needed at the end of a quotation, should the mark be placed inside or outside the quotation marks? Answer: It depends. Here are the rules for the placement of the various punctuational marks inside or outside of closing quotation marks:

-- In the United States, periods and commas (illogically) are always to be printed *inside* the quotation marks;

-- In Great Britain, periods and commas (illogically) are always to be printed *outside* the quotation marks;

-- In either country, question marks and exclamation points (quite logically) are printed within the quotation marks if they are part of that which is being quoted and outside the quotation marks if they are not part of that which is being quoted.

-- Since colons and semi-colons can never logically end a quotation, they are always printed outside the quotation marks.

The logical rules, by definition, make sense. We are not at all sure why the British chose to make the exception for periods and commas; but it is quite possible that the United States chose to reverse that convention simply to demonstrate its independence from its former mother country.

In order to put this matter to rest, therefore, a writer need simply understand the logical rule and then memorize the aberrant convention concerning periods and commas. It is necessary, of course, to know on which side of the Atlantic Ocean you are at any given time.

Only rarely will an error in this regard affect the communicated sense of a sentence. Most of the time, readers take no note whatever of where the punctuation mark appeared in relation to the quotation marks. Given that, should we expend any energy at all to get it right? Of course we should -- not for moral purposes ("Always do the right thing") but because there will inevitably be some readers out there who choose to take notice. They will do so because they care about such things. They can care for good reasons or for bad reasons. Whatever the reasons, such an error will cause these readers to spend their valuable reader energy being distraught with you instead of being engaged in the substance of your message. For that moment at least, communication stops. To take the best care possible of your text and of your readers, conform to the conventional details so both you and your readers can get on with the real business at hand -- communication. There is always an exception to generalized advice: If you have need to annoy! disrupt; and otherwise plague your -- reader, put your punctuation [marks] wherever you like.

The Apostrophe: Whose Who's Are What's What

The Complex Life of an Airborne Comma

From a distance, you might expect that the apostrophe -- a minimal mark that without causing confusion can be printed straight, slanted, or curved -- would be among the most clearly defined of all punctuation marks. As it turns out, the comma gone afloat has historically been asked to do too many unrelated tasks that have mistakenly (and therefore confusingly) been taken to be related. The rules for its use, therefore, are of necessity confusing and at times almost conflicting. On the one hand, misuses of the apostrophe probably account for the greatest number of publicly displayed grammatical mistakes; on the other hand, a great majority of those mistakes interfere little or not at all with the reader's comprehension.

Of the many uses of the apostrophe today, two are the most common: (1) its use to form a contraction by indicating an omission; and (2) its use to signal possession. These two uses, seemingly distinct, are quite closely related, but only by a curious historical error.

Contraction: What's What

The contractional use came first. The ancient Greeks used the mark to indicate an elision -- a linguistic moment when a sound disappears because of its neighbors, leaving only an apostrophe behind to indicate its former presence. As such, it functioned as a kind of punctuational gravestone. The Aldine Press revived that ancient usage in its 1501 edition of Petrarch; it has been with us ever since. Shakespeare's colleague and rival Ben Jonson devoted the first chapter of the section on syntax in his *English Grammar . . . for the Benefit of All Strangers* (1640) to what he called the Apostrophus:

> *Apostrophus* is the rejecting of a vowel from the beginning or ending of a word. The note whereof, though it many times, through the negligence of writers and printers, is quite omitted, yet by right should, and of the lerneder sort hath his signe and marke, which is a *Semi-circle* ' placed in the top.

Note that he makes no mention of the apostrophe indicating the possessive: For him it only indicated a missing letter. Note also that "writers and printers" were having trouble getting these things right in 1640. Perhaps not much has changed over the years.

Most often when we employ the apostrophe to indicate missing letters, it is in the service of creating contractions. *Can't* and *don't* are straightforward substitutions of the apostrophe for the missing *no* and *o* in *cannot* and *do not*. *Shan't* and *won't* are more complicated: The original *shall not* is missing two *l*'s (before the *n*) as well as its *o* (after the *n*); and the original *will not* is missing both the –*ill* and the original *o*, but has somehow picked up an extra *o* earlier in the word. (Clearly the logical alternatives -- the visually troubling *sh'n't* and the orally unacceptable *willn't* -- have been unable to engage our affections.)

For the most part, we have done away with poetic apostrophic omissions like *e'en* for *even* or *forc'd* for *forced*. These were usually intended to indicate unambiguously that the word was to be pronounced as one syllable (*forc'd*) and not as two (*forc-ed*). We have a few vestiges of the original practice, like our surprisingly quaint *o'clock*, which is the short form for *of the clock*. Might we someday wave goodbye to the Teutonic god Woden by suppressing his name visually (as we have orally) from the day named after him? It would then become *W'ensday*. Eventually it just might become *Wensday*. Such a transformation is highly unlikely, unless we as a country opt for organized and far-reaching spelling reform. *Wednesday* is so common a word and has caused all of us so much effort in the learning of its spelling that we are likely to require all future generations to share our burden.

The presence of contractions in the language has given rise to a number of socio-grammatical questions. For a great many decades, to contract or not to contract was one of the main distinctions between informality and formality. One just didn't use contractions in formal prose, at any time. Proper young men and young ladies could be distinguished from those lower in class and delicacy by the number of apostrophes they did *not* use -- even in spoken language. Contractions tended to round that which they thought should be kept straight and narrow. That uncomfortable uncontracted sound is still available to us today in the computer-generated messages that reach us from places like shuttle trains in airports: "YOU -- ARE -- NOW -- COMING -- TO -- CONCOURSE -- B. -- PLEASE -- STAND -- CLEAR -- OF -- THE -- DOORS." Apparently blockish rhythm and formality are still somewhat interconnected.

The rule used to be an easy one: Never use contractions in formal prose. Today we are not quite as formally attired as we once were, in either our clothes or our punctuation. It is possible to appear at very fine restaurants or in very high-level intellectual publications without a tie and with an apostrophe. But though the rules may have weakened, the old communicative signals are still there. There are now occasions on which a necktie is, if not inappropriate, at least uncongenial; similarly, there are moments in even the most formal pieces of prose when the lowering of the high style by the use of a contraction establishes the right colloquial tone for the moment. Since the rules are no longer clear, it is unwise either to employ or to avoid contractions merely on the basis of what feels good to you at the moment of composition. You would do better instead to consider your work in light of its probable reception by your reader. Does your reader *want* you to assume a more chummy pose at that particular moment? What is to be gained? What is to be lost?

You needn't be a purist about the matter, either -- mistakenly presuming that total abstinence is always the safest route. The language is and has always been in continual change. If you insist on banning the apostrophic contraction altogether, then you had better be prepared to refer to the time of day as "six of the clock," instead of "six o'clock." How would your reader like that?

Possession: Whose Who's Are Who?

A Genitive Misconception

Curiously, the apostrophe that indicates contraction was responsible for creating the apostrophe that indicates possession. In Greek and Latin, possession was signaled by a word ending that indicated the possessive case -- the genitive. By the fourteenth century, Middle English had dispensed with most of the old case endings, keeping only a treasured few -- mainly the accusative case (*whom* instead of *who*), the plural (by adding *–s* or *–en*), and the genitive (possessive) case (by adding *–es*). (*Brid* was the word for "bird." *Briddes song* meant "bird's song.")

In the sixteenth century, we made a mistake. We assumed that the *–es* genitive ending was actually an elision -- that it indicated something was missing. "Johnes book," we decided, was actually a shortened form for "John, his book." We therefore took to writing "John's book," using the apostrophe to do what it did best -- to indicate something was missing from the original form. We therefore presumed that the apostrophic possessive was part and parcel of the apostrophic contraction. Unfortunately, we were wrong. A feminist consciousness, had it been available at the time, might have saved us the error: If "John, his book" was to become "John's book," then surely "Jane, her book" should have become "Jane'r book."

For all of Ben Jonson's criticism of the inconstancy of others, he seems not to have made up his own mind concerning the apostrophe and the possessive. On a single page in his section on the possessive he uses an *s* without an apostrophe ("Out of all other birds sight"), an *s* with an apostrophe ("the Duke of Mysia's men"), and, for a word ending in an *s* sound, no *s* and no apostrophe ("which is endured for righteousnesse sake").

When scholars finally decided that the "John, his book" theory was false, why did they allow this misuse of the apostrophe to persist in the language? Probably because the apostrophe had become quite useful in distinguishing the possessive from the plural. Since both end in *s* most of the time, the presence of an apostrophe could neatly and clearly distinguish one from the other. But in turn, it gave birth to a different set of sticky problems in which the plural and the possessive became once again confounded. Where the long-term development of language is concerned, little remains neat and clear for long. What was intended to be clear -- and what still seems so clear from a distance -- became a muddled set of exceptions, a grammatical pot-hole waiting to disturb the alignment of both writer and reader.

The apostrophe (sometimes) denotes possession. Possession, in turn, denotes either ownership (Jane's book), or close relationship (Jane's mother), or both (Jane's dog). In general, there are three main ways a reader is informed of the concept of possession: (1) by the verb ("Jane owned the book"); (2) by the preposition "of" ("The wrath of Atilla"); or (3) by the apostrophe ("Jane's book," "Atilla's sword"). Occasionally, some of these may be combined: "This is a favorite book of Jane's."

So far, so good. But there is a major exception -- major because it is so common: Personal pronouns avoid the apostrophe, even when they employ the genitive –s: yours, his, hers, its, ours, theirs. That is enough of a bother by itself; but because "its" is in this list, we suffer the yet further confusion of there being an "it's" that is *not* a possessive but rather a con-traction for "it is." Bother, indeed. This has produced one of the most com-monly encountered grammatical errors. It still escapes many a publisher's proofing efforts. However, it's still worth the effort to get it right, because there will always be certain readers out there who note the error and become temporarily distracted from your text or permanently disap-pointed in you. Unreasonable or not, that is the reality of the situation.

Selected Possessive Difficulties

1. Note that there are instances when the error of an omitted apostrophe changes the meaning of the word, causing real momentary confusion (e.g., won't/wont; can't/cant). In both of these cases, the contraction is common, and its look-alike is rare.

2. There is still some disagreement as to whether proper names that end in s require an 's or just a final apostrophe to form the possessive. Most handbooks comfortably rule that something owned by Frances is "Frances's," while Jesus, Zeus, and Moses are granted an exception. Based probably on their high status and the frequency of their appear-ance in print, these three are granted more quietly reduced possessives: Jesus', Zeus', and Moses'.

3. When should you use the possessive form with apostrophe ("the coun-try's Constitution") as opposed to the longer form of the propositional phrase ("The Constitution of the country")? Counter-intuitive though it may seem, this is not exclusively a matter of the less formal versus the more formal. Part of the choice should be based on rhythm and other auditory considerations: One choice may fit the sound better than the other.

28a. We will be left to wonder whether the country's Constitution will prove equal to the tasks put upon it.

28b. We will be left to wonder whether the Constitution of the country will prove equal to the tasks put upon it.

The difference here is subtle, but still functional. All those *w* sounds in (28a) (we will . . . wonder whether) make the *c* sounds in "country" and "Constitution" a couple of clunky concatenations. The more leisurely arrival in (28b) of the second *c* sound reduces somewhat the awkward rhythm/alliteration problem. Get rid of a couple of the *w*'s and add a couple of extra *c*'s, and we might well choose the (a) version over the (b):

29a. Captain Crichton wondered whether the country's Constitution will prove equal to the tasks put upon it.

29b. Captain Crichton wondered whether the Constitution of the country will prove equal to the tasks put upon it.

And then again, we might not. The point here is that the sound differs; with that difference comes a distinction in signification -- although that distinction may be differently perceived by different readers.

More importantly, and more controllably, deciding between apostrophe and preposition will alter the structural location of the terms involved and thereby alter the interpretive signals sent to the reader. Recall the discussion in Chapter 2 concerning the nature of the Stress position. There we noted that anything that arrives for the reader at a moment of full syntactic closure is likely to invite a slightly greater sense of emphasis than anything else in the sentence. With that in mind, compare the following two sentences:

30a. When we consider the chances of this new democracy lasting beyond its infancy, we must in no way underestimate the importance of the country's Constitution.

30b. When we consider the chances of this new democracy lasting beyond its infancy, we must in no way underestimate the importance of the Constitution of the country.

This difference is a telling one: While they both indicate that the next sentence is likely to focus on the Constitution, sentence (30a) does a better job of heralding and of building that momentum. It ends by leaning forward on the most important word, "Constitution." The structure of sentence (30b) undercuts the ringing importance of "Constitution" by the energy-depleting downward turn, all too tame, of the almost insignificant verbal tag "of the country."

The same kind of difference in intensity can result if the possession in question appears at the beginning of the sentence, in the "whose story?" position:

31a. The country's Constitution is likely to be the focus of attention during the next session of Parliamentary debates.

31b. The Constitution of the country is likely to be the focus of attention during the next session of Parliamentary debates.

By allowing "Constitution" to be the first word of weight, (31b) manages for most readers to spotlight "Constitution" and downplay "country." In (31a), the force is more evenly distributed to "country" and "Constitution." Which is "better"? It depends on how you want your reader to focus the available reading energy and attention.

Plurals and Possessives

As noted above, everyone below the rank of respect afforded Jesus, Zeus, and Moses needs both an apostrophe and an *s* to indicate the possessive. The thunderbolt may be Zeus', but the book is Frances's and the assignments at the end of its chapters are the class's. When pronunciation becomes a problem for singular nouns, we still tough it out on paper -- *Dickens's* -- even though orally it is perfectly acceptable to leave off the final *s* when pronouncing it as if it were spelled *Dickens'.*

The plural is a different story altogether. When the singular *class* becomes a plural *classes* and the plural gets to possess something, we choose not to expand the all-too-noticeable symphony of hisses. We do not require yet another *s* to indicate the possessive; a mere *s*-less apostrophe will suffice. *Classes' gifts* will do fine; we need not struggle with **Classes's gifts.*

For plurals not ending in *s*, we add *'s*: *children's books.* We just cannot do without that genitive *s*. The role of the apostrophe is not to signify possession all by itself but rather to assist us in perceiving the true function of a neighborhood *s*. Is the *s* a mark of the plural? Or is it the mark of a possessive? Or is it just the last letter of a word? The presence of an apostrophe (in most but not all cases) tells us that this *s* is a possessive *s*.

Compounding the Problem

Compound words compound the problem and again lead us to confuse plurals and possessives. For compound words or terms (whether hyphenated or not), the plural form attaches itself to the main noun, while the possessive apostrophe always attaches itself to the last word in the phrase: So we refer to

mothers-in-law (many of them)

but also to

mother-in-law's prerogative (belonging to her).

When the noun ends the phrase, everything happens at that point:

her in-laws' insistence (belonging to them)

Where all these sticky matters are concerned, it is particularly hard to take your reader into account. Both your ear and your eye prove fallible, for two main reasons: (1) Since the apostrophe makes no sound, you cannot *hear* that anything is going wrong; and (2) since your head already knows what is *supposed* to be there, your eye is all too willing to see it, whether it is there or not. Unfortunately, there are some grammatical problems -- though far fewer than is usually assumed -- where sheer memorization of convention and astute vigilance in proofreading are required. The apostrophe presents us with one of the best examples of this unfortunate state of affairs.

The plural-or-possessive problems continue: What if you have to refer to two people who can be taken either as individuals or as part of a single team? Example: You get an e-mail from a colleague who tells you with enthusiasm that she has just finished reading "Jones's and Smith's articles." How many articles has she read? More than one. How many authors are concerned? Two. But how many authors were involved with each article? One. Assuming your colleague's grammar is correct, the two apostrophes indicate she has read one or more articles by Jones and one or more articles by Smith. Had Jones and Smith been the joint authors of all the articles, then she would have had to omit the first apostrophe: "Jones and Smith's articles." The work was that of Jones-and-Smith -- but we do not use the hyphens to denote their collaboration.

You can almost always get around these annoying problems by beating around their bush: "You really must look at those two articles by Jones -- and don't forget that great one by Smith, too." You perhaps have heard of the St. Louis zookeeper who wrote his colleague in San Diego,

Dear Sir:

Please send me one mongoose. And while you are at it, please send me another.

So if your colleague had read six articles -- two by Jones, two by Smith, and two by the collaboration of Jones and Smith, she would have done well to alter her language to allow the ambiguity to flourish, even if that concealed for a moment the facts of authorship: "I have just finished a bunch of articles on the cerebral cortex by those intellectual wizards, Jones and Smith." You want to know who wrote what? If she is a truly helpful colleague, she will have sent you the necessary bibliographic citations. If not, go look them up for yourself. The language cannot be expected to solve all problems gracefully and concisely.

Other Plurals and Other Uses

The apostrophe has a number of other uses, usually concerned with the setting off of a term from something that happens to the term. We have noted above that the apostrophe creates possessives, but not plurals; but with numbers and with words treated as words, we do indeed use the apostrophe to form the plural. An amateur golfer loves to record a few 3's on the scorecard during a round; the professional golfer should seek professional help if too many 6's begin to appear. But most grammarians are not distressed by either 3s or 6s -- presumably because there is little danger of misidentifying 3s and 6s as being anything other than 3's and 6's. We should all be able to count the number of *i*'s in *Mississippi* (4) and be interested in the number of "Thou shalt's" and "thou shalt not's" in the *Five Books of Moses* (613). And Boeing surprised us all when their 757's and 767's turned out to be smaller than their 747's.

It is true that the major manuals of style -- both those published by the Modern Language Association and the University of Chicago -- insist that this apostrophe should not be used. However, its constant usage in publications, especially newspapers, makes it so available to the public that we know how to read it -- despite the disapproval of the formal taste makers. You are safer writing "the 1970s" than "the 1970's"; but no one will misunderstand your "the 1970's." This is a matter of orthography, not of rhetoric. When writing for publication, or for approval (such as an application for a job or a grant,), be safe and use "the 1970s."

The same dual option is available for the pluralization of words treated as words: "How many Shakespeare's have been produced in all of European culture?" (Of course, many of us would argue that you have no need to speak of "Shakespeares"; there is only one Shakespeare.) When you are using the name as a metaphor or as a standard, feel free to use an apostrophe to indicate the plural. Or not.

The apostrophe is required, however, when it indicates the loss of numbers -- as 1996 will often be seen as '96 but rarely (in prose, as opposed to tables) as 96. In the case of words, as opposed to numbers, the apostrophe can eventually disappear (just like the hyphen) after we have become so accustomed to the truncated form that we consider it both normal and formal. All those violoncellos first became 'cellos, but eventually were transformed into cellos.

So the apostrophe is a mess. How strange that such a little mark should cause such great, unending, and hair-splitting confusion. What started out merely and clearly indicating elision came (through an interpretive error) to signal possession. Once the error was discovered, the apostrophe retained its possessive qualities because it did such a good job distinguishing between the possessive and the plural. But then it got mixed up in the production of plurals as well. It's its own worst enemy.

We need not follow suit and be our own worst enemies where grammar is concerned. Understanding that part of grammar -- the largest part -- which is logical and helpful, both to us and to readers, can alter the power relationship between us and our language. Instead of our feeling that we must conform to grammatical standards for the sake of being judged by others, we can learn to employ those standards to control the interpretive acts of our readers and auditors. Occasionally we happen upon those relatively few parts of grammar, like the apostrophe, whose complex histories have made them controllable only by rote memory. If we recognize that state of affairs, we can free ourselves to see that the problems lie in the grammar, not in some inadequacy of our own. Memorizing the rules (and knowing when to ignore the rules) becomes easier, less threatening. A little memorization never hurt anyone; but constant mystification can be disabling.

The Ellipsis . . . Now You Don't

Ellipsis is a term that has fulfilled a great many functions over the years. It is a figure of speech that refers to the omission of anything -- from a single word to a whole logical step in an argument. When the philosopher Schopenhauer tells us (albeit in German) that "Everybody's friend is nobody's," it is easy enough to supply the missing word: "Everybody's friend is nobody's friend." The ellipsis here qualifies as a figure of speech because of the effect it can have on the reader. The very missingness of the second "friend" suggests the friendlessness that results from too much friendliness. It also allows the climactic "nobody's" to occupy the Stress position. The rhetoricians of Roman times and of the European Renaissance delighted in subdividing categories for the different kinds of possible ellipses, producing wonderfully impressive terms to denote the new subfigures: *zeugma, syllepsis, absolute ellipsis, scesis onamaton, anapodoton, aposiopesis, aporia, praeterition, praecisio,* and even *enthymeme.* These breathtaking terms may be new to you; but you would recognize the function of each were there room here to offer you examples. Since my personal favorite is praeterition, I will use it to show you how unthreatening are the concepts that hide behind these imposing terms.

Praeterition (or preterition) describes the rhetorical act of mentioning something by professing not to mention it. You take the microphone to speak about your opponent: "I do not mention how he lies on his tax forms, how he beats his dog, and how he cheats on his wife. I pass over these things; I do not mention them." Cicero was particularly good at this. Take a look at his orations against the villainous Catiline.

Though the term *ellipsis* was born of a figure of speech, our concern here is with its usage to describe a punctuation mark. Even that has changed over time. *Ellipsis* used to refer to the dash or series of dashes that were supplied to indicate the number of letters being omitted in a word, usually in a proper name. Alexander Pope, the English satirist poet of the eighteenth century, could escape libel suits by omitting so many letters of the name of the person he was attacking that positive identification would be at least arguably impossible. (At the same time, since each dash represented one missing letter, almost everyone would know whom he meant.) The notorious scoundrel Charters appears in Pope's poems as Ch _ _ _ _ rs. Of course, when Pope's detractors wrote about him, he quickly became P_ _ _, or P_ _e, or even P_ pe.

We have changed the reference for ellipsis since then. Now it refers to the three dots we supply to indicate that we have left out words or even sentences within a quotation. The dots are separated by single spaces. If the omission is a whole sentence, the three dots follow the period, making a total of four dots. You can tell the difference between an omission at the end of a sentence (ellipsis + period = 4 dots) and the omission of an entire sentence (period + ellipsis = 4 dots) by whether or not there is a space between the final letter and the first dot:

Omission of the end of a sentence:

> If the omission is of material at the end of a sentence, a space follows the final word, which is then followed by the three dots, leaving the period to appear as a fourth dot . . . .

Omission of an entire sentence:

> If the omission is of a whole sentence, the period comes immediately after the last word and is then followed by the three dots. . . .

The proper grammatical use of an ellipsis sounds easy enough. If you leave something out of a quote, you put in three dots to let your readers know you have done so. But the effective rhetorical use of the ellipsis is a more complex matter. At times, readers are annoyed to know that something is being kept from them. Their attention can wander from considering what you are saying to wondering what you have hidden from their sight. You have to balance the advantages gained from omitting something against the dangers risked by raising suspicion of inappropriate or ill-advised authorial suppression.

There is another danger, often far more serious than this. When you leave something out of a quotation, you change its *structure*. Since that structure is responsible for supplying important instructions for the reader's interpretive process (see all of Chapter 2 and Chapter 3 above), you must take care that the omission will not alter those structural instructions in a misleading way.

To demonstrate both of these dangers, I borrow the example that one of the best-selling grammar handbooks uses to demonstrate ellipsis. It offers an original quotation and follows it first by quotation of that source with a mid-sentence ellipsis and then a quotation of it with a whole-sentence ellipsis.

32a. Original Source

> Personal space is not necessarily spherical in shape, nor does it extend equally in all directions. (People are able to tolerate closer presence of a stranger at their sides than directly in front.) It has been likened to a snail shell, a soap bubble, an aura, and "breathing room."
>
> (Robert Sommer, *Personal Space: The Behavioral Bases of Design*, p. 26)

32b. Quotation with Words in a Sentence Omitted

> Sommer says, "It has been likened to . . . breathing room.'"

32c. Quotation with Sentence Omitted

> Sommer uses similes to define its dimensions: "Personal space is not necessarily spherical in shape. . . . It has been likened to a snail shell, a soap bubble, an aura, and 'breathing room.'"

In (32b), I find myself wondering what *else* Sommer likened to personal space. Those three dots actually call my attention to my ignorance -- or to the author's intentional suppression of something I am not to be permitted to know. It is clear what can be lost from *quoting* Sommer saying "It has been likened to"; it is not clear that anything could possibly be gained from it. The ellipsis here causes more trouble for the reader than it is worth. Solution:

32d.   Sommer likens personal space to "breathing room."

A writer has to know when *not* to use an ellipsis. A great part of that decision should be based on the question of whose voice needs to be heard. In general, a writer does well to keep his or her voice dominant throughout, deferring to the voice of a recognized expert only when that expert's presence will support the writer's own perceptions. To string quotes together with minor introductory phrases of your own is to cede most of your authority to your sources and to lose the power of your own voice. Use of the ellipsis is often prompted by the sensed need for the voice of others to predominate. When that is the case, better to eradicate part or all of the quote and seize the moment in your own voice -- with, of course, the appropriate footnotes when necessary.

Example (32c) is yet more serious: The ellipsis makes nonsense of the sentence that follows it. By omitting the last clause of the first sentence and the entire second sentence, the ellipsis not only removes from the quote the whole concept of directionality but also creates a Stress position for "not necessarily spherical in shape."[10] Those words, which now end the new first sentence, suggest the next sentence will carry on with the work of exemplifying that non-spherical shape; but while a snail shell might or might not qualify, a soap bubble is recognizably "spherical in shape"; and both an aura and "breathing room" are essentially shapeless. In the original quote, the first sentence ended with "nor does it extend equally in all directions." That Stress position occupant sure-handedly led us to the directional concerns of the original second sentence. As a result, the similes of the original third sentence made far more sense: They offered comparisons based both on spherical shape, nonspherical shape, and on directionality. The alteration in structure created by the ellipsis resulted in a false Stress position occupant that seriously misleads the reader and makes nonsense of what follows.

Ellipsis, by its very nature, changes the shape of prose structure. The shape of structure, in turn, can result in profound differences in perceived meaning. The writer who leaves out a part of a quotation has a great advantage over the reader of the resulting elliptical prose: The writer knows what has been omitted, while the reader is left to grapple with the clues provided by the new, shape-changing, shape-changed structure.

In using the ellipsis, therefore, you would do well to check the resultant quotation for at least these two concerns: (1) Is more gained or lost by signaling the omission? and (2) Does the resultant structure send the reader the same interpretive instructions as those sent by the original structure? In other words, abandon your writer's perspective, from which you are permitted to know what is missing; instead, read the new quotation from the reader's perspective, which can deal only with that which is actually left on the page.

When is it wise and helpful to your reader to use an ellipsis? Use one when the material you are omitting would cause confusion, distraction, or unnecessary interruption. As an example, here is the full quotation from a source you wish to use:

33a. If you faithfully follow the detailed procedure, in the order it is stated, especially if you have never done this before, you will always produce the same helpful result.

You happen to be writing for readers who have "done this before"; the "especially" clause is therefore of no use to you or them. Using an ellipsis will clean up the sentence nicely for both of you:

33b. If you faithfully follow the detailed procedure, in the order it is stated, . . . you will always produce the same helpful result.

T *he Period: A Comfort Zone*

Light at the End of the Tunnel

The period is a great comfort to readers. When used properly, it sends a clear message:

This sentence is now complete.

If you have reading energy left over, now is the time to let it go.

Summon a fresh, new breath of energy so you can read the next one.

None of the other punctuation marks provide such unmitigated comfort: The comma performs so many functions that we have to proceed beyond it to discern retroactively which function it had been trying to serve; the semi-colon sends us in two directions at once, cautioning us to cling backward even as we lean forward; and the colon joins as much as it separates. But the clean period, the crisp period, the comfortable period lets us know that one of life's many tasks is at an end. It congratulates us. The pleasure or relief of such closure can even be increased when the size of the unit being closed increases: The pleasure of ending a sentence is exceeded by that produced by the ending of a paragraph, which is in turn outdone by that which ends an entire document, which in turn pales in comparison with that which ends a complete book. Endings please.[11]

The problems arise when the period fails to do what it promises to do. That can be the result either of grammatical impropriety or of rhetorical insufficiency. The former, being a noticeable error, announces its failure with the shock of an unforeseen interruption. For example, the sentence fragment. The latter is more subtle, but more damaging. Its very grammatical correctness disguises its unhelpfulness. Since these are quite separate concerns, we shall look at them separately.

Periodic Problems and Improprieties

The Sentence Fragment

The "frag" in *fragment* comes from the Latin verb *frangere*, "to break." A fragment is literally something broken off from a whole greater than itself. The sentence fragment is therefore a bit of a sentence that seems broken off from what should have been a whole sentence.

It is this broken quality that characterizes the fragment, for better and for worse. The "worse" is easier to characterize: It is, quite simply, a sudden violation of a reader expectation. A sentence fragment is usually caused by the absence of one of the primary requirements of an English sentence -- the verb:

34a. *The sentence fragment, a blight on the grammatical landscape.

In Chapter 2 we noted that a common problem at the sentence level is caused by the separation of a subject from its verb. Here is an example (5a) from Chapter 2:

35. The combination of such confidence in understanding situations and such unwillingness -- or perhaps inability -- to step forward and be assertive was completely new to her.

We have to hold onto the subject "combination" for 19 words (and a set of dashes) as we await the arrival of the verb, which turns out to be the relatively unrewarding "was." Think how much more disappointing -- and disruptive to the point of shocking -- it must be to encounter a period while you are still waiting for the verb to arrive.

34b. **The sentence fragment,** [there's the subject; but the comma tells me that I will have to wait until I see another comma before the verb will have a chance to appear; but I can do that, because I've read lots of interrupted sentences like this before; so here we go . . .] **a blight on the grammatical landscape** [Ah yes, that sounds like the kind of interruptive phrase I was expecting; so now there will be a comma, after which the verb will appear]. [Wait a minute -- was that the period? I was looking for a comma! How could I be betrayed like this? That's the last time I trust *this* writer.]

The sentence fragment does worse than interrupt us; it ends our motion through the sentence prematurely. Sentence elongatus may be exhausting; but it is not nearly as painful as sentence interruptus.

There are, of course, occasions on which just such an interruption makes a good deal of dramatic sense; but the key to that minor phenomenon is the nature of and need for that drama.

36a. I warned them that they would not succeed if they continued to function with that impossible, egocentric attitude. Not one bit. They
would be rejected by all those around them.

The fragment ("Not one bit.") works precisely because it functions as
an act of punctuation, not as a fulfillment of syntactic expectation. "Not one
bit" might as well be replaced by an exclamation mark -- except that the
three words take longer and therefore extend the duration of the fortified
emphasis. The fragment works best when it is a phrase that might have
been added to the previous sentence by means of a dash:

36b. I warned them that they would not succeed if they continued to function with that impossible, egocentric attitude -- not one bit. They
would be rejected by all those around them.

In these cases, the creation of a fragment allows the reader two Stress
positions instead of one. The dashes in (36b) place only the "not one bit"
in the Stress position; but the sentence fragment in (36a) creates a Stress
position for both the descriptive "impossible, egocentric attitude" and the
exclamatory "not one bit."

Most grammar handbooks warn against the sentence fragment but
suggest it can be effective if used sparingly. Here are the reader-based considerations for judging when that sparing use might be effective:

a) Does the material in the Stress positions of the fragment and of the sentences that surround it truly deserve those Stress positions?

b) Does the shock quality of the fragment (usually caused by a lack of
verb) create an effect that is in some important way productive?

c) Does the fragment, if short, act as a substantive mark of punctuation?

d) Does the fragment make its impact because its very sound imitates
and therefore suggests something is fleeting or dissipating or foreshortened?

The Run-on Sentence

The correlative of the sentence that stops short of its own expected closure
is the sentence that runs on past its appointed stopping place. Many sentences run on; but the term *run-on sentence* refers to a particular grammatical error, often known by the more anatomically descriptive term *comma
splice*. To create that error, a comma must splice together two independent
clauses without the presence of the necessary coordinating conjunction. To
rephrase that without the jargon, we can fault a comma for joining two
clauses that could each stand by itself as a full sentence -- if there is no connecting word like *and* present.

There well may be no way to teach the run-on sentence (or comma
splice) by ear. "You silly person -- can't you *hear* that it's a run-on?" will
rarely work. If this person, silly or otherwise, could have heard it, he would
never have produced the mistake in the first place. It can be taught and

learned, at least in part, in terms of how many Stress positions are required to get all the appropriate information properly emphasized. A detailed example of this is explored on page 223.

There are a number of reasons why some writers tend not to put a period where needed:

-- Their train of thought is sometimes an express, which does not stop at local stations;

-- There might be a compelling (even if subconscious) fear of not having yet said enough of substance to deserve the rest and fulfillment offered by the arrival of a period;

-- The writer might have learned the "one-thought-one-sentence" rule so well in the fifth grade that he or she must retain it, even after the mature thought process has become too complex for a single Stress position.

-- The writer trusts too unquestioningly in the *ear*, which often cannot adequately distinguish between the need for a comma and the need for a period.

Abbreviated Functions

The period seems to be the simplest of all punctuation marks -- until we start to notice its non-sentence-ending functions and the resultant possible ambiguities. For example, we use the period to indicate a shortened word, an abbreviation. *Mister* is far more recognizable in its abbreviated form *Mr.*; few people know how to spell the elongated form of *Mrs.*; and there is no elongated form for *Ms.*, which was created by combining the older terms *Miss* and *Mrs.*

Periods are "allowed" to signal abbreviations because they rarely create visual ambiguities by doing so. If a *Ms.* or a *Mr.* is immediately followed by a surname, a reader has no problem whatever in understanding what function the period is performing. The same recognition is available for the periods used in other abbreviations: A.M.; P.M.; B.A.; Dr.; etc.; and so forth.

It is wise to stay away from constructions that will raise ambiguities that otherwise would not exist. Here, for example, is a sentence from two paragraphs back:

37a. *Mister* is far more recognizable in its abbreviated form *Mr.*; few people know how to spell the elongated form of *Mrs.*; and there is no elongated form for *Ms.*, which was created by combining the older terms *Miss* and *Mrs.*

Had the sentence ended at *Ms.*, both the sentence *and* the abbreviation would have to share the same punctuation mark. One expectation tells us that the period is functioning as an indication of abbreviation; another tells us the period is a sign that the sentence is over. It is best to avoid the problem, either by adding a word or by restructuring the sentence altogether. The main exception to this advice is the ending of a sentence with *etc.*[12]

We do not double periods when an abbreviation ends a sentence, even though logic might prompt us to do so.

37b. *There is no elongated form for the relatively new *Ms.*.[13]

We prefer a cleaner ending.

37c. There is no elongated form for the relatively new *Ms.*

Sometimes conventions change for the sake of mere simplicity, of mere laziness, of the cost of typesetting or newsprint, or of the need to look "modern." We often see *am* and *pm* after numbers, especially in tables; Massachusetts, for a long time abbreviated as *Mass.*, is now *MA*, thanks to the economic needs of the Post Office. These economic forces continue to cause change. The MLA Handbook, 4th Edition, remarks that there is now a trend toward omitting the period at the end of abbreviations -- and even the spaces in the midst of abbreviations. Ph. D. is fast becoming PhD, before our very eyes. Language is always in the process of change. Do not mourn the passing of such conventions if the change reflects reality and helps readers to do their job more efficiently.

Indirect Questions
It is clear that an indirect question must end with a period, not a question mark.

38a. I asked if he had ever heard of the semi-colon.

The whole "if" clause plays the role of direct object, just the same as if it were a word. In the progression from
(1) subject - verb - object
        to
(2) subject - verb - indirect object - direct object
        to
(3) subject - verb - indirect object - direct object - qualification
        to
(4) subject - verb - clause,

the "objectiveness" of the object remains visible and audible:
1) I asked a question.
2) I asked him a question.
3) I asked him a question about the semi-colon.
4) I asked if he had ever heard of the semi-colon.

The implied question mark has to become visible only when the clause being quoted becomes a fully independent one.

38b. I asked, "Have you ever heard of the semi-colon?".

By the way, that is why you need the capital letter at the beginning of the quote: It signals the reader to expect an independent clause -- that is, a clause that could stand by itself as a sentence.

There is a possibility this may be changing as a result of the widely accepted intonation pattern known as *upspeak*. The term refers to the ending of a spoken non-question as if it were a question, which seems to guard against the statement sounding too aggressive. This new oral question mark seems to invite a response; at the least, it tries to recognize the existence and personal value of the listener. It was bred in California; but it has many ancestors, notably in Ireland. It sounds like this:

39. *This new oral question mark seems to invite a response?

No matter how definitive you might prefer an upspeak person to sound, they will usually continue to respond in a quasi-interrogative manner:

40a. (Lost traveler:)

How do I get to Elm Street from here?

40b. (Helpful upspeaking citizen:)

You take your first left? And then the third on the right? And if you pass the Post Office, you've gone too far?

Some people feel this is a positive step toward better interpersonal relations. Others are driven by it to the brink of minor acts of violence.

Polite and Impolite Requests
It is not so clear whether you should use a period or a question mark after a polite request. It depends on how polite you want the request to appear. Both of the following examples are "correct"; but they convey different tones of voice and imply different power relationships between writer and reader.

41a. Would you please be especially careful how you use that wonderful punctuation mark, the semi-colon.

41b. Would you please be especially careful how you use that wonderful punctuation mark, the semi-colon?

The period in (41a) seems to indicate that no reply from the reader is necessary; the question mark in (41b) seems to demand from the reader a complying (even if silent) "yes" or "no" response. (41a) tends toward demonstrating politeness; (41b) tends toward demonstrating annoyance.

Similar to the difference between an indirect question and a direct question, the presence of a period suggests an intellectual distancing:

42a. Would you please be especially careful how you use that wonderful punctuation mark, the semi-colon. There now, that's enough on that subject. Turning to the question of tomorrow's weather, . . .

The presence of a question mark, on the other hand, suggests a distinct invitation to dialogue:

42b. "You -- (are you listening?) -- you -- would you PLEASE be especially careful how you use that wonderful punctuation mark, the semi-colon? And now what do you have to say for yourself?"

So if you know how you want your reader to feel, you know whether to use the period or the question mark at the end of a polite request.

Periodic Rhetorical Failure

As suggested at the beginning of this discussion of the period, it is entirely possible to use the period correctly but unhelpfully.

Since the period brings a sentence to full syntactic closure, it creates what we have been calling a Stress position. (See Chapter 2.) The period therefore indicates the final resting place of that effort to create emphasis. Conversely, it also implies the relative lack of primary emphasis for all of the previous information in that sentence. Here are the first two consecutive sentences, none too helpful, from the section of a well-known grammatical handbook that tells us how to use the period.

43a. Periods are used as end punctuation primarily in sentences that make a statement, but they may also end other kinds of sentences.
43b. In addition, periods are part of many abbreviations, and they have some special functions in quotation and dialogue.

These two sentences are grammatically correct but rhetorically not as helpful as they could be. Sentence (43a) states the general rule in its main clause, but allows us no period (nor colon nor semi-colon) to bring this bottom-line definition to closure. Instead we find a comma, followed by a "but." The very lack of that closure and emphasis warns us that this important-sounding rule is probably less important than the exception(s) about to be articulated. We needed more than a comma's worth of rest in order to finalize the main clause, to allow it to reverberate momentarily before the succeeding sentence began. Moreover, the actual Stress position of sentence (43a) leads us to believe that "other kinds of sentences" is of great importance. Since that importance is not immediately self-evident, we are led to expect that a consideration of "other kinds of sentences" will follow immediately. Unfortunately, that does not happen. Sentence (43a) is followed immediately by sentence (43b).

Sentence (43b) presents us with a similar kind of stylistic unkindness. It buries the more broadly applicable information about abbreviations both by refusing it a Stress position and by following it with a second independent clause that concentrates on something less broad. Note also how the information is presented as merely additive: The first clause of (43b) is marked as being "in addition"; the second clause is introduced by "and." Sentence (43b), in turn, leaves us leaning forward in the expectation of discovering more about the contents of its Stress position, the "special functions in quotation and dialogue"; that, too, proves not to be forthcoming.

As a result, these two sentences merely stockpile information instead of packaging it in a way that instructs readers about its relative values, its interconnections, and the immediate future development of its thought. But for the fear of being judged wordy, the author might as well have produced the following equally unhelpful single sentence:

43c. Periods are used as end punctuation primarily in sentences that make a statement, but they may also end other kinds of sentences, appear as part of many abbreviations, and have some special functions in quotation and dialogue.

In some ways, sentence (43c) is more honest. It signals to our eye and ear that a whole lot of information has been piled together for us to unpile as we may. At least we would know up front the amount of work we were supposed to do for ourselves.

For the period, as with all other marks of punctuation, it is important to know not only its correct usage but also the effects it tends to have on its readers. Since the period is indicative of final and full syntactic closure for the sentence, it also calls forth the kind of primary emphasis we should be giving to the material that has just led up to it.

One of the most common writing problems today is the sentence that begins with a main clause and ends with a subordinate clause. This is not wrong in any grammatical way and often is not wrong rhetorically; but it can burden readers unnecessarily. Why do we see this so often? I can offer an explanation.

In middle school and high school, when we are learning how to write, we are producing sentences of one clause only. We therefore *begin* our composition of the sentence by choosing the subject of the main (and only) clause, soon to be followed by our choice of the verb. When we graduate and go to college, we are given reading assignments that constantly present us with prose that sounds very professional -- and very different from our own. We soon perceive (although more unconsciously than consciously) that the professional prose differs from ours in two aspects: (1) It uses fancy words that we did not previously know; and (2) the sentences are about twice as long as ours. To improve ourselves, therefore, we do two things: (1) We learn some of the hard words, so we may use them in our own writing; and (2) we double the length of our sentences. We accomplish this doubling by writing our normal sentence and then substituting for the expected period a comma; after that we add another clause. We now "sound" more professional; but we have lost the opportunity to give our first clause the Stress position it probably needs. We have therefore handed our readers a main clause -- with no Stress position -- and then another clause. Main clauses usually require a Stress position. If they do not, most often they should be demoted to the lower status of a subordinate clause or a phrase. I have seen this as a pervasive problem in more than 50% of this country's professionals.

T he Comma: It Gives One Pause

The Choicest Cut

The word *comma* comes from the Greek *komma*, meaning "segment" or "cut." It divides things, and by dividing, joins them. It is the only mark of punctuation that does not definitively announce its function at the time of its arrival. You always have to go past the comma to find out what its function is supposed to be. Since readers, therefore, are naturally less certain every time they see a comma what function that comma will fulfill, it is entirely understandable why writers (who after all are just readers turned around) also feel confused about them.

Example: Take a sentence that begins with the name *Pat* followed directly by a comma. Consider what a large number of possibilities we might expect to encounter:

a. Pat, Mike, and Alice went . . .

b. Pat, leaving Mike and Alice behind, went . . .

c. Pat, without Mike or Alice, went . . .

d. Pat, not Mike, went . . .

e. Pat, under a great time constraint, went . . .

f. Pat, who could not have cared less about the matter, went . . .

g. Pat, alas, went . . .

h. Pat, at exactly 4:03 P.M., went . . .

i. Pat, representing Mike and Alice, went . . .

j. Pat, an M & A representative, went . . .

Those are just some of the possibilities we might expect when the opening word of a sentence is followed immediately by a comma. What if the sentence begins with a full clause followed by a comma? What kinds of structures might we then expect to develop?

a. Although I am unable to grant your request, ???????? . . .

b. Although I am unable to grant your request, which you have submitted three hours too late for the deadline, . . .

c. Although I am unable to grant your request, despite my normally good-natured sense of generosity, . . .

d. Although I am unable to grant your request, give you any hope for success, or even promise to return your phone calls, . . .

e. Although I am unable to grant your request, and I cannot imagine changing my mind at any time in the near future, . . .

f. Although I am unable to grant your request, now or ever, . . .

g. Although I am unable to grant your request, I am happy to invite you to ask me again next week, when I may be in a better position to be of help.

The comma is the most common mark of punctuation. Some handbooks claim it occurs twice as often as all other marks combined. Others tell us its misuse comprises about one quarter of all the grammatical errors most commonly encountered. It serves a larger number of functions than any other mark, some distinctive, some overlapping. Here is a partial list:

-- to distinguish nonrestrictive elements from restrictive elements

-- to mark the boundaries of interruptive material

-- to mark transitional material

-- to mark contrasting material

-- to separate the members of a series

-- to separate clauses in a sentence

-- to separate introductory material from the main cause

-- to separate adverbs and adjectives that together modify a single noun

-- to mark direct address

-- to introduce direct address after a verb that identifies the speaker

-- to keep in order dates, addresses, numbers, and titles

That list is hard enough to compile; it is more than challenging to memorize; and it is impossible to retain in mind at all times both it and the rules that accompany it unless one is a full-time paid professional in the field of teaching the use of the comma.

As a result, it has long been clear to researchers of language that a series of "rules" for each, to be memorized and held ready for summoning when the need arises, is of minimal help at best. There are too many uses, too many conflicts, and too much disagreement among experts for the mass consumers of commas to be well enough served by the rigor of rote. It may help a great deal, however, to explore what readers are likely to do when they encounter this common squiggle at the foot of a letter. As the various uses start to overlap, the common comma command "pause" begins to sound like a theme upon which many variations are constantly being played.

The World of Series

Rules are particularly difficult to apply when they are the object of professional disagreement. Example: In a series of items, should there be a comma before the *and* that signals the end of the list? Which of the following is "correct" in answer to the question "What colors do you have in stock for the 540X sedan model?"

    a. red, white, and blue

        or

    b. red, white and blue.

According to all the standard textbooks, both of these are acceptable. According to readers, however, the first is preferable to the second because it allows for no ambiguity. How many cars are there to choose from here? Answer (a) tells us there are three and only three: One is red, one is white, and one is blue. Answer (b) suggests there might be either three or two: Either (i) one is red, one white, and one blue, or (ii) one is red and the other is a two-toned white-and-blue model. The best "rule" to follow, in these and all other writing matters, is "Do what is best for your reader." If you consistently omit the comma before the *and* in a series, sooner or later you will produce a series in which the missing comma creates an ambiguity and thus confuses your reader. If you consistently use the comma before the *and*, no such ambiguity can intrude.

To Begin With, Separate the Introductory Material from the Main Clause

Unless they are otherwise informed, readers tend to expect that a sentence will begin with the subject of its main clause. When introductory material precedes the main clause, a comma "informs us otherwise," saying to the reader, "You were expecting the main clause at the beginning; it didn't happen; but now it's coming right up." So here we have a fallback expectation: That is, if the initial expectation (that the sentence will begin with main clause) fails, then the arrival of a comma re-kindles that expectation. It tells us that the delayed main clause should be following immediately. This reader expectation will be your best guide in any case where the "correct" usage is not clearly defined.

Here is a simple sentence that fulfills the default value expectation of the subject of the main clause arriving immediately.

44a. He opened the door.

And here is an only slightly more complex sentence in which the fallback expectation kicks in. Because we do not get the subject of the main clause right away, we expect it to appear right after the first comma we meet.

44b. With great trepidation, he opened the door.

When such a comma lies about the immediate appearance of the subject, a number of effects are possible, both positive and negative. One positive effect can be the increasing of expectational tension. In (43c), the second comma repeats the expectational pull of the first one, heightened by the yet further delay in its sense of tension:

44c. With great trepidation, unwilling to admit what might be revealed, he opened the door.

However, when the intervening material is lengthy and does not add to the buildup constructively, it can function destructively, so that by the time the main clause finally appears, the reader is worn out.

44d. With great trepidation, noticing the clock on the shelf above the door had stopped and was still displaying 9:42, just as it had done earlier that day when he had thought it really was 9:42, he opened the door.

If no comma separates initial material from the grammatical subject, then the reader naturally tends toward bonding that initial material with the subject as a single, necessary unit. Note how the "only" bonds with the "she" in (44e), suggesting that her door-opening knowledge was unique:

44e. Only she knew how to open the door.

The grammar handbooks do not agree on whether or not you can omit a comma after material that precedes the grammatical subject if that material is only a word or an extremely short phrase. Once again, consideration of the reader will lead to the best decisions. It all depends on how much you want the reader to make that word or phrase part of the clause that is about to begin.

44f. Without hesitation, he opened the door.
44g. Without hesitation he opened the door.

The (44f) version "hesitates"; the (44g) version does not. Both are possible; but they "mean" in different ways.

To decide whether a sentence has become overloaded, it is usually best to base your judgment on what a reader can handle -- rather than on what the writer wishes to discharge. If you consider, at a slow-motion pace, the demand on your reader's endurance, you will often be able to recognize serious information overload when it happens. In the following example, a sentence is allowed to unfold in pieces, with the comments in square brackets representing natural readers' responses as they occur.

45a. Similarly, . . . --

["Fine. An introductory adverb. I can handle that. But now I want the subject of the main clause, please."]

45b. Similarly, in a situation like this one, . . .

["OK. But I really would like my subject now, please.]

45c. Similarly, in a situation like this one, which cannot be reduced to a simple or quick solution, . . .

["I WANT my subject! Now, please!"]

45d. Similarly, in a situation like this one, which cannot be reduced to a simple or quick solution, given all the problems that usually

["AAAAARGH!"]

It is not a question of too many words or too many commas; it is rather a question of not delivering what was promised at the first comma, when the reader still had enough energy to invest and was primed to do the act of investment.

Look what happens to the same information when it is preceded by such a main clause:

45e. Similarly, we should refer the question to the Student Council in a situation like this one, since it cannot be reduced to a simple or quick solution, given all the problems that usually arise from these complications.

That sentence can be comprehended on first reading without a sense of sheer exhaustion. The main difference between (45d) and (45e) is this: In (45d), we are continually waiting for the arrival of that which will make greater sense of material we have already been handed; but in (45e), nothing arrives in the sentence that we cannot handle at that moment of its arrival.

As I have said before, every Reader Expectation can be violated to good effect. There will be times when, as a special effect, you may *want* to tantalize and overburden your reader. Sometimes making the reader wait for the resolution at the end can make that moment even more powerful. "So, my friends, if you want government that cares about the people instead of itself, if you want a senator that will look out for your interests instead of vested interests, if you want someone in Washington who values family more than family values, and if you want someone with courage, tenacity, imagination, and character, then you must cast your vote this November for Barbara T. Birtwhistle." The candidate's name arrives with thunder.

A comma (or its lack) after short introductory information also tells the reader something about the relative importance or markedness of the introductory phrase. Both of the following sentences are "correct"; but the presence or absence of the comma after the second word makes the reader think differently about the relationship of those two words to the rest of the sentence.

46a. After breakfast, the sculptor returned to the task at hand.

46b. After breakfast the sculptor could return to the task at hand.

In sentence (46a), the "after breakfast" acts mainly as a temporal marker, telling us *when* something happened. But in (46b), the lack of comma warns us not to separate the breakfast from the rest of the sentence because it will play some more important, integrating role: It is preparing us for the "could." It suggests that it was *because* of breakfast, not merely "after" breakfast, that the sculptor could get to work. This is the restrictive/nonrestrictive difference we have encountered before. (See Chapter 1.) In (46a), the first two words are helpful but not essential to the sentence's making sense; but in (46b), the omission of the first two words denies the reader essential information.

If we took the "could" out of this sentence, would a lack of comma make the sentence function the way (46b) functions above?

46c. After breakfast the sculptor returned to the task at hand.

Yes; but since there is no word like "could" to reinforce the suggestion of breakfast "helping" the sculptor to return to work, this sentence does not offer as strong a set of interpretive clues as (46b), where the lack of comma and the "could" work together to direct the reader's attention.

Here is another example of comma usage distinguishing the restrictive from the nonrestrictive -- the necessary from the helpful-but-additional. (It is much less important to know these technical terms than to understand the distinction they are trying to make. That distinction has everything to do with that important person, the reader.)

Compare these two:

47a. The sculptor standing in the doorway called for more breakfast.

47b. The sculptor, standing in the doorway, called for more breakfast.

In both of these sentences, more breakfast was called for by a sculptor; but each suggests a different number of sculptors were present at the moment in question. In (47a), with no commas to set off the identifying material "standing in the doorway," most readers will read the entire phrase as a nonstop event -- "the-sculptor-standing-in-the-doorway." This, in turn, will distinguish this sculptor from others present at that time. This is *not* "the-sculptor-standing-by-the-fireplace" nor "the-sculptor-looking-out-the-window"; it is, most distinctively, "the-sculptor-standing-in-the-doorway." In (47b), there is only one sculptor on location. By the way, she was standing in the doorway.

Bad Advice: Use a Comma When You Need to Take a Breath

A majority of people, if pressed for an answer to the question "When are you supposed to use a comma?", would answer something like "When you need to take a breath." Unfortunately, the comma sends too many complex signals for it to be used effectively on a "whenever-I-want-to-use-it" basis. The comma becomes a serious problem for the reader when the writer allows it to imitate speech -- that is, the writer's sense of speech:

48. *No one answered, so I left a message on the machine, and wondered if they would get it, before it was too late, or not.

This "comma where a breath is needed" concept usually refers to where the *writer* needs to take a breath. No reader cares about the writer's breathing habits; but all readers are intensely concerned about their own breathing opportunities. Readers need to know not only they *can* take a "breath" at a comma but also precisely which *kind* of "breath" to take. That instruction, as noted above, is never complete until *after* the arrival of the comma, when the continuing text informs us retroactively what kind of a comma it had been. Given that necessary delay, we should try to limit possible ambiguity whenever we can. Ambiguity on a constant basis will eventually exhaust the reader. Exhausted readers eventually abandon texts.

The Comma Splice: A Matter of Stress

The comma splice is aptly named. It refers to the splicing of two independent clauses without the aid of a connecting conjunction coming between them. The comma (incorrectly) replaces the conjunction, it acts as splicing tape to hold the two clauses together. (The sentence that precedes this one is an example of a comma splice.)

That is the definition. It is accurate, specific, and (if the terms used are known to the reader) clear. Why, then, do so many people commit this common comma flaw? And why do even more people nervously wonder if they are doing so, even when they are not? Apparently, clear rules do not suffice, especially if writers have to recall them, which seems rather an artificial task. Avoiding that artificiality, they rely on the more natural aid of the ear. The splicing comma "sounds" to them significant enough to create the kind of pause necessary to separate one independent clause from another. It is very hard to help people avoid this error if they are particularly prone to committing it. As suggested above, you cannot say to them, "Can't you *hear* it's wrong?" If they could have heard it, they would not have done it.

What bothers a reader about a comma splice? True, there are some readers who are knowledgeable enough about grammar and fierce enough in their defense of its proprieties that the presence of a single comma splice will distract them significantly or even send them into a minor rage. But those who harbor no such feelings of protectorship for the language can also be disturbed by this comma problem. It has something to do once again with expectations concerning the Stress position.

Here is a delightful comma splice from a freshman student of mine:

49a.   *If I am not sure, I will revise the sentence using a conjunction, then I know where to put the comma.

Pride goeth before a fall: In the very sentence in which he boasts of his control of the comma, he commits a comma flaw. He could not "hear" the problem; so telling him to listen harder would have been futile. Instead, I asked him a structural question: Which pieces of information in this sentence did he want his reader to emphasize? Which therefore deserved a Stress position? He chose both "using a conjunction" and "where to put the comma."

49b.   *If I am not sure, I will revise the sentence *using a conjunction*, then I know *where to put the comma*.

I challenged him to create the necessary second Stress position. He reluctantly divided the sentence into two shorter sentences:

49c.   If I am not sure, I will revise the sentence *using a conjunction*. Then I know *where to put the comma*.

"Baby prose," he said, throwing down his pen in disgust. I asked why he was distressed. He insisted that the two halves of his original sentence were so closely related that they belonged in the same sentence. I said I never told him he needed to make two sentences; rather, he needed to make two *Stress positions*. He quickly came up with the solution -- a semi-colon.

49d.   If I am not sure, I will revise the sentence *using a conjunction*; then I know *where to put the comma*.

This student's comma-spliced sentence (like most comma-spliced sentences) was "too long" -- but not because it contained "too many" words. The final revised version, (49d), contains exactly the same number of words; but it does not strike us as "too long." This takes us back to the new definition of when a sentence is too long, offered at the end of Chapter 2: "A sentence is too long when it has more viable candidates for Stress positions than it has Stress positions."

Because it is the only mark of punctuation that never reveals its function at the moment of its arrival, a comma is never capable of producing a

Stress position. Periods, colons, semi-colons, question marks, exclamation points, and even most dashes tell us what they are doing the moment they arrive. No comma, however, can be understood without going *beyond* it to see how it is connected to the material that follows. Since the comma is always urging us forward in a continuous motion -- despite its "breathing" or "separating" function -- it can never create a Stress position.

By obliterating comma splices, we can greatly reduce a reader's mid-sentence crisis.

New Three Bartenders: The Problems of Multiple Modifiers

Do you or do you not put commas between two adjectives or between adjectives and adverbs? Well, it depends whether you want your reader to consider the two terms as a unit or as functioning independently.

There are a number of possible tests:

Test #1: Could the modifiers be separated by the word *and* without ruining the sentence? If so, inform the reader of that by using a comma.

50a. A small and shy voice was heard after several endless moments of silence.

50b. A small, shy voice was heard after several endless moments of silence.

Test #2: Does the first modifier modify the second modifier? or does it modify the noun? If it modifies the next modifier, then the *lack* of a comma will notify the reader not to stop, not to separate those two terms from each other:

51a. They hired three new bartenders.

That treats your reader better than

51b. *They hired three, new bartenders.

On the other hand, if the adjective in question modifies the noun directly, then the comma is necessary to inform the reader that both of those words take an equal shot at attaching themselves to the noun they share in common:

51b. They hired large, powerful bouncers.

Test #3: Can the order of modifiers be reversed? A comma tells the reader "yes."

51c. They hired large, powerful bouncers.
51d. They hired powerful, large bouncers.

We may think the word order of (51c) less elegant, less smooth; but we can still make good sense of the sentence in this inverted form.

On the other hand, the lack of a comma between modifiers suggests that reversing them would produce an unidiomatic usage:

51e. They hired three new bartenders.

51f. *They hired new three bartenders.

51g. *They hired powerful, large, three bouncers.

The same instructions to the reader could be delivered by a system of brackets, were that our way of doing things:

51g. They hired three [large powerful] bouncers.

But since we do not do that, we need to send the reader the appropriate message by using the appropriate comma.

51h. They hired three large, powerful bouncers.

A special case worth noting: When a whole phrase becomes a modifier that *contrasts* its contents to the material it modifies, commas help warn the reader that such a contrast is taking place.

52a. Given the scandals of the previous year, the majority of the voting public was willing to settle for honest, even if not highly intelligent, town council members.

When the comma after "honest" here is not followed by another adjective, the reader is informed that the noun to be modified by "honest" will not appear until this new interruption is over and a second comma appears. When that second comma arrives, readers expect the noun will arrive immediately thereafter. If it fails to do so, the sentence structure becomes harder to decipher:

52b. Given the scandals of the previous year, the majority of the voting public was willing to settle for honest, even if not highly intelligent, not to mention adequately competent, town council members.

Such a structure is not "wrong"; it only runs the risk that some readers will not quite be up to the task the first time around. To ensure reader failure, just keep postponing the promised arrival beyond endurance:

52c. Given the scandals of the previous year, the majority of the voting public was willing to settle for honest, even if not highly intelligent, not to mention adequately competent, although in some cases it was difficult to tell, town council members.

Here are two additional examples of these contrastive, interrupting commas giving clear signs to the reader. The first qualifies the subject of the sentence; the second offers a clarification of a verb. In both cases, the reader is well informed by the first comma what kind of words to expect just after the arrival of the second comma. In (53a), we expect the verb to appear immediately after the comma that closes the interruptive material:

53a. The pilots, unlike the flight attendants or the mechanics, were willing to strike in order to secure the 23% pay raise.

In (54a), a similar delayed arrival is functioning, this time to complete the motion of the verb:

54a. The principal emphasized that students should walk, not run, to the nearest exit when the fire alarm sounded.

In both of these cases, we can again exhaust the reader, even to the point of noncomprehension, if we refuse to produce the expected words after the second comma as promised:

53b. The pilots, unlike the flight attendants or the mechanics, but along with ticket sellers in all cities of more than 300,000 population, except west of the Rocky Mountain range, and in Kansas and Maryland, were willing to strike in order to secure the 23% pay raise.

54b. The principal emphasized that students should walk, not run, especially on the third floor where the corridors had been narrowed by the construction of the new locker units that had been added just after the Thanksgiving break, to the nearest exit when the fire alarm sounded.

Nothing is grammatically "wrong" with either of these unfriendly sentences; but both of them treat the reader badly, just because the writer wanted to include a certain amount of presumably important information. That information can be included in a reader-friendly fashion simply by rearranging the structure of the sentences so the promises made by the commas can be kept:

53c. The pilots, unlike the flight attendants or the mechanics, were willing to strike in order to secure the 23% pay raise. The pilots were joined in that opinion by the ticket sellers who worked in Kansas, in Maryland, and in all cities east of the Rockies that were home to more than 300,000 people.

54c. The principal emphasized that students should walk, not run, to the nearest exit when the fire alarm sounded. He emphasized the special importance of this for those on the third floor, since after the Thanksgiving break those corridors had been narrowed by the construction of the new locker units.

These rearrangements also supply enough Stress positions for all the stressworthy material.

Clauses and Comma Promises

The more sophisticated your thinking becomes, the more sophisticated structures you must employ in your writing. The average sentence of first-year college students contains between 13 and 15 words; the average published sentence contains between 24 and 26 words. This does not mean that longer is better but rather that better is oftentimes longer. Most 18-year-olds still think primarily in terms of the single declarative statement:

> Here is an idea.
>
> Here is another idea.
>
> Now here is yet a third one.

The ordering of these three statements, the writer thinks, will imply the connections between them. Recall, though, for whom this 18-year-old writer is writing -- for an audience (a teacher) who presumably knows in expert fashion how to combine these materials. If the student produces the data, the teacher will be able to perform the more complex act of synthesis.

No professional, however, can afford that luxury of intellectual dependence. Think what would happen if a lawyer relied on the judge to do the act of intellectual synthesis:

> Your Honor --
>
>> Here are the facts in our case.
>>
>> Here are some previously decided cases.
>>
>> Therefore, we win.

"We" would probably not win. Professionals are people who are paid to articulate the connections. The lawyer here has to show *why* the existence of the previous decisions should force the judge to conclude that "we win." In order to do that, professionals are constantly led to *combine* more than one parcel of thought *in the same sentence*. This produces a large number of sentences that contain more than one clause. Important synthesizing words like *because* or *as a result of* are used to make the wished-for connection available to the reader. If you constantly write sentences containing a single clause only, you will tend to produce sentences that average between 13 and 16 words; if you often combine two clauses or a clause and a significantly weighted phrase in the same sentence, then your sentences will tend towards averaging between 24 and 26 words in length.

A number of "readability formulae" were formulated in the 1930s and 1940s, the most famous being that of Dr. Rudolph Flesch. His "Flesch Test" demonstrated, he argued, that sentences become too hard to read when they exceed 29 words. Good research; bad conclusion. (If the average published sentence is 24 to 26 words long, just think how many sentences of more than 29 words have had to be published in order to balance off all the

8-, 10-, 12- and 14-word sentences that exist in print.) Flesch was right to see that *something* tended to happen after the 29-word mark. After 29 words or so, the writer is getting into a *third* clause or other major unit of discourse; and three clauses are far more difficult to handle than two. Therefore, after 29 words, a sentence does not, as Dr. Flesch claims, become harder to *read*; it merely becomes harder to *write*.

We can control longer sentences by ensuring two things: (1) that every Stress position is filled with something stressworthy; and (2) that everything stressworthy has its own Stress position. That is so, of course -- (No Rules! No Rules!) -- unless there is a good reason for doing otherwise.

It is not enough to "know the rules." Prose that is "correct" but unreadable is yet worse than prose that makes itself clear but contains an "error." Indeed, when correcting an error seems to make a sentence harder to follow rather than easier, it is time to restructure the sentence altogether. Here is a lengthy and complex but helpful example from a graduate student's Ph.D. thesis:

56. *Bishop Tutu was a skillful and self-aware rhetorician, and it would be a mistake to assume without argument, as many church historians have done, that we can ignore the occasions on which he wrote and spoke, and treat his words as transparent windows into his personal belief system.

In this case, the comma before the "and treat" is incorrect; but if you take it out, it creates yet greater difficulties of comprehension. "Treat" begins to sound like it belongs to "he" instead of "we"; and in so belonging, it creates the sound of a grammatical error -- "he wrote and spoke and treat. . . ."

The problem here cannot be narrowed to the single grammatical "error" in the sentence; the structural problems, while not technically errors, are far more troublesome. Look at the number of jobs the commas here are expected to perform:

1. The first comma (". . . rhetorician, and it . . .") connects two independent clauses. This [_____, and _____] structure is often unhelpful to readers. At one and the same time it suggests (a) that since the first clause is an independent clause, it contains something worthy of emphasis, but (b) because the comma cannot offer the clause a Stress position, there is not opportunity for the reader to apply emphasis. Already the sentence is in trouble.

2. The second comma ("to assume without argument, as many ...") signals an embedded phrase that will separate the infinitive ("to assume") from its direct object (the "that" clause). Unfortunately, we have already had exactly such an interruption (the phrase "without argument") *without* commas and are therefore doubly burdened and confused.

3. The third comma ("historians have done, that we ...") ends the interruption begun by the second comma. At least now, despite the interrupted interruptions, we feel, perhaps, although not with great

confidence, that maybe the sentence, which has already seemed rather long, will perhaps proceed in an orderly -- and no more to be inter-rupted -- fashion to its end. (You can see from my last sentence how annoying sentences can be when they do not take into account how readers will unpack them.)

4. The fourth comma ("on which he wrote and spoke, and treat . . . ") does us in. Coming just before the word "and," it signals us that yet another independent clause is about to begin; but instead of finding the expected grammatical subject, we find ourselves confronted with a verb ("treat"). We have been so burdened already by this structure that most of us would probably give up the good fight at this point, either by returning to the beginning of the sentence or by fast-forwarding to its end. If we do make the effort to find out to which previous verb the new arrival belongs, we discover two persuasive candidates -- "assume" and "ignore" -- only one of which can be the right one.

The problem here goes beyond the improper use of a comma, or even beyond the use of too many commas; it concerns the number of *kinds* of comma use we are asked to deal with in the confines of a single but multi-layered sentence. It is simply too difficult for us to recognize all the levels of modification at the moments when they arrive and reappear. Sometimes the traffic is directed by the word "and"; sometimes it is directed by com-mas; and sometimes a subordination or resurfacing from one level to another is merely implied by the relationship of one term to another. Here is a schematic map of our journey:

1 He was a
    2 skillful and self-aware
1 rhetorician [comma]
      and
1 it would be a mistake to assume
      3 without argument [comma]
        4 as many church historians have done
          [comma]
1 that we can
    2 ignore the occasions
      3 on which he wrote
      and
      3 spoke [improper comma]
      and
    2 treat his words as transparent windows
      3 into his personal belief system.

Too much reader energy must be expended on figuring out the sentence's *structure*; therefore, too little energy can be retained to contemplate its *substance*.

A Short List of Common Commas

There is no simple rule, nor any simple set of rules, that will make the multiple uses of the comma clear and easy. That little squiggle of punctuation serves too many purposes for us to keep them continually and distinctly in focus. However, there is one question you can ask yourself that will keep you on the right side of "correctness" most of the time: Ask not what the comma rules demand of you but rather how you can use the comma to take better care of your reader's needs. Like any other mark of punctuation, the comma simultaneously separates and combines that which lies on either side of it. Knowing what degree of separation you want your reader to experience will usually lead you to make the best choice.

Here again is the list of the most common uses of the comma, this time with brief examples.

-- To distinguish nonrestrictive elements from restrictive elements

> Ludwig van Beethoven, bereft of the power of hearing, composed his greatest compositions at the end of his life.

> Ludwig van Beethoven bereft of the power of hearing was able to free himself from the limitations of conventional musical sound and produce his greatest compositions at the end of his life.

>> (The first sentence would still make sense if we omitted the phrase within the commas. The second would not.)

-- When used in pairs, to mark the boundaries of interruptive material

> Ludwig van Beethoven, who was to die an embittered man, composed his greatest pieces after he suffered a complete loss of hearing.

-- To mark transitional material

> Despite this loss of hearing, Ludwig van Beethoven composed his greatest pieces toward the end of his life.

-- To mark contrasting material

> It was Beethoven, not the more popularly acclaimed Ludwig Spohr, who eventually claimed the title of the greatest composer of his era.

-- To separate the members of a series

> One cannot do better than to spend an evening listening to Monteverdi, Mahler, and Beethoven.

-- To separate independent clauses from dependent clauses

> When she discovered his extreme dislike for Beethoven, she detested him for it.

> She knew of his extreme dislike for Beethoven and detested him for it.

-- To separate introductory words, phrases, or clauses from the main body of the sentence

> Without the late string quartets of Beethoven, life would be insupportable.

-- To separate adverbs and adjectives that together modify a single noun

> Even on such an extremely hot, wet, steamy evening, the exquisite, uplifting, soaring music of Beethoven made us forget our physical discomfort.

-- To mark direct address

> O Beethoven, what would we do without you?

-- To introduce direct address after a verb that identifies the speaker

> He said, "O Beethoven, what would we do without you?"

-- To keep in order dates, addresses, numbers, and titles

> On December 16, 1770, at 12 Heiligemusikstrasse, Bonn, Germany, was born that one in 100,000,000 genius, Beethoven, the prince of composers.

As is so often the case, the best practice is to consider the needs of your reader first and foremost. If you do that consistently, you will usually be staying within the "rules" of comma usage and be providing for your reader the pause that refreshes.

Now that you have finished this chapter, take another look at its opening exercise. See if it makes more sense now.

Endnotes

1. Our semi-colon was used by the ancient Greeks as the equivalent of our question mark. By the seventh century c.e. it had attained approximately its modern use. From the eighth through the fifteenth centuries, an inverted semi-colon was used to signal a pause with the force of slightly more than a comma but slightly less than a semi-colon. That inverted mark has not been in use for the past five centuries.

2. *Dewriting* is a term I use for the rewriting of a text that retains all the original material but changes some of its locations.

3. For a definition and discussion of the Stress position, see Chapter 2.

4. For a deeper and more leisurely journey into this subject, explore M. B. Parkes, *Pause and Effect: An Introduction to the History of Punctuation in the West.* Berkeley: University of California Press, 1993. Both its scholarly text and its wonderful photographic illustration are illuminating. Much of the historical information in this section can be found there.

5. A barbarism is the use of forms or constructions borrowed from other languages and therefore considered alien to good usage. A solecism is an outright error, impropriety, or inconsistency.

6. The ambiguity of leaning is a bit tricky to exemplify in English, which is so different in construction from Latin, but the word *only* might prove helpful as an example. Imagine *only* position between the statements "I would do [X]" and "You should do [Y]." Without punctuation, it is impossible to tell with which statement the *only* is to be associated. It could mean "I would do [X] only. You should do [Y]"; or it could mean "I would do [X]. Only you should do [Y]."

7. Please understand that I am not taking a stand or even inferring a stand for or against abortion here. I use this controversial topic only to highlight what striking differences can be achieved by a choice of different punctuation marks.

8. In reading the advice I give about avoiding line-ending hyphens, you might be wondering why this book is so chock full of them. My original manuscript contained not a single one -- except for the intentionally annoying ones in the paragraphs that prededed this one. It would be an unbearable burden for printers of books to have to make do without these hyphens. Books look better when both the left and right margins are justified. If hyphens were not used freely, many lines would look either swollen (with too many characters scrunched together) or unnaturally stretched (with too much space between letters in individual words). So when you have control over the setting of the text, you can choose between the annoyance of lots of hyphens or the less professionalized look of varying the right margin.

9. With apologies to *Star Trek*.

10. The mistake in judgment here is compounded by a grammatical error: The first dot after "space" should not be located directly after the letter *e*, because that suggests erroneously that "space" is the final word of the original sentence. If the first dot had been delayed by one space, at least some readers might note that the word "space" was not intended to occupy the Stress position of the original sentence.

11. As noted earlier, this is particularly the case in Western cultures, and especially so in North American culture. This is not the case in many other parts of the world, where people are not as obsessed with closure.

12. On the other hand, in most cases I would advise against using *etc.* at the end of a sentence -- not because of the ambiguity of the punctuation mark but because the trailing off or dismissive handwaving effect of *etc.* is usually an inappropriate choice for the Stress position, which most often ought to contain something worthy of emphasis.

13. Another detail: If a term like "Ms." appears at the end of a sentence in italics, two periods would cause little distress. The first, in italics, would clearly belong to the italicized term; the second would clearly belong to the sentence as a whole.

Works Cited

Austen, Jane. *Pride and Prejudice*. New York: Oxford University Press, 1970.

Bain, Alexander. *English Composition and Rhetoric*. Enlarged edition. New York: American Book Company, 1887.

Baron, Dennis E. *Grammar and Good Taste: Reforming the American Language*. New Haven, Conn.: Yale University Press, 1982.

Benjamin, Walter. "Unpacking My Library." *Illuminations*. Trans. Harry Zohn. New York: Harcourt Brace, 1968.

Borges, Jorge Luis. "Blindness." *Seven Nights*. Trans. Eliot Weinberger. Mexico, D.F.: Fondo de Cultura Economica, 1980.

Burke, Kenneth. *Counter-Statement*. Berkeley: University of California Press, 1968.

Chesterton, G. K. "A Piece of Chalk." *Collected works*. New York: Ignatius Press, 1986.

Demos, John. "The American Family Then and Now." *Past, Present, and Personal: The Family and the Life Course in American History*. New York: Oxford University Press, 1986.

Didion, Joan. "Goodbye to All That." *Slouching Towards Bethlehem*. New York: Farrar, Strauss&Giroux, 1973.

———. "Quiet Days in Malibu." *The White Album*. New York: Noonday Press, 1979.

Eighner, Lars. *Travels with Lizbeth: Three Years on the Road and on the Streets*. New York: St. Martin's Press, 1993.

Flesch, Rudolph. *The Art of Clear Thinking*. New York: Harper's, 1951.

———. *The Art of Plain Talk*. New York: Macmillan, 1962.

———. *The Art of Readable Writing*. New York: Harper&Row, 1974.

———. *How to Write Plain English: A Book for Lawyers and Consumers*. New York: Harper&Row, 1979.

———. *How to Write, Speak, and Think More Effectively*. New York: New American Library, 1964.

Ford, Larry. *Cities and Buildings: Skyscrapers, Skid Rows, and Suburbs*. Baltimore: Johns Hopkins University Press, 1994.

Gleick, James. *Chaos: Making a New Science*. New York: Viking Penguin, 1987.

Gottlieb, Beatrice. "The Emotional Role of the Family." *The Family in the Western World from the Black Death to the Industrial Age*. New York: Oxford University Press, 1993.

New York: Herb Lubalin Study Center of Design and Typography. *Period Styles: A History of Punctuation*. Cooper Union for the Advancement of Science and Art, 1988.

Jonson, Ben. *The English Grammar Made by Ben Jonson for the Benefit of All Strangers Out of His Observation of the English Language Now Spoken and In Use* (1640). London: Lanston Monotype Corporation Ltd., 1928.

King, Martin Luther, Jr. "I Have a Dream." Speech delivered at the Lincoln Memorial, Washington, D.C., August 28, 1963.

Lakoff, Robin Tolmach. "We First." *Talking Power: The Politics of Language*. New York: Basic Books, 1990.

Lanham, Url. *Origins of Modern Biology*. New York: Columbia University Press, 1968.

Lincoln, Abraham. "The Gettysburg Address." Speech delivered at the consecration of the Cemetery at the Battlefield at Gettysburg, Pennsylvania, November 19, 1863.

Lopate, Philip, ed. *The Art of the Personal Essay: An Anthology from the Classical Era to the Present*. New York: Anchor Books, 1994.

Ong, Walter. "Historical Backgrounds of Elizabethan and Jacobean Punctuation Theory." *PMLA* 59 (1944): 349–60.

Parkes, M. B. *Pause and Effect: An Introduction to the History of Punctuation in the West*. Berkeley: University of California Press, 1993.

Snow, C. P. "The Moral Un-Neutrality of Science." *A World of Idea*, 2nd ed. Ed. Lee A. Jacobus. New York: Bedford Books, 1985, 416ff.

Sommer, Robert. *Personal Space: The Behavioral Bases of Design*. Englewood Cliffs, N.J.: Prentice-Hall, 1969.

Thomas, Lewis. *The Lives of a Cell: Notes of a Biology Watcher*. New York: Viking Press, 1974.

———. "Notes on Punctuation." *The Medusa and the Snail: More Notes of a Biology Watcher*. London: Allen Lane, 1980.

Turner, Frederick Jackson. *The Frontier in American History*. New York: H. Holt 1920.

Weaver, Richard M. *The Ethics of Rhetoric*. Chicago: Henry Regnery, 1953.

Williams, Joseph. *Style: Ten Lessons in Clarity and Grace*, 7th ed. New York: Longman Publishers, 2002.

Woolf, Virginia. "The Pastons and Chaucer." *The Common Reader*. New York: Harcourt Brace, 1958.

Index